Advance Praise for *Hunting the Caliphate*

"With the complementary insights of a general and his senior enlisted man, along with an insider's eye for detail and an unshakeable belief in their mission, Pittard and Bryant expertly pull back the curtain on the front line fight against ISIS. From Iraq to Afghanistan and Syria, Pittard and Bryant describe the development of a devastating air campaign waged from a distance, where rapid life or death decisions must be made with limited information and murky rules of engagement, and where ultimate success hinges on coordination between a state-of-the-art operations center with a small group of highly-trained Americans led by Pittard and Bryant, and their indigenous allies battling ISIS on the ground. Eye-opening, candid, and at times deeply human, *Hunting the Caliphate* is a must read for understanding a new kind of war told by two men who not only fought that war, but helped define it."

—DAVID BROYLES, former USAF Pararescueman (PJ) and co-creator of History Channel's combat drama, *Six*

"From mass executions to pinpoint air strikes, political and military frustrations and the politics of coalition warfare, *Hunting the Caliphate* is a compelling blend of military history and first-person memories of the war against terror—the complex battlefield, the joys of victory, the tragedy of loss, and the sacrifice of the men and women who carried out the mission. An insider account from a senior Army ground commander and a front line battlefield airman, the book is a gritty, compelling read for all who hope to understand America's longest war."

—DEBORAH LEE JAMES, 23rd Secretary of the Air Force, author of *Aim High: Chart Your Course and Find Success*

"Simply excellent. *Hunting the Caliphate* is the first account to give sustained insights into the events and personalities shaping the war on ISIS that academics and journalists have been unable to capture except in snapshots. Effectively written, and with editing nothing short of first-rate, it is a descriptive and gripping narrative from two contrasting yet intersecting perspectives that offers readers a broader view of the US military campaign against ISIS. As a historian of modern combat operations, I applaud the insightful observations appearing throughout that serve to accurately convey an important history—and dispel its myths."

—MARK J. REARDON, Senior Historian, US Army Center of Military History

HUNTING THE CALIPHATE

AMERICA'S WAR ON ISIS
AND THE DAWN OF THE STRIKE CELL

DANA J.H. PITTARD and WES J. BRYANT

Post Hill
PRESS

A POST HILL PRESS BOOK

Hunting the Caliphate:
America's War on ISIS and the Dawn of the Strike Cell
© 2019 by Dana J. H. Pittard and Wes J. Bryant
All Rights Reserved

ISBN: 978-1-64293-055-9
ISBN (eBook): 978-1-64293-056-6

Cover art by Cody Corcoran
Interior design and composition by Greg Johnson, Textbook Perfect

This is a work of nonfiction. All people, locations, events, and situations are portrayed to the best of the authors' memory.

Post Hill Press
New York • Nashville
posthillpress.com

Published in the United States of America

DEDICATION

This book is dedicated to the men and women, military and civilian, who answered the call to protect American interests and support the Iraqi and Syrian people in the fight against ISIS—and continue to do so.

To Lucille, Taylor, and Jordan. Thank you for your unwavering love and support. You are my inspiration.

—Dana J. H. Pittard

For the path that I've been fortuned to walk, there are a few people to whom I am eternally grateful. Grandmaster Pak Chi Moon, who gave me an enduring gift, and a different set of eyes from which to view the world. My loving Aunt Judy, who in my darkest hours and without judgment lifted me from the abyss. My amazing wife Katie, who endured the hardships and sacrifice of America's longest war by my side and who, no matter what, was always a light. And Jerry "Skip" Haile, who became a father when I needed one most, and who was always there for us.

I dedicate this book to my angels, London and Berlynn—everything I've done was for you. It is my hope that one day you will see this book as something greater than a collection of Daddy's war stories. Through understanding the hard lessons of the past, we can mindfully shape our future; and I long for one in which you and your generation realize a more peaceful humanity.

—Wes J. Bryant

TABLE OF CONTENTS

Foreword

In the summer of 2014, two-and-a-half years after the withdrawal of the last of the U.S. combat forces from Iraq, President Barack Obama authorized a small U.S. task force to return. The mission of the task force was to help Iraqi and Kurdish Forces protect the capitals of Iraq and the Iraqi Kurdish Region from the relentless advance of the terrorist "army" of the Islamic State of Iraq and al Sham[1] (ISIS), and also to help secure the U.S. Embassy in Baghdad and the U.S. Consulate in Erbil.

Hunting the Caliphate provides a vivid, first-hand account from two key members of the U.S. task force. In so doing, it describes what began as an effort to reconstitute and support Iraqi forces and evolved into a revolution in how the U.S. fights wars against extremists like those in Iraq, Syria, and Afghanistan.

In the months leading up to the task force's deployment in mid-2014, ISIS had established a *Caliphate* in an extensive area of western and northern Iraq and northeastern Syria. It was administered in accordance with an extreme interpretation of Islamic law. In conquering such a vast area, ISIS elements had demonstrated both enormous brutality and impressive skill on the battlefield. ISIS elements also used social media and the internet to share their successes—and barbaric actions—with the rest of the world, seeking to recruit Muslims from the region and beyond to join them. ISIS worked particularly skillfully in exploiting a sense of Sunni Arab alienation in Syria and Iraq. Initially, in fact, its fighters were welcomed by the Sunni communities they'd "liberated" from predominantly Shia Syrian and Iraqi forces—a welcome the communities would quickly learn to regret as the brutal, repressive nature of ISIS became increasingly evident.

---

1   Al Sham is Arabic for the *Levant*.

ISIS grew out of the extremist group Al Qaeda in Iraq (AQI), which had been destroyed by elements of the Multinational Force-Iraq and Iraqi Security Forces during the "surge" of 2007 and 2008, a period during which I was privileged to be the Multinational Force commander. In the years that followed, U.S. and Iraqi special operations and intelligence elements continued to pursue the remnants of AQI until the departure of American combat forces in late 2011. The lack of subsequent focus on the remaining AQI cells allowed them an opportunity to reconstitute, an effort that was given a significant boost when the highly sectarian actions of the Iraqi prime minister, in the wake of the departure of U.S. combat forces, alienated the Sunni Arab population and prompted enormous Sunni demonstrations—which were put down by very heavy-handed, often abusive, Shia-led Iraqi forces.

For those who had served in Iraq, especially during the surge and beyond, it was tragic to watch the fabric of the Iraqi society that we had worked so hard to bring back together be torn apart once again by the actions of the Iraqi government. As before the surge, Sunni Arab provinces once again became disenchanted with the government in Baghdad, and they turned into breeding grounds for Sunni extremists. ISIS took full advantage of the situation as it rebuilt its capabilities.

A similar dynamic arose in Syria in late 2011, as the repressive, brutal Alawite/Shia government of Bashar al-Assad violently put down peaceful Sunni demonstrations when Arab Spring discontent with "kleptocratic" leaders spread to Syria. The brutal actions of the Assad regime forces led to growing resentment and violence in the Sunni areas of Syria, and ultimately led to the start of the Sunni-Shia Syrian Civil War that has raged so horrifically for the past eight years. ISIS rightly assessed that it could exploit the anger in Syria and gain additional fighters, leaders, and resources in the Sunni areas—especially in the north and east (which also contained the bulk of Syria's oil production). They subsequently did just that.

By the summer of 2014, ISIS had already seized Mosul—the largest city in northern Iraq—and a number of cities in western Iraq. It was spreading down the Tigris and Euphrates River valleys like a virulent plague, threatening Ramadi and Baghdad in central Iraq, and also Erbil— the capital of Iraq's Kurdish Regional Government—in northern Iraq.

And it controlled a vast area of northeastern Syria that was contiguous to the areas it controlled in Iraq.

It was the threat to Baghdad and Erbil, in particular, that led President Obama to approve deployment of U.S. forces to those cities. They would become the hubs of the U.S.-led coalition that sought to help Iraqi forces halt the advance of ISIS and then to advise, assist, and enable the Iraqis as they conducted an increasingly impressive counter-offensive against heavily armed, dug-in ISIS elements. Though the U.S. task force was initially modest in size, it grew over time and ultimately became very lethal and effective in support of the Iraqi forces on the ground. And it did so with a fraction of the 165,000 American men and women in uniform that deployed in Iraq during the height of the surge.

The counter-ISIS effort included numerous strange bedfellows, among them forces from dozens of the countries that comprised the U.S.-led coalition, Iraqi military and police forces, Kurdish Peshmerga, Sunni tribal elements, and even Iranian-supported Shia militia. Over the ensuing several years, a new way of waging war evolved, largely unprecedented in its methodology and application of modern technology. The employment of an enormous constellation of manned and unmanned intelligence, surveillance, and reconnaissance assets together with air- and ground-launched precision strike munitions—all guided by the industrial-strength fusion of all forms of intelligence—in order to enable host nation forces with whom coalition advisors were located, has been a path-breaking approach. And, over time, the ability to conduct precise airstrikes on a significant scale without forward controllers on the ground added a hugely important component.

Hunting the Caliphate tells the story of this effort—of the men and women of the U.S.-led coalition that enabled Iraqi Security Forces to halt the advance of one of the most barbaric and extreme forces the world has ever seen, and then commence the counter-offensive operations that would ultimately lead to the defeat of ISIS in Iraq and in Syria.

We read of this fight from two different vantage points—that of the task force's commanding general, Major General Dana Pittard, and that of one of the special operations forces' most experienced Joint Terminal

Attack Controllers,[2] Wes Bryant. Both were highly talented professionals who had served with distinction in Iraq and elsewhere previously, and already had achieved enviable reputations as accomplished warfighters and leaders. They knew Iraq and the Iraqis well, and they served the citizens of the "Land of the Two Rivers,"—and our own country—with extraordinary skill and competence.

The resulting narrative offers a riveting, no-holds-barred account—hitherto untold—of what transpired as new approaches for battling a determined, highly capable (and extremely barbaric) enemy were developed while American and coalition elements sought to help Iraqi and other partners in the fight against ISIS from Iraq to Syria to Afghanistan. This is a compelling, important story—and *Hunting the Caliphate* captures it vividly and clearly.

—*General David H. Petraeus*,
    U.S. Army (Ret.), Arlington, Virginia

---

2   See Glossary for full definition and description of "Joint Terminal Attack Controller."

Introduction

In this book, we will use the name *ISIS* to refer to the terrorist force that has also been widely known as *ISIL*, *IS*, or *Daesh*. In August of 2014, ISIS controlled more than 34,000 square miles in Iraq and Syria—from the Mediterranean coast to the south of Baghdad. Eight months later, they'd lost almost half of that land. The authors are proud to say they were among the small group of U.S. service members to affect that.

An old military adage states "artillery is the king of the battlefield, while infantry is the queen." Indeed, ground forces are maneuverable and able to utilize countless methods of warfare and insertion, while artillery—though not nearly as maneuverable—packs a punch come rain or shine. But as true as that adage is, it was coined far before the days of airpower. An entirely new player in the game of chess that is war, airpower is both far-reaching and devastating. In the war against ISIS, it was the combination of airpower and ground forces provided by the Iraqi military, Kurdish Peshmerga, Shia militias, Syrian Kurds, and other entities that would eventually defeat ISIS.

Airpower was expertly synergized in support of ground combat forces, with most of the airstrikes directed and controlled from remote operations centers—"war rooms" that would come to be known as *Strike Cells*. The strike cell soon became the dominant method of hunting and killing one of America's most brutal and elusive enemies. By August of 2017, as part of *Operation Inherent Resolve*, the United States and its coalition partners had conducted nearly 25,000 airstrikes in Iraq and Syria,[3] most all controlled from strike cells operated by the U.S. military.

---

3 "Special Report: Operation Inherent Resolve," *U.S. Department of Defense*, accessed April 23, 2018, https://www.defense.gov/OIR/.

During the decade or so prior to the rise of *ISIS*, throughout the long-standing wars in Iraq and Afghanistan, remotely controlled strikes were accomplished but on quite a limited basis in comparison. In the initial U.S. invasion of Iraq in 2003, some of the first strikes against Saddam Hussein's army were executed from remote cells. Over the years to follow, remotely controlled strikes onto "high value" targets became fairly routine in Iraq, Afghanistan, and other select locations in the Middle East. Still, the majority of airstrikes were coordinated and controlled by JTACs on the ground and in the direct fight.

America's new war on ISIS changed things. The Obama administration restricted U.S. military combat action against ISIS almost solely to an air campaign, and in so doing inadvertently wrote a new chapter in U.S. military operational history. The scope of close air support, and the military's implementation of it, soon evolved. The strike cell was born.

In the summer of 2014, Dana Pittard and Wes Bryant infilled into Baghdad as a part of the small task force sent by President Obama to protect the U.S. Embassy and other facilities from the threat of ISIS and, if necessary, evacuate thousands of American citizens from Iraq. Little did they know the mission would soon evolve into a devastating and intense military campaign against ISIS.

A year earlier, in 2013, Major General Pittard was deployed to the Middle East as the deputy commander of operations for the U.S. Army Central Command. When President Obama authorized the reaction force to enter Baghdad to respond to the ISIS threat, Pittard was quickly designated the Joint Forces Land Component Commander-Iraq. He infilled into Baghdad and commanded the first military forces to enter Iraq in a military capacity since the American withdrawal in 2011.

While General Pittard took charge of the Iraq crisis in Baghdad, Master Sergeant Bryant was tasked to the Kingdom of Bahrain as the senior JTAC for the Joint Special Operations Task Force-Gulf Cooperation Council—the headquarters element that would oversee the special operations mission against ISIS. Soon after, Bryant infilled into Baghdad as the senior enlisted JTAC for the Special Operations Task Force-Iraq, and the noncommissioned officer in charge of its fires cell.

From the moment Pittard's headquarters team hit the ground, he was determined that more needed to be done to stop ISIS. He persisted in levying the senior military chain of command to put pressure on Washington, and eventually gained authorization from President Obama to direct the first airstrikes against ISIS after ISIS attacked Iraq's Kurdish Region.

The airstrike campaign kicked off with a fury. Once the administration and senior military leadership realized the results, a virtual Pandora's box was opened. General Pittard soon directed Army Colonel Tim Kehoe and his 17th Field Artillery Brigade staff to establish a new strike cell at the Baghdad International Airport (BIAP) that would come to be known as the *BIAP Strike Cell*. With its multiservice team of conventional and special operations forces, the BIAP Strike Cell would safeguard central Iraq and the capital.

From his position at the special operations task force in Baghdad, Master Sergeant Bryant became the senior enlisted JTAC at the forefront of the establishment of the BIAP Strike Cell; and was the tactical lead for the team of special operations JTACs tasked to carry out the mission. Within weeks, the BIAP Strike Cell had prosecuted the first airstrikes against ISIS in the Baghdad region, pushed back the ISIS advance on the capital, and laid the foundations for how America would continue to wage its war against the caliphate. Over the months and years to follow, the BIAP Strike Cell and others like it would come to decimate ISIS ranks on a massive scale throughout Iraq and Syria.

By spring of 2015, Dana and Wes had gone their separate ways. Dana was serving as the deputy commander of the Army's Central Command in Kuwait and preparing for his upcoming retirement from active duty. Wes was back in the States at his Special Tactics unit, training and evaluating the unit's special operations JTACs while at the same time keeping himself sharp for what would become two more deployments to hunt ISIS in Syria, then Afghanistan, before his own retirement three years later.

It was around then that Dana began writing a book, initially about the U.S. infiltration into Iraq in 2014 and the first few months of the campaign against ISIS. In spring of 2016, Dana reached out to Wes to gain his JTAC perspective for the book. After some reconnection and collaboration, the two quickly found that the same synergy that had made their strike cell team so successful back in 2014 was still between them a year-and-a-half later. They soon made the decision to co-author a book on the war against

ISIS, and *Hunting the Caliphate* was born into a joint endeavor that would come to be over three years in the making.

Dana and Wes felt that the unique and unprecedented blend of perspectives between the political, strategic, and operational insight of the senior commanding general on the ground combined with the first-hand tactical experience of the senior enlisted special operations JTAC to carry out the mission would be very impactful and resonate with a wide spectrum of readers.

Dana and Wes wanted to record a vital piece of history and do it in a way that was gritty and real—not just as a legacy to those who served in the fight against ISIS, but to educate the public on the inside story of a very unique campaign. They believe the American people deserve to know and, perhaps more importantly, that policy makers and government officials must better understand the warfighter's point of view since they make the decisions that guide America's military efforts across the world while often never having had any personal military experience.

There are a lot of standout aspects about *Hunting the Caliphate*: It is the first definitive account on the war against ISIS straight from two of the key men who waged it. It is one of the few books co-written by a general and a senior noncommissioned officer (from two different services, at that). And, it is the first major book written by a Joint Terminal Attack Controller.

First and foremost, *Hunting the Caliphate* is a story. It is a perspective on the campaign against ISIS from the eyes of two warriors, and it is *their* story. The authors could not possibly include enough in one book to highlight the amazing work that so many others accomplished in the fight against ISIS, including their teammates. Nevertheless, it is their hope that this story reflects the service and sacrifice of all who served in the initial months of the Iraq crisis of 2014, have deployed to hunt ISIS since, and continue to fight ISIS and other threats to this day.

—*Dana J.H. Pittard and Wes J. Bryant*

Reference Maps

The following pages contain CIA resource maps pertinent to the context of this book.

Political Map of the World, October 2016

CIA Political World 2016

Source: United States Central Intelligence Agency, "Political Map of the World," Washington, D.C. Central Intelligence Agency, 2016, https://www.cia.gov/library/publications/resources/the-world-factbook/docs/refmaps.html.

Antarctica

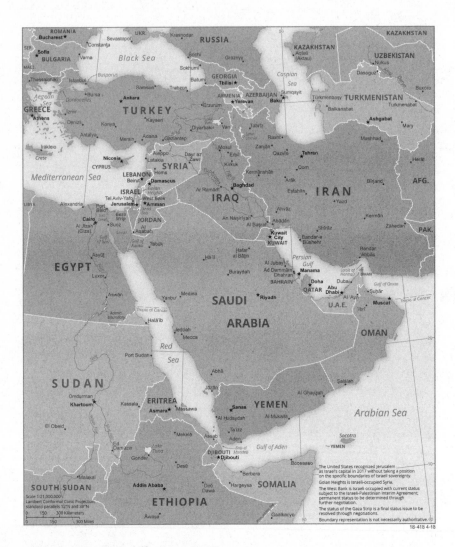

CIA Political Middle East 2017

Source: United States Central Intelligence Agency, "Middle East Political," Washington, D.C. Central Intelligence Agency, 2017, https://www.cia.gov/library/publications/resources /the-world-factbook/docs/refmaps.html.

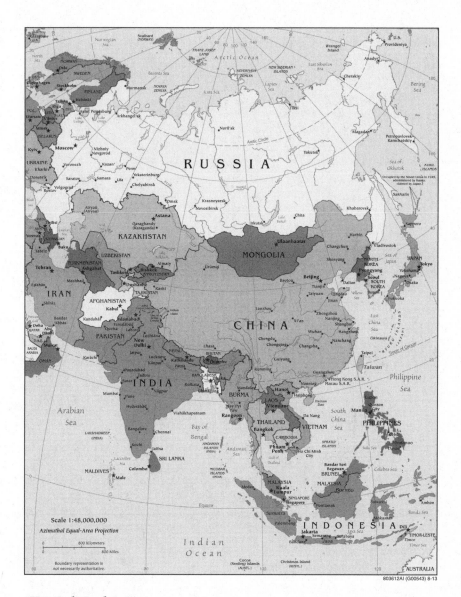

CIA Political Asia

Source: United States Central Intelligence Agency, "Asia Political," Washington, D.C. Central Intelligence Agency, https://www.cia.gov/library/ publications/resources/the-world -factbook/docs/refmaps.html.

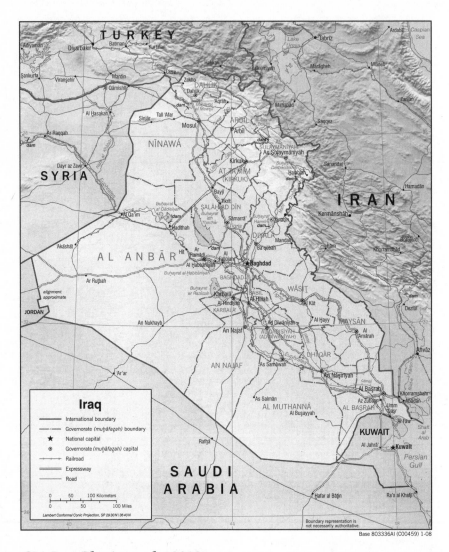

CIA Iraq Physiography 2008

Source: United States Central Intelligence Agency, "Iraq Physiography," Washington, D.C. Central Intelligence Agency, 2008, https://www.cia.gov/library/publications/resources /cia-maps-publications/Iraq.html.

CIA Syria Physiography 2007

Source: United States Central Intelligence Agency, "Syria Physiography," Washington, D.C. Central Intelligence Agency, 2007, https://www.cia.gov/library/publications/resources /cia-maps-publications/Syria.html.

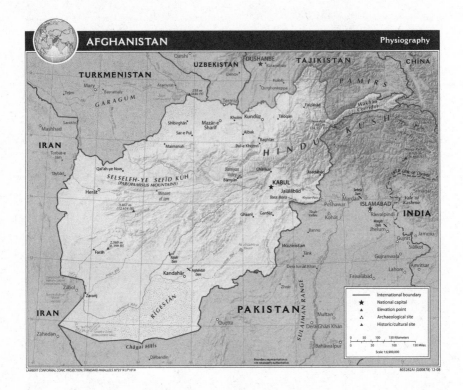

CIA Afghanistan Physiography 2009

Source: United States Central Intelligence Agency, "Afghanistan Physiography," Washington, D.C. Central Intelligence Agency, 2009, https://www.cia.gov/library/publications/resources/cia-maps-publications/afghanistan.html.

We do not merely destroy our enemies;
we change them.

—GEORGE ORWELL, *1984*

Good Hunting: The Iron Fist of Fallujah

DANA PITTARD

Early October 2014

Abu Ali, a local ISIS commander in Fallujah, was a proud leader and fighter, and with good reason—he'd helped ISIS take over the Sunni-dominated city of Fallujah earlier that year. It was a key victory that had positioned ISIS in Fallujah along the ancient Euphrates River just sixty-nine kilometers west of the Iraqi capital of Baghdad.

Abu Ali's name was a *nom de guerre*, meaning "Father of Ali," and he ruled eastern Fallujah with an iron fist. He levied harsh taxes, enforced Sharia law, and virtually enslaved Iraqi citizens. Unfortunately for him, such notoriety and status earned him a prime target position for our strike cell, which had the mission of coordinating all airstrikes in central and western Iraq.

ISIS leaders knew the United States took great care to avoid killing civilians and hitting religious structures, so they tried to use our respect for humanity to their advantage. Ali lived in a densely-populated neighborhood, with houses connected and literally on top of each other, hence he was nested amidst hundreds of innocents.

We knew where he lived; his home was one of four houses on a small compound surrounded by a five-foot mud brick wall with a large metal gate. Through the gate was a driveway that led to the side of a three-story house with a flat patio roof. All the houses on the small compound were connected and well protected by stationary and walking guards. We could not hit Abu Ali at his home with an airstrike due to our concern for civilian casualties as well as the potential for collateral damage to the homes of family members in the compound and scores of adjacent houses. Instead, we kept him under constant surveillance, and bided our time.

With a religious mosque on nearly every major street corner and intersection, Fallujah is known as the "City of Mosques." ISIS often used the mosques as shelter for their illicit activities, knowing that the religious centers were normally not targeted by airstrikes. Abu Ali felt safe traveling in the middle of Fallujah because of the large civilian population and its high number of mosques. Ali and his fellow ISIS leaders seemed to think the American military's unwillingness to slaughter civilians and destroy their property was a weakness—yet another reason why ISIS would prevail over the West (they believed). The reality was much different.

Ali and his ISIS fighters traveled with seeming impunity throughout Fallujah's winding streets and alleyways. However, we constantly observed them from the air with our Predator drones—twenty-seven feet long, with a wingspan of forty-eight feet and flying 14,000 feet overhead.

We watched…and waited patiently.

Our Predator drone followed Abu Ali as he took his family to the market, his four bodyguards trailing behind in their vehicle. We watched as he got out of the back seat of his car with his wife along with their elementary-school-aged son and daughter and his bodyguards. They walked into a crowded outside market, with vendors selling their goods from makeshift wooden stalls.

Ali was of medium height and had a long beard. He wore sandals and a flowing *dishdashi*—robes that we often referred to as a "man dress." Abu Ali was intermittently on his cell phone while his wife—who was covered in a scarf or *abaya*—shopped and bartered with vendors in the dense market. Their two children ran around, playing with each other and other nearby children. Different men greeted Abu Ali, shaking his hand and giving him a traditional kiss on each cheek, left then right.

We couldn't hit Ali with an airstrike in the crowded marketplace, but we noted the routes he and his two-vehicle convoy took going to and from the market and other locations. A pattern emerged, and we drew up a tentative plan.

A few days later, we lured Abu Ali into a trap. One night we blew up an ISIS checkpoint in eastern Fallujah with an airstrike. Such checkpoints were a key symbol of ISIS' power in towns and villages. They used the checkpoints to subdue the population by controlling traffic and exacting tolls and taxes from commercial trucks.

The checkpoints usually consisted of a small wooden shack that looked like a large tollbooth. They normally had black ISIS flags displayed and were manned by three to six ISIS fighters. This particular one was located at a key road intersection less than ten kilometers from Ali's house. His turf.

We killed at least three of his ISIS fighters in the airstrike.

Within twenty minutes of the explosion, our Predator drone's video feed showed several ISIS vehicles carrying Ali's top lieutenants rushing to his home to confer. From their scattered behavior, and the communications we intercepted, it was apparent that they were unsure of the cause of the explosion that had destroyed their checkpoint. We continued to monitor them.

After talking with some of our intelligence personnel, Colonel Tim Kehoe—the adept field artillery officer I'd chosen to direct our new strike cell at the Baghdad Airport—advised me. "Sir, I think we may get a chance to strike *Objective Rio* tonight."

Objective Rio was our codename for Abu Ali (the actual codename remains classified).

"Good," I replied. I'd been reading updates from the staff and eating pistachios. Some people drank coffee, chewed gum, or smoked cigarettes to stay alert; I ate Turkish pistachios.

We watched on the main screen in the strike cell as Abu Ali came out of his house to meet his lieutenants. He was wearing sandals and a man dress as he listened to the reports from his men. From our intercepts, we learned that he wanted to see the damage firsthand so he could describe it to his ISIS superiors. We knew his going to the scene of the checkpoint explosion would also be a show of bravado meant to impress his subordinates—an ISIS leadership trait we'd happily capitalize on.

Ali had taken the bait.

He would take one of two distinct routes to get to the destroyed checkpoint. All we had to do was choose the optimal place to hit him. He and his security detail piled into two black Mercedes sedans. Ali was with three of his men in the lead car, sitting in the back seat. The second car carried five more men. The small convoy snaked its way through the narrow back streets of Fallujah while our Predator drone patiently tracked them from high overhead. Our ears in the sky listened as Abu Ali called his subordinates on his cell phone and demanded updates.

Our strike cell was on full alert, preparing to attack. The JTACs called in a pair of coalition strike aircraft. As expected, the enemy convoy drove through the most heavily populated areas of Fallujah where they felt safe from our airstrikes. But we had counted on that. Colonel Kehoe and the JTACs discussed the best options to hit the convoy.

Vern—a JTAC-qualified Navy F/A-18 pilot and the lead officer in charge of the JTACs in the strike cell—used a red laser pointer to highlight Abu Ali's expected route on the Google Maps display screen in front of us. "This long, wide boulevard in the middle of Fallujah would be the best place to engage," he told us.

Colonel Kehoe replied, "Okay, that looks like a possibility, but how does it look from a collateral damage perspective?"

Our collateral damage analyst, a seasoned army staff sergeant seated immediately to my right, had a quick answer. "Hmm, the route only has short segments where we could safely pull off a strike without risking significant collateral," he came back. "The intersection Vern is pointing at could work, even though there's a large mosque within four hundred meters. It has a thick stone wall around it that will probably shield it from damage, but the missiles would have to hit the convoy head-on from the front."

I groaned. I knew a front-angle missile shot at a moving vehicle would not be easy for any pilot.

As if he read my thoughts, Vern chimed in, "The coalition aircraft have a really accurate missile. We can get the aircraft to position themselves to hit the target head-on with their missiles. I'm confident."

There wasn't much more time to decide. The team looked to me. I looked each of them in the eyes, then I turned back to Vern, "Do you really think you can get the pilots to hit both cars from an exact front angle?"

Vern replied quickly, "Yes sir, I do. I have a lot of confidence in these coalition pilots. They're almost as good as our own."

The room was silent. All eyes turned toward me, but I still took a few more seconds to observe the live video feed on the main screen as Abu Ali's convoy made its way through Fallujah. I finally turned to Tim Kehoe, "Okay, the strike is approved."

It was a tough decision. Albeit slight, there was a possibility of causing collateral damage or civilian casualties. I knew many of my more risk-averse colleagues would not have made the same call. However, we had an opportunity to kill an ISIS leader, and those opportunities were fleeting. It was a decision I did not make lightly, but I had faith in our strike cell team's abilities to assess the situation accurately.

We watched the live feed from our Predator drone as Abu Ali's convoy moved toward our anticipated target area. Abu Ali probably felt safe in his car surrounded by his men, with so many civilians walking along the sides of the wide boulevard. The convoy approached the intersection near the mosque with the stone wall around it, about 1,000 meters from the checkpoint we'd destroyed earlier.

The JTACs sitting in front of me controlling the coalition pilots over the radio kept their eyes on the two vehicles. Our coalition jets had moved from 20,000 feet in the air down to 15,000 to prepare for the strike. The pilots confirmed the targets, skillfully tracking them as the two vehicles approached our designated target engagement area.

Thirty men and women in the strike cell went silent, with all eyes on the huge screen linked to our overwatching Predator drone. Seconds passed. Abu Ali's two-vehicle convoy moved slowly toward the engagement area. The coalition aircraft were now positioned so their missiles would glide in directly to the front of the ISIS vehicles.

Our JTACs coolly gave the pilots clearance to strike. Seconds later, two missiles launched almost simultaneously.

BOOM! BOOM!

I imagined the last thing Abu Ali and his bodyguards likely heard was a crackling and whistling sound just milliseconds before the missiles hit them.

Both vehicles were hit violently between the headlights. They exploded into a mist of smoke and debris in rapid succession. The tremendous dual explosions caused a huge orange and red fireball. The shockwave blew debris in all directions from the impact, and we could see pieces of metal and human remnants flung a hundred meters down the road.

A heavy plume of smoke obscured everything from our aerial view, so much that we couldn't see the large mosque with the stone wall to assess if it had been affected by the strike. Our initial thought, and fear, was that the mosque had been inadvertently damaged. Waiting for the smoke to clear, we all silently watched the Predator screen. After a few excruciatingly long minutes, the smoke began to dissipate. It was obvious the stone wall surrounding the mosque had been hit with debris, but it was well intact and the mosque was unscathed. The strike had caused no major collateral damage—it was a clean hit! The strike cell went wild with cheering, and our JTACs radioed congratulations to the coalition fighter pilots.

At the location where Abu Ali's vehicles had been hit, the scene on the ground was utter chaos. People ran everywhere. The violent explosions had caused panic along the wide boulevard. Civilian bystanders ran up to the burning remnants of Abu Ali's vehicles but they could not reach the bodies within the flames. A fire truck arrived quickly and poured water on the wreckage.

Clearly, no one survived.

The Aftermath

The celebration was still loud and raucous in the strike cell when I received a call from an Air Force brigadier general from the United States Central Command (CENTCOM) in Tampa, Florida. During the strike, our Predator drone's live video feed had been viewed by multiple U.S. headquarters both in the Middle East and the United States.

"General Pittard, sir, we are concerned about how close that strike came to the mosque. On something as close as that, I recommend you let us make the call from CENTCOM," the junior-ranking general advised me.

I chuckled. "Really? I don't think so," I replied. "As the target engagement authority here on the ground in Iraq, I will continue to make those difficult calls when I can." I could tell the brigadier general was unhappy with my response. I continued, "Look, that airstrike was a calculated risk, and there was no collateral damage. Our record speaks for itself—we've been successful in killing thousands of ISIS fighters over the last few months without a single civilian casualty...but thank you for your call and concern." I said goodbye and hung up.

The next call came immediately from my boss, Lieutenant General James Terry, from my higher headquarters in Kuwait. "Dana, congratulations—that was a damn good strike!"

"Thanks, sir," I said. "Tim Kehoe's staff and the special ops JTACS have really been doing some good work."

"I agree with that, Dana," he replied. "You and the entire team up in Iraq are making history helping the Iraqis defeat ISIS," he continued. "Just, please—try to do it without stirring up so much fuss with our Air Force friends in the future."

I laughed. "Will do, sir!"

"Good hunting," Terry finished.

PART 1

The War on Terror: ISIS Rising

CHAPTER 1

Awakening the Eagles

DANA PITTARD AND WES BRYANT

Dana Pittard
September 11, 2001

I was on the campus of Harvard University serving a one-year War College Fellowship at the John F. Kennedy School of Government when Osama bin Laden's al-Qaeda terrorist organization attacked our country. Another student stopped me as I walked to class. He told me that a plane had just hit the World Trade Center. I slipped into a building called the *Forum* inside the main entrance to the Kennedy School.

About 300 students and faculty members in the auditorium were watching CNN in horrified silence as it projected images on a giant video screen. I arrived right as the second plane struck the second tower. A collective groan came from the crowd and several "Oh my Gods!" Most of the students in attendance were mortified. I was stunned when a couple of Middle Eastern students actually clapped! I just about lost it. If that had been at Texas A&M in my home state of Texas, rather than Harvard, there would most certainly have been a brawl. Instead, I just turned and glared at the Middle Eastern guy nearest me who'd clapped.

He saw the look of sheer rage on my face and stopped.

At the time—as a West Point graduate, a veteran of *Operation Desert Storm,* and a lieutenant colonel in the U.S. Army—I knew we were going to war. I ached to get into the fight. Our country had been attacked. I felt a duty to step up and help protect the nation.

The 9/11 attacks on American soil came at a time when I was preparing to take command of an Army brigade combat team in Germany. I was also contemplating a return to civilian life once I completed that command. To be honest, the slow bureaucratic processes of the military had left me feeling frustrated.

The attacks gave me renewed motivation and inspiration, and any lingering thoughts of retirement were lost in the events over the following years that would eventually lead me to face one of the most formidable foes America had yet seen.

From my days at West Point and through the War College at Harvard's Kennedy School, nearly all of my training had been in traditional conventional warfare. However, there was nothing traditional about the fanatical terrorist army that I would come to face in just a few short years.

In the summer of 2002, following my year at Harvard, I moved my wife Lucille and our two young sons, Taylor and Jordan, to Vilseck, Germany. I took command of a combat unit of nearly 4,000 soldiers. The 3rd Brigade, 1st Infantry Division—with six combat-ready battalions—was an armored brigade known as the "Dukes."

Soon after assuming command, I deployed most of the brigade to Kosovo for nine months of peacekeeping operations. Once we re-deployed back home to Germany, we had a brief six months to quickly refit, re-equip, and re-train before deploying to combat in Iraq in 2004, for over a year.

Our mission in Iraq was to stabilize Diyala, a province just northeast of Baghdad. Diyala Province was a microcosm of Iraq, with a large Sunni and Shia Arab population as well as a sizeable Kurdish population. Our brigade became known locally as the "Dukes of Diyala."

Soldiers and units in the Duke Brigade experienced tough and gritty fighting. One of my Soldiers, Staff Sergeant David Bellavia, would become the first living recipient of the Medal of Honor in the Iraq War for his actions in Fallujah in 2004.[1]

---

1   Meghann Myers, "This soldier is about to be the Iraq War's first living Medal of Honor recipient," *Army Times*, June 7, 2018, accessed June 8, 2019, https://www.armytimes.com/news/your-army/2019/06/07/this-soldier-is-about-to-be-the-iraq-wars-first-living-medal-of-honor-recipient/.

We fought Sunni insurgents and Shia militias throughout Iraq in Baqubah, Muqdadiyah, Khalis, An Najaf, Fallujah, and Mosul. We stabilized Diyala Province and helped it achieve the highest percentage of Sunnis among any province to vote in Iraq's first democratic election in early 2005. Our success came at a profound cost, though: we lost thirty-six fellow soldiers and had nearly 300 wounded that year.

After returning home from Iraq in 2005, I was selected for promotion to brigadier general and moved with my family to Fort Riley, Kansas (Lucille's hometown was Junction City, just outside of Fort Riley). Unfortunately, my stay home with my family was not destined to be long. I was ordered to deploy back to Iraq in 2006 as the commanding general of the Iraq Assistance Group.

During that year tour, I oversaw advisory teams embedded in every Iraqi division, brigade, and most battalions. I worked for the Multi-National Corps-Iraq commander, Lieutenant General Pete Chiarelli, and the Multi-National Force-Iraq commander, General George Casey. By 2007, Chiarelli and Casey departed Iraq and I then fell under the command of Lieutenant General Ray Odierno and General Dave Petraeus. Both Petraeus and Odierno would help to defeat the Sunni insurgency over the following two years.

I departed Iraq in the summer of 2007 to become the commanding general of the U.S. Army's National Training Center (NTC) in the Mojave Desert at Fort Irwin, California. General Petraeus was instrumental in my selection to command the prestigious NTC. I thanked him, but also warned him politely that I would be innovatively changing things at the NTC to make the training even more realistic.

General Petraeus merely responded, "That's why we're sending you there, Dana!"

We soon made the training at NTC more focused on the counterinsurgency warfare our forces had been waging in Afghanistan and Iraq. I departed Fort Irwin in 2009 and spent a brief year working for General Martin Dempsey at the Training and Doctrine Command (TRADOC) at Fort Monroe, Virginia. There, I received my promotion to a two-star major general.

In 2010, I took command of Fort Bliss, Texas and a year later the 1st Armored Division in my hometown of El Paso, Texas. Commanding the base and unit in my hometown was truly a dream come true. My family and I enjoyed our tour at Fort Bliss, and both my sons graduated from high school in El Paso. I thought Fort Bliss would be my last operational assignment before retirement. Developments in the Middle East proved me wrong.

Twelve years after the attacks of 9/11, I came to have a much bigger fight on my hands. I was deployed again to the Middle East as the deputy commanding general for operations in the U.S. Army Central Command. I was fifty-four years old, with both sons in college, and I'd moved my wife and mother to Virginia and deployed to the country of Jordan in 2013 for what I thought would be a final year-long tour. Soon, I found myself a part of the senior command element leading the fight against an even more radical Islamic terrorist group than al-Qaeda and the Taliban.

In June of 2014, I deployed from Kuwait to Baghdad to become the senior ground commander in Iraq and lead the first months of the fight against ISIS—an enemy I hadn't even heard of before 2013. Due to the gravity of the threat that ISIS posed to the region and the world, my tour of duty was extended from one year to two.

Wes Bryant
September 11, 2001

"Someone better have fucking died to call us back inside right now!" I exclaimed to no one in particular.

I was newly married, in my early twenties, and about three years into my career in the Air Force as a Tactical Air Control Party (TACP) specialist. I was stationed in northern New York at the U.S. Army's Fort Drum, attached to the 10th Mountain Infantry Division in the 20th Air Support Operations Squadron (ASOS).

Back in 1998, after a brief stint on my own after high school and some failed community college classes which only proved I had absolutely no idea what direction I wanted to take in life, I enlisted in the U.S. Air Force to enter one of its relatively unknown ground combat career fields. At the time, I would have joined for room and board only, not even a paycheck. Having had a pretty adverse childhood and adolescence, I was ready to leave my life behind and give everything to a new one in the military. I enlisted as an E-1, an Airman Basic, and by 2001 I'd been promoted two more grades to Senior Airman.

And I was full of piss and vinegar.

It was early fall, a little after 9 a.m. on a clear, cool morning in northern New York. I was in a grassy field situated right off my squadron's main building, doing some tactical training with my battalion TACP team. We'd just finished morning PT (physical training), and we were going through our standard weekly radio communications checks on our two jungle-camouflaged Humvees—ensuring the high-powered radio pallets in the Humvees were ready for combat deployment at a moment's notice.

A minute or so prior to my exclamation, Sergeant Cox, the noncommissioned officer in charge of our team, had poked his head out the door of our two-story squadron building about fifty meters away from where we were set up in the field.

"Hey everyone, get in here ASAP!" he yelled.

Finally, begrudgingly, I stormed back inside with the rest of the guys; though I was sure in my mind that there was nothing in the world detrimental enough to interrupt the training we'd been doing. I walked in to find one of the old tube televisions that we had scattered around the unit turned on. It was set on a desk in the middle of the long room of sectioned-off office spaces where we normally ran our mission planning for training and exercises. All the guys in my entire brigade TACP team were gathered around it, watching in silence.

On the screen, a New York City skyscraper burned.

Shortly after, the news stations put out word from Washington that our nation had succumbed to a multi-pronged terror attack by way of hijacked airliners. We watched in disbelief at the aftermath of the Pentagon crash, then the collapse of the north tower, the separate crash in Pennsylvania that fell short due to the heroic actions of its crew and passengers, and finally the collapse of the south tower. I will always remember watching, in shock, the desperate people jumping and falling from the towers as they burned.[2]

---

2 History.com Editors, "9/11 Timeline," *History*, June 21, 2011, accessed September 11, 2018, https://www.history.com/topics/21st-century/9-11-timeline.

"Pack your bags," Sergeant Cox, a veteran of *Operation Allied Force* in Kosovo,[3] bellowed as we continued to watch with eyes glued to the screen. "We're going to war."

As the minutes dragged on, we asked one another how *any* of what we were watching could be happening in America. We knew the U.S. had recently waged *Operation Desert Storm* in the early '90s,[4] but most of us young guys were just starting high school back then. None of us believed anyone would be stupid enough to mess with the United States anymore.

We had no idea who'd perpetrated the attack at the time, but we knew soon after that it was a confirmed act of terrorism, and that our government was surely going to make someone pay. Even so, as we watched the carnage on the screen play out, we had no idea where that event would take all of us in the ensuing years. We could scarcely foresee that the attack on the Twin Towers that day would lead us into the longest war in our nation's history—a war that would, at times, come to consume our lives.

By late September 2001, Army Special Forces and Ranger teams were already on the ground in Afghanistan, working with the *Northern Alliance* to root out the Taliban government and al-Qaeda networks that U.S. intelligence quickly correlated as being responsible for the attacks. Alongside those teams were Air Force special operations JTACS, at that time known as *ETACs* (Enlisted Terminal Attack Controllers). One of my good friends and mentors, Billy, was among the first on the ground as a TACP attached to one of the elite Ranger units.

By December, the well-known special operations *Battle of Tora Bora* was hard-fought in eastern Afghanistan in a valiant but unsuccessful attempt to capture Osama bin Laden, who was by then revealed as the mastermind behind the 9/11 attacks.[5] Around that same time, my unit sent some of the first conventional force ETACs to Afghanistan attached to an infantry brigade from the 10th Mountain Division. By March

---

3   Capt. Gregory Ball, "1999 – Operation Allied Force," *Air Force Historical Support Division*, August 23, 2012, accessed January 27, 2019, https://www.afhistory.af.mil/FAQs/Fact-Sheets/Article/458957/ operation-allied-force/.

4   Dr. Deborah Kidwell, "1991 – Operation Desert Shield/Desert Storm," *Air Force Historical Support Division*, December 02, 2011, accessed January 27, 2019, https://www.afhistory.af.mil/FAQs/Fact-Sheets/Article/458965/operation-desert-shielddesert-storm/.

5   John Swift, "Battle of Tora Bora," *Encyclopaedia Britannica*, accessed September 11, 2018, https://www.britannica.com/event/Battle-of-Tora-Bora.

2002, our 20th ASOS TACPs became the first conventional ETACs to see combat in Afghanistan, fighting bravely in *Operation Anaconda* in the Paktia province of southeastern Afghanistan—to this day one of the largest and bloodiest battles of the war.

During Anaconda, as our conventional forces battled it out with Taliban in the *Shah-i-Kot* valley, special operations teams met fierce Taliban resistance in the mountains to the southeast. In what came to be termed the *Battle of Takur Ghar*, more famously known as the "Battle of Roberts' Ridge" after the first casualty of Anaconda—Navy SEAL Neil Roberts[6]—Air Force Combat Controller John Chapman would later become the first airman awarded the Medal of Honor since the Vietnam War. Chapman was killed in action endeavoring truly heroic feats to save his SEAL and Ranger teammates.[7]

To my eventual dismay, I hadn't been tasked for that first deployment to Afghanistan. I'd already laid alternate career plans in place months before 9/11 had happened, and that unfortunately took me out of any chance to get in on the early fighting in Afghanistan. It was something that I always regretted. But, I suppose, it led me on a path that I otherwise may not have taken.

In January of 2002 I attended the elite U.S. Army Special Forces Combat Diver Qualification Course (CDQC) in Key West, Florida—the Army's equivalent to the combat dive program of the Navy SEALs but without the underwater demolitions. Getting my combat dive "bubble" was a goal that I'd set out to accomplish three years before, after I'd first gone and failed while in the Air Force's special operations training pipeline shortly before I became a TACP.

Strangely, the winters in Key West can get quite cold. During our initial week of pass/fail underwater confidence events, the imposing, black-clad Special Forces cadre had to periodically pull us out of the water, put us under steaming hot showers and feed us hot, overly-salted soup in

---

6 "Report details SEAL's last stand in Afghanistan," CNN, May 17, 2002, accessed January 27, 2019, http://www.cnn.com/2002/US/05/17/ret.seal.death/index.html.

7 Stephen Losey, "'Extraordinary sacrifice': Air Force Tech. Sgt. John Chapman posthumously awarded the Medal of Honor," *Air Force Times*, August 22, 2018, accessed January 27, 2019, https://www.airforcetimes.com/news/your-air-force/2018/08/22/extraordinary-sacrifice-air-force-tech-sgt-john-chapman-posthumously-awarded-the-medal-of-honor/.

order to prevent hypothermia and dehydration among our small group of Army and Air Force special operations trainees. They were short-lived breaks, though, and it was always right back in the frigid water.

I'd prepared for the course for three years, but still I lost consciousness underwater during one of those pass/fail events. In the dreaded "one-man confidence" test, instructors creatively conjure an experience of rough seas while the trainee—breathing from his SCUBA gear with a blacked-out mask while at the bottom of an eighteen-foot pool—must remain calm and go through emergency procedures while getting tossed and twirled around, his gear pulled and yanked, and his air source taken. By "creatively conjure"—I mean they beat and wrestle the crap out of you and rip off your straps, tanks, regulator, and even sometimes your shorts. They do everything they can to see if the trainee will panic under duress while underwater. It is for that reason and more that the combat diver's course is known throughout the Special Forces community as the "toughest school in the Army," above even Ranger School and the Special Forces Qualification Course.

Because of all my training, I remained calm and didn't panic; even though the instructor jerked my regulator from my mouth, tied the air hose in a knot, and shoved that mess somewhere behind me in the tank manifold so effectively that, despite my avid attempts, the modest breath-hold I'd managed to gasp in before having my air source stolen didn't last long enough for my blind hands to find the regulator in time to feed myself more much-needed air.

I remember the burning in my diaphragm, then going numb, the peaceful blackness closing in, and then waking up flopped on the pool deck to a concerned cadre bent over me with an oxygen mask shoved in my face.

The next day, though a bit shaken from my first underwater black-out the day prior, I got back into the pool and passed my final test with flying colors. A few weeks later I became among the handful of TACPs in the history of my career field to graduate from the Army's CDQC, earning the coveted combat dive bubble.

For me, dive school was among the truest tests of the warrior spirit I ever had in my career; and I would carry that spirit with me throughout my time in the military.

Plans already long in place, soon afterwards I left the TACP career field to fulfill my original dream of becoming a Pararescueman or "PJ"— the special operations combat rescue specialists of the Air Force. In my first few years in the military, I'd made it through the brutal Air Force special operations Indoctrination Course, accomplished TACP training and apprenticeship, graduated the Air Force Survival, Evasion, Resistance and Escape (SERE) School, Army Air Assault School, and had gutted through a cold and muddy Army Ranger selection course. To top it off, I'd just graduated from the elite Special Forces Combat Dive school. I was hungry for even more challenge, and I saw becoming a PJ as a way to get it.

I spent the next couple of years in the Pararescue training pipeline gaining even more specialized instruction. I graduated from the Army Airborne and Special Forces Military Freefall (MFF) schools as well as the Pararescue special operations Paramedic course. It was all very valuable training but, for me, there was still something missing.

During all that time, my brothers from the TACP community were fighting across the world in Afghanistan, and then in Iraq once that war kicked off in spring of 2003.[8] Previously as a young TACP, I had gotten a taste of the world of ground combat and combat tactical air control, and my friends from that world were now coming back from Afghanistan and Iraq as seasoned warriors; but I was still in training. After hearing their exhilarating tales of killing the enemy with airstrikes time and again, I realized that I had taken the wrong path. As honorable a job as it was to be a Pararescueman, I finally came to grips that it just wasn't for me.

I wanted to be the predator...the *hunter*.

By spring of 2004, I went back to my former career as a TACP and never looked back. By fall of that year I became certified as a JTAC, completed advanced training as an Enlisted Battalion Air Liaison Officer (EBALO) and, shortly thereafter, was sent on my first deployment to Iraq attached to the Army's 1st Cavalry Division conducting combat operations in the famed "triangle of death" south of Baghdad. Over the next few years I would deploy to Iraq and Afghanistan attached to maneuver

---

8   History.com Editors, "War in Iraq Begins," *History*, November 24, 2009, accessed January 27, 2019, https://www.history.com/this-day-in-history/war-in-iraq-begins.

units from the 82nd Airborne Division, 173rd Airborne Brigade, and 1st Armored Division.

Then, in 2007 I was tasked with a remote, year-long tour to South Korea that I sorely did not want. I'd been dealing with what, years later I would learn, was significant combat PTSD stemming from my first deployment to Afghanistan two years prior. It had been manifesting itself as a real problem with anger and aggression in my life and was severely affecting my career and my personal relationships. Compounding that, my wife and I were having a lot of trouble financially—we'd just bought our first home and were admittedly over-extended, our mortgage in constant jeopardy. Facing the long, unaccompanied tour was just not something either of us were ready for, but we had no choice.

I'll never forget the feeling of dread I had the day I left her at the airport; facing the year away while our life and relationship was in shambles. Still, somehow strangely, my tour to South Korea soon turned into one of the best things that had yet happened in my life and career.

I'd grown up training in the traditional martial arts. They'd helped pull me out of a childhood filled with hardship and juvenile delinquency. To make the best of the remote tour, early on I had resolved to seek out a Korean martial arts teacher at my first opportunity.

On hitting the ground, I arrived at a small Army base at the northern edge of South Korea, close to the demilitarized zone buffering North Korea. There, I was lucky enough to find an old Korean man who taught Chinese Kung Fu. He was a humble man, in his late seventies, and it didn't take long for me to learn that he was the real deal—a true Grandmaster. I couldn't believe my luck. I soon dedicated my time outside of my military duties solely to training.

Grandmaster Pak was a native North Korean and a combat veteran of the Korean War. Nearly sixty years earlier he'd been among the handful of North Korean guerilla forces that had fought alongside the South and the United States against the Communists. Today, such men are celebrated by the South Korean military as the forbearers of Korea's special operations forces.

My time training under Master Pak and listening to the wisdom gained from his life before and after the war was life-altering. The horrors that he and his family had endured through Japanese-occupied Korea, the division of north and south following WWII and subsequent Russian occupation, and the Korean War—with the tough years that followed the Armistice—few people today could comprehend.[9]

"Be lucky you born strong country," he would so often say to me in his broken English after relaying a story from those hard times. He loved America for what it did for his country. And he always reminded me of the opportunities that we have as Americans and what it means for America to be the pillar of light and hope for the rest of the world.

My time in Korea made me a stronger person and, really, a more competent warfighter. I went back to the States more grounded and focused, and with an even deeper, more *intelligent* patriotism for the nation I served. Embarking to a new duty station, and soon after another deployment to Iraq, I simultaneously set my mind toward the singular goal of becoming a special operations JTAC.

I'd graduated from some of the toughest and most prestigious ground combat schools in the military and, more importantly, I knew I was a damn good JTAC. I wanted to be the best of the best, a Special Operations Forces (SOF) TACP—the close air support expert on the ground bringing combat airpower to special operations teams.

Over the next couple of years I assessed for the special operations component of my career field over and over, but was denied at every turn. Of course, my time back in Korea had not been without strife. I'd gotten an administrative punishment known as an Article 15 after an angry and heated run-in with the bitter captain in charge of my remote detachment. (I was never one for the rank-based hierarchy of the military, and that hurt my career many a time.) In the eyes of the special operations assessment boards, the infraction was perceived as enough of a "character flaw" to bar me from acceptance. Still, I persisted, and reassessed every chance I got. By 2011, I was finally accepted into the special operations branch of my career field.

As a conventional force TACP, I'd been part of a small community of no more than 2,000 men. When I became a SOF TACP, I joined a much smaller brotherhood of around 100. I became part of the Air Force's Special

---

9   "The Korean War: Timeline," CBS News, July 6, 2018, accessed September 11, 2018, https://www.cbsnews.com/news/the-korean-war-timeline/.

Tactics, working alongside my career field's brethren, the Combat Control Teams (CCTs). CCTs were also a small community of around 500 men who specialized in forward airfield, landing, and drop zone establishment and forward air traffic control. With the onset of the war in Afghanistan, CCTs became increasingly qualified as special operations JTACs as the skillset came in high demand by U.S. Special Forces teams.

Upon my acceptance into special operations I underwent even more specialized training—demolitions, advanced tactical shooting, CQC (close quarters combat), helicopter alternate infiltration techniques, and JTAC tactics specific to special operations. I'd also become qualified as an Army Pathfinder just before transitioning into special operations, and that further broadened the capabilities I could bring to the teams that I'd soon be attaching to.

In the years to follow I deployed with Special Forces teams in the ongoing fight against the Taliban and al-Qaeda in Afghanistan. By 2014, I was a well-vetted and experienced JTAC with solid conventional and special operations experience under my belt. My rocky path over the years—striving, fighting, and sacrificing in both my life and career so many times—seemed to finally have a purpose.

That summer, I was picked as part of the small special operations force dispatched by President Obama to secure Iraq against the urgent threat of ISIS. Demonstrating an evolved brand of terrorism more brutal than anything any of us had ever seen, ISIS was then proving itself to be among the most cruel and ruthless villains in recent modern history.

From 2014 through 2017 I deployed as the senior Air Force special operations JTAC for Army Special Forces and Navy Special Warfare (Green Beret and SEAL) task forces throughout the Middle East. As the war against ISIS progressed into a multi-nation campaign spread across Iraq, Syria, and Afghanistan, I'd have the honor and privilege of hunting the caliphate on all three fronts.

CHAPTER 2

Through the Eyes of a JTAC

WES BRYANT

Fall 2005

The sun shined over southern Afghanistan as we pushed north through the center of Kandahar city in a small convoy of lightly armored Humvees that comprised our infantry company headquarters element.

Alex, my partner and JTAC-in-training (termed *ROMAD*), had gotten us some coffee from the *Green Beans* coffee shop on Kandahar Air Base just before we'd rolled out. A big fan of the dichotomies found in life, I enjoyed driving through the war-torn city on a combat operation while indulging in the wholly American luxury of a hot caffé mocha. It was a long drive, though, and the coffee was a short solace.

Kandahar was a bustling Afghan metropolis. It had large multi-lane roads, tall buildings, restaurants, coffee shops, and markets—it was the definition of "urban sprawl" with people seemingly on top of one another. It seemed to me like a Mad Max version of civilization—trying to copy the West, but not quite getting it right. If you added in war-ravaged infrastructure and incredibly weary and suspicious citizens, then you'd have the complete picture.

Alex drove us along as our convoy made its way to the other side of Kandahar to begin the long trek north on dry desert roads. A witty Japanese-Hawaiian with a thick islander accent and a penchant for jokes and banter, Alex entertained the two of us with a string of simultaneously insensible and deep conversations about nothing in particular, while blaring songs from *The Killers* and *Fall Out Boy* from his iPod through one of our truck's radio speakers.

We trudged on, and the hours eked by.

We headed through a small village called *Pada*. Pada was in a bit of a green belt—the main road lined equally with mudded huts and walls with lush vegetation. The village was backdropped on nearly all sides by mountains. I thought to myself how beautiful Afghanistan would be were it not for the state of the country.

A few old men glanced our way. Elementary school-aged kids, dirty-faced and disheveled, darted in and out of the huts and jumped on top of a short wall lining the road to get a look at our convoy as it passed. We made our way fairly slowly, since by that point the roads were hard-packed dirt and not paved as they had been through the city. To complicate the drive more, we were being funneled into a narrow gauntlet lined by sturdy mud walls, on a road system never made for the huge width and weight of American armored Humvees.

Northeast of Pada, estimated to be about an hour's drive, was our objective area. There, in a valley characterized by two small villages of *Gumbad* to the north and *Gumbaz* to the south, we would establish our "blocking position." Two other infantry companies were simultaneously advancing into the region via separate avenues of approach tens of kilometers separated from us. Once they got in place and cleared their objectives, our company would then take the "main effort" and push east. Because of that, I had no air assets tasked to me at the time, but things were quiet anyway.

We had a special team in our convoy whose job it was to intercept and monitor enemy communications. As we exited Pada to the north, our interpreter picked up enemy chatter between two men discussing our convoy movement.

"*The Americans have reached Pada,*" a scout relayed.

We knew, then, that at least one individual was watching our activity in Pada and reporting our movement to a Taliban team somewhere north of us. It was a regular tactic of the Taliban—to place scouts masked as villagers to forward-warn about movement of U.S. forces. I requested air support from higher headquarters in order to give us some cover. The communications intercepts continued, and we soon heard them coordinate for an unknown team to "*set up the ambush*" and "*ready the bombs.*"

Our company commander was relatively young, just a first lieutenant. He was the acting company commander while the captain was back home on leave. But he was aggressive. He passed his plan over the radio: Instead of becoming prey, we would be the predators. We would draw the enemy in as they continued to watch and report our movement, making them believe they could easily ambush our slow-moving convoy. Meanwhile, dismounted fire teams—squads of infantrymen—would traverse the rocky terrain above, parallel to the convoy, and intercept the embedded enemy positions. We'd then hit them with heavy weapons from the trucks while I obliterated their positions with airstrikes.

After an hour or so we had no enemy contact and no further communications intercepts had come in. We decided to call their bluff. Since it was nearing nightfall, the company commander finally gave the order to collapse the squads back to the convoy and continue our movement at normal speed. He wanted to get to our blocking position before sundown in order to establish a secure patrol base in the valley while we still had daylight. We pushed ahead with the convoy to pick up our infantry squads that had been shadowing us along the ridgelines. Alex and I were pretty damn disappointed we wouldn't be getting into a fight, after all.

"Pussies," Alex said, referencing the Taliban who must have decided that attacking us was too risky.

I agreed.

The convoy slowed as we linked with our infantry squads. Just then, the platoon sergeant for the platoon that was attached to our headquarters element came running down the road from the north. The truck in front of us stopped. A weathered and experienced fighting man with a dark and swarthy complexion, the platoon sergeant yelled something at the driver I couldn't quite make out. The driver slammed on the gas and raced ahead.

Then the platoon sergeant turned and ran to us. Alex pushed down his armored window. "Get the fuck up there! We've made contact!" the sergeant yelled. Just then, two RPGs (rocket-propelled grenades) impacted the ground to our front-left, about thirty meters away, just as enemy rifle and machine gun fire came inbound.

Here was our ambush.

"Let's go, man!" I yelled to Alex.

Alex was already on the gas. I was head-down in my map sending an update on the ground situation to the set of A-10 Warthogs overhead that I'd called in after the intercepts.

"Hawg, this is *Gunslinger Four-Two*, we're in contact from the north!" I told the pilots.

As I talked the lead pilot's eyes onto where I thought the enemy positions might be, in the back of my mind I registered the strange fact that even though my adrenaline was up, I felt pretty damn controlled. My training took over—I was simply doing the job I was trained to do. The outside influences of a screaming platoon sergeant, rocket-propelled grenades, and gunfire became mere distractions.

I felt stone cold and focused, with no doubt in my mind that we would decimate the enemy before us. We pushed on a few hundred meters. Alex jerked the wheel back and forth to avoid more incoming RPG rounds as they impacted to our sides and front. Then, the convoy abruptly halted.

We were in a wide, open valley. Tall ridgelines to our sides bracketed us east and west. In front, to the general north a couple hundred meters, two mountain peaks towered where the east and west ridgelines terminated. The road cut between them, creating a saddle effect. I had no idea why we stopped. We seemed to be right in the heart of the *kill zone*.

RPG rounds and gunfire blasted around us. I saw the company commander and mortar team sergeant jump out of the truck in front of us. They started running toward the northeast ridgeline, but no one came over the radio to say what the hell the plan was.

"Grab your shit and get out!" I yelled to Alex.

I made sure my radio was seated in its pouch on my body armor and threw open the heavy armored Humvee door, fully intent on catching up with the company commander. Alex and I got out of the truck. We saw other soldiers up and down the convoy doing the same.

We were taking fire from at least three directions, but the enemy was so dug in on the high ground and concealed behind rocks we couldn't make any of them out. We tried to return fire on an enemy we couldn't see, on a ridgeline far above us. Worse, the company commander was nowhere to be seen. He'd run toward the rocky terrain at the foothills of the northeast ridge and was out of sight.

"Alex, get the L-T on the team net!"

I needed to get in touch with the ground commander. I continued to work to find any enemy locations as Alex tried to raise him on his FM radio, but the lieutenant never answered. I instructed the pilots to try to make out any enemy positions on the ridgeline. I passed distances and directions to locations I thought we were taking fire from, but the pilots had a hard time pinpointing the origin of any enemy fire or making out anyone at all on the ridgelines. (If you've ever tried to pick out a couple of robed men hiding among man-sized rocks on a desert mountain ridgeline from 15,000 feet in the air while flying 270 knots—you'd understand why.)

My ground commander—the lifeline to my awareness of friendly force locations and ability to pinpoint enemy positions with information from our most forward soldiers—was nowhere to be found. And he wouldn't answer the net. I didn't see any point in running blind into the foothills to figure out wherever he had scrambled off to. If we didn't find him, then we'd risk being completely disconnected from the rest of the force.

Rounds continued pelting the ground around us. We ran for cover in a *wadi*—a small ditch—along with the mortar team that had stayed back when their sergeant ran off with the company commander. A couple of our Afghan Army soldiers got in the *wadi* along with us. They fired their AK-47s blindly into the ridgelines.

One of the Afghan soldiers looked at us then yelled, in broken English, "I am going to fire!"

Before we could register what he'd said, the ear-numbing boom of the backblast from his RPG launcher slammed into both of us. He'd fired at the northwest ridgeline while standing right next to us and hadn't taken the time to clear his backblast area before pulling the trigger. Alex and I took the brunt of the auditory shock.

"Fuckin' idiot!" Alex yelled.

The Afghan soldier realized his mistake and gestured an apology in the Afghan way—nodding his head toward his shoulder in an effort to feign "*sorry*."

Alex and I weren't wearing the nice, cushy closed-ear communications headsets with advanced hearing protection that would become standard issue years later—my unit couldn't afford those back then. We were still using old "H-250" radio handsets, straight from the Vietnam era, that you had to hold up to your ear and use like a phone with a push-to-talk button.

The incoming fire had already been doing a number on my ears. With the shock of the RPG, I realized that if I got much more I wouldn't be able to talk to my pilots on the radio because I'd be temporarily deaf. As ridiculous as it felt, I kneeled in the *wadi* for cover as I put my earplugs in. I needed to ensure my ability to continue doing what I was paid to do.

The three-pronged attack, the chaotic disarray of our soldiers' locations, the loss of contact with my ground commander, and the blast to my ears created a mess of shit that I'm not sure I was quite ready for, but I kept on nonetheless.

"Get *Legion Six* on the net, Alex. We need to find out where his guys are!"

"He's not answering on the company or platoon net!" Alex came back, just as frustrated.

Rounds still hammered all around, and I had yet to figure out where all our guys were let alone where the enemy was. Half the platoon was out of sight, and the other half was scattered up and down the road along our convoy right in the kill zone.

THWAP! A sixty-millimeter mortar round launched from its tube next to us. The mortar team had quickly "laid-on" one of their 60mm mortar tubes in order to get at least some effects up on the ridgelines.

SCHWACK! The high-explosive round hit near the top of the northwest peak.

I ran up to the mortar team leader. "Wha' d'ya got up there?!"

"Taliban on top of that ridge, for sure," he replied through scores of incoming and outgoing gunfire. "They're the ones firing the RPGs. I saw the last one come from there!" He pointed at a spot up on the peak.

"Do you have comms with Legion Six? We haven't been able to raise him!"

"Yeah…at least I got him a bit ago!" He tried again to raise the lieutenant on his radio but got no response.

At least we had an enemy location, I thought. I could work on getting the pilot's eyes on the position and ready to strike while Alex kept trying to raise the lieutenant on the net to lock down all our friendly locations and get final approval to clear the strike.

THWAP! The mortar team sent another round up on the northwest ridge.

My lead pilot got his eyes on the general location, even though he couldn't make out individual fighters. Still, I couldn't approve a strike without go ahead from the lieutenant and up-to-date information on where all his guys were. For all I knew, some of them could have been making their way up the northwest ridge on the north side that was masked from our vantage point. In a worst-case scenario, I would risk a strike inadvertently going long of the target and hitting them, or at the least sending fragmentation their way.

"We can throw some *Willie-Pete* down for marking," the lead Warthog pilot came back as an option.

Willie-Pete referred to air-to-ground rockets used primarily for marking rounds. They ignited an incendiary, toxic, white phosphorus smoke. They were great for marking targets, but could be very dangerous to any nearby friendly troops. They were also unguided and known to stray off course. I didn't want to risk throwing marking rounds down.

"Stand by, I'm still not in comms with the ground commander," I told him.

SHEEEEWWWWW...SMACK!

Another enemy RPG whistled over our heads. It struck the low-lying rocks just a few meters in front of us off the west side of the road. The only thing that saved us—it was a dud.

Thank the gods for expired Communist ammunition, I thought.

Gunfire rang continuously.

Then, the platoon medic came running toward us with a look of urgency and despair. With him—the company commander and mortar team sergeant.

"JTAC!" the medic yelled. He slowed as he approached, leaned with his hands on his knees and huffed for a few seconds.

"JTAC...I need you to pass up a MEDEVAC. The MEDEVAC net isn't answering."

I wasn't surprised. We were out of range for the FM frequency that the MEDEVAC net worked on, and our location in the low-lying valley would preclude any chance of making communication anyway. I knew we needed to use my satellite communications to send up the MEDEVAC request to higher headquarters.

The company commander interjected long enough to tell us that one of his infantry fire teams had been pinned down on the northeast ridge by enemy fighters up on the peak. I told him that we were ready to strike that location on his call, but he told me he still didn't know where his other squad was, and some of the guys were making their way to the top of the ridge in a counterassault—they'd be too close to risk a strike. He ordered me to just concentrate on the MEDEVAC.

The medic ran back to tend to our casualties. I asked the lead Warthog pilot if he could relay the MEDEVAC request to save the time it would take for me to set up my portable satellite antenna and make the call myself. After all, he was flying a multi-million-dollar communications and weapons platform. He was right on it.

In the time it took me to coordinate the MEDEVAC, the lieutenant had run off again.

A couple of our truck gunners were firing .50 caliber machine guns toward the east from the turrets of two Humvees.

"Aaaay!" I called through the gunfire. "Where did Legion Six go?!"

One of the soldiers pointed to a ridgeline to our southeast. "Headed to the top of that ridge!" he yelled.

Alex and I started running to the foothills of the southeast ridge to catch up with the ground commander. Then, the medic came running up again from behind us, this time with one of the young infantrymen.

"JAYYY-TAC!"

We stopped as he approached, heaving.

"JTAC…" the medic huffed, "change the MEDEVAC to two wounded, one KIA."

The young infantry private stood next to him, a glazed look of shock on his face. Quietly, the private interjected. "Doles' been hit," he said, despair gripping his voice.

Alex and I looked at one another. I felt a choking in my throat. I gathered myself.

"Alright. I'll pass the update, man."

Meanwhile, the rest of the squad on the northeast ridge—along with two French commandos who'd attached to our unit for the operation—assaulted the enemy position on the northeast peak and killed two Taliban fighters. Gunfire eventually calmed down as the rest of the fierce Taliban ambushers withdrew into the mountains, easily evading us.

Alex and I made our way to an overwatch position on the southeast peak. I continued to control the A-10s while he controlled two Apache gunship helicopters, scanning the valley and ridgelines for any more enemy fighters as the MEDEVAC helicopters made their approach.

Two Blackhawks landed in the valley below, spinning rotor blades blasting desert sand in a gritty whirlwind. Medics and security elements kneeled, protecting the littered casualties. Alex and I exchanged solemn looks. We watched our casualties, in black covered litters, loaded onto the helicopters.

All in all, two U.S. and two Afghan soldiers had been hit during the fighting. One Afghan was wounded in the arm and the other shot in the neck, dying instantly. Of our Americans, one took a through-and-through gunshot to his lower back from a sniper we later discovered was likely hiding among an Afghan nomad caravan in the valley to the southeast. He miraculously survived—the medic thanking me for the rapid MEDEVAC, insisting the soldier had only made it because he'd gotten to surgery before he bled out. I didn't take credit, I was just glad for it.

Our second American casualty was hit by the same sniper while charging the northeast peak, in a brave counterassault on the Taliban fighters holding the position at the top. He died on the battlefield. Staff Sergeant John Doles was an esteemed infantry squad leader. He had been among the few soldiers to parachute into Iraq during the initial invasion in 2003. America lost a valiant soldier and family man that day.[1]

Over the course of the next few months I would rain down fire with airstrikes across the Taliban-infested mountains and valleys in the Kandahar region. But that wouldn't bring back anyone we lost on that day or any other. I blamed myself for the casualties. A JTAC's existence was to

---

1   Joseph Giordono, "Italy-based soldier killed fighting Afghan insurgents," *Stars and Stripes*, October 5, 2005, accessed September 11, 2018, https://www.stripes.com/news/italy-based-soldier -killed-fighting-afghan-insurgents-1.39160.

be the firepower that rained death on the enemy and protected the lives of his brothers (and sisters). I was on the ground not just to hunt the enemy, but to safeguard friendly forces, and I felt I'd failed at both.

On every mission throughout the years following, the scars from that day always burned brightly in the back of my mind. The memories never left me; but drove me to be better. I became determined that my most succinct goal as a JTAC was to kill as many of the enemy as I could while never allowing another friendly casualty to happen on my watch. That attitude would stay with me through more deployments over the years and become reinforced when I transitioned into special operations.

I scarcely could have known at the time, but almost a decade later I would carry those same lessons and that same determination into an entirely different fight using an evolved method of war fighting. In 2014, as we hunted the brutal enemy known as ISIS in Iraq, the echoes from years past in Afghanistan resounded loudly in my mind. I may then have been controlling airstrikes from a strike cell miles away from our partner Iraqi forces on the ground—but I was still there with them. In their moments of need, they were my brothers just the same.

In the scope of my job as a JTAC, I saw no difference. When our partner forces battled ISIS, I understood their perspective, emotion, and urgency for the close air support they counted on. Most importantly, I understood damn well the consequences of getting it wrong.

CHAPTER 3

A Stage Set in Syria

DANA PITTARD

July 2013

I deployed to the Middle East for the final time in my career for what I thought would be a one-year tour as the deputy commanding general for the U.S. Army Central Command (USARCENT).

My commander was Lieutenant General James Terry, based at Shaw Air Force Base in South Carolina. Lieutenant General Terry reported to General Lloyd Austin, the CENTCOM commander. As Terry's senior forward-deployed subordinate, I had responsibility for over 18,000 U.S. Army personnel in eighteen countries across the Middle East and Southwest Asia. We were headquartered in Kuwait, about forty-five minutes from the capital of Kuwait City.

I was simultaneously the commander of CENTCOM Forward in Jordan (CF-J), reporting to General Austin in Tampa, Florida. My headquarters for CF-J was near Jordan's capital of Amman. As the leader of CF-J, my mission was to provide support and training for the Jordanian armed forces, support humanitarian operations for refugees, support the U.S. ambassador to Jordan as needed, and work with Jordanian and U.S. agencies as necessary to closely monitor the situation in Syria.

My original plan was to spend three weeks at my headquarters in Jordan and one week in Kuwait each month. However, tensions in Syria changed that plan swiftly, and I ended up spending nearly all of my first five months in Jordan.

Jordan was a fascinating country. It had an extremely dry climate and was, in fact, the fourth most arid nation in the world. There were few natural resources in Jordan, so it was a relatively poor country with a population of only six million—over half of them Palestinian. Jordan was officially a constitutional monarchy ruled by King Abdullah II, whose father, the late King Hussein, had been revered by both the military and the people of Jordan. By sharing borders with nations such as Israel, Syria, Iraq, and Saudi Arabia, Jordan was strategically placed in a very rough neighborhood of the world.

The outbreak of the Syrian Civil War in 2011 made living in that "neighborhood" even tougher for Jordan.[1] The Syrian Civil War was a multi-sided conflict fought primarily between the government of President Bashar al-Assad and his allies and at least 1,100 different armed opposition groups. Millions of Syrians had fled to other countries, primarily in the Middle East and Europe.

The civil war placed an unbelievable amount of political, economic, military, and humanitarian pressure on Jordan. When I arrived in 2013, Jordan was in a full-blown humanitarian crisis due to the arrival of between 500,000 and 750,000 Syrian refugees who'd fled the violence in Syria. The Zaatari refugee camp in Jordan, administered by the United Nations, became the second largest refugee camp in the world.

I sometimes felt like I was in the calm before the storm. The Jordanian leadership, led by King Abdullah II, was rightfully concerned about the civil war across the border in Syria spilling into northern Jordan. I visited the Jordan-Syria border several times. Jordanian border guards could watch, from their towers and checkpoints, the ongoing fighting between the Syrian Army and various rebel factions in southern Syria.

The powerful Muslim Brotherhood, which had taken control of Egypt during the "Arab Spring" of 2011, had a following in Jordan.[2] However, King Abdullah's secret police fully infiltrated the Muslim Brotherhood

---

1   The Editors of Encyclopaedia Britannica, "Syrian Civil War," *Encyclopaedia Britannica*, July 6, 2011, accessed April 24, 2018, https://www.britannica.com/event/Syrian-Civil-War.
2   NPR Staff, "The Arab Spring: A Year Of Revolution," *NPR*, December 17, 2011, accessed April 24, 2018, http://www.npr.org/2011/12/17/143897126/the-arab-spring-a-year-of-revolution.

and kept dissent way down. That, coupled with some effective reforms, actually helped the Jordanian people to stay loyal and not turn against Jordan's royal family.

The U.S. ambassador to Jordan at that time was Stuart Jones—a career diplomat originally from the Philadelphia, Pennsylvania area. I enjoyed listening to his Philly accent because my mother and many members of my family were originally from Philadelphia. I liked Ambassador Jones, and I appreciated the way he accepted our small but growing U.S. military footprint in Jordan.

In Amman we found common ground with the U.S. embassy staff. As the commander of CF-J, having access to the embassy staff was very helpful as we pieced together a picture of the ongoing conflict in Syria.

The U.S. government provided low-level support to moderate Syrian rebels. The program was well-run by some very professional and experienced people who I thought very highly of. They pushed the moderate Syrian rebels through a three-to-six-week training cycle. It was a small program that was making some gains in southern Syria.[3]

I asked some of the people running the training program if they thought the program could be expanded to increase the flow of trained moderate Syrian rebels. I surmised that even more trained and equipped moderate rebels could make a difference in the fight against Bashar al-Assad. The personnel patiently answered that they were training as many recruits as possible, but there simply weren't enough moderate Syrian recruits who wanted to return to Syria and fight.

The trainers mentioned that many U.S. politicians wanted to see the program expanded, but the trainers had adamantly responded, in not so many words, "We can't 'shit' new moderate Syrian recruits willing to fight."

There were simply not enough military-aged males in the Syrian refugee population interested in returning to Syria to fight Bashar al-Assad's regime—not to mention the other enemy rebel factions such as al-Qaeda-linked al-Nusra Front and the early seedlings of ISIS.

---

3   Fabrice Balanch, "The End of the CIA Program in Syria," *Foreign Affairs*, August 2, 2017, accessed January 27, 2019, https://www.foreignaffairs.com/articles/syria/2017-08-02/end-cia-program-syria.

The number of rebel factions in Syria that could be considered "moderate" was dwindling fast. There were also huge potential logistical challenges that would have to be overcome, and questions needed to be answered with the prospect of expanding a U.S.-trained rebel force in Syria: Who would lead it? How would they be sustained? Would we provide the moderate rebels with heavy weapons such as machine guns and mortars so that they could adequately respond to the Syrian Army in a firefight? Would we provide close air support? Would we provide medical evacuation capability in Syria? Without U.S. advisors accompanying them, the moderate rebels likely wouldn't get air support, artillery support, or medical evacuation capability.

I greatly admired and respected the trainers. They were dedicated American patriots who were tough, committed, and skilled. I believed them when they said it would be damn near impossible to expand the program without significantly more moderate recruits—and those numbers were just not available.

The Guns of August 2013
Wednesday, August 21, 2013

That morning, as we closely monitored the situation in Syria, it became evident that something was wrong. During our early morning update brief we were informed there was a possible chemical attack in the Damascus suburb of Ghouta.[4]

Soon, videos of the aftermath of the attack surfaced and were seen by the entire world. The scenes of innocent dead civilian men, women, and children were sickening. Syrian rebels immediately blamed pro-Assad forces, and the Syrian government blamed the rebels. Russia and Iran disputed whether the Syrian government was to blame, but the rest of the world nearly universally condemned the Assad regime.

At CF-J, the reports of the chemical attack in Syria raised our eyebrows. We spoke to our higher headquarters at both USARCENT and

4   Joby Warrick, "More than 1,400 Killed in Syrian Chemical Weapons Attack, U.S. Says," *The Washington Post*, August 30, 2013, accessed April 24, 2018, https://www.washingtonpost.com/world/national-security/nearly-1500-killed-in-syrian-chemical-weapons-attack-us-says/2013/08/30/b2864662-1196-11e3-85b6-d27422650fd5_story.html?utm_term=.48600701b60a.

CENTCOM who were also watching the situation closely. A week earlier, we'd had a visit by General Martin L. Dempsey, the U.S. Chairman of the Joint Chiefs of Staff and principal military advisor to President Barack Obama. He'd reiterated the U.S. policy that America would act if Assad used chemical weapons. In fact, only a year previous in 2012, President Obama had stated that the regime's use of chemical weapons would constitute a "red line" that would draw us into action.

We consulted with our Jordanian military counterparts who had some amazing contacts in Syria. Their sources told them the chemical attack was real, and that over 1,000 Syrian Sunni Arabs and their families who were opposed to Assad had been killed. Further, they said the order probably came from someone high up in the Assad regime.

Over the next nine days, CENTCOM and the American military sprang into action. Video-teleconferences between the CENTCOM commander and all component commands, including mine in Jordan, went from weekly to daily. We reviewed contingency plans, consulted our allies, and moved naval ships and aircraft into strike positions. Our Arab allies were absolutely behind us and supported America striking Syria.

I felt it was our moral obligation to keep our word. Our President had said that the use of chemical weapons by the regime would cross a "red line." Bashar al-Assad and the Syrian regime had crossed that red line by conducting a chemical attack that killed an estimated 1,400 innocent civilians.

During the nine days between August 21 and August 30, we received more VIP visits than we'd had in the previous six months. The Special Operations Command (SOCOM) Commander, Admiral Bill McRaven, stopped by to visit our special ops troops. I had a lot of respect for him as the senior military leader behind the raid into Pakistan that had killed Osama Bin Laden in 2011.[5] He was very personable, and he gave us some advice and context. Republican Senator Bob Corker from Tennessee and other congressional leaders visited as well in order to become better informed on the situation in Syria and the region.

General Lloyd Austin, the CENTCOM commander and a man who I greatly admired, came through Jordan to assess our status. We were the

---

5   Nicholas Schmidle, "Getting Bin Laden," *The New Yorker*, August 8, 2011, accessed September 12, 2018, https://www.newyorker.com/magazine/2011/08/08/getting-bin-laden.

closest American military forces to the Syrian border. If Syria tried to retaliate against the U.S. following an American strike, it was most likely going to be against our personnel in Jordan and possibly U.S. military personnel in Turkey.

We went over our internal defensive procedures with GEN Austin as well as our mutual defense procedures with the Jordanian military force responsible for outer security of our compound. We consulted closely with the senior leaders of the Jordanian military.

Toward the end of his one-day visit, General Austin took me aside and gave me his view of what would probably happen against Syria: America would likely conduct a punitive strike—only the size and scale of the attack was then being discussed within the White House and the Pentagon. He and I went over possible procedures and countermeasures in the event of a Syrian response to our attack. I also discussed contingency procedures with LTG Terry.

Before he departed Jordan, General Austin's last words to me were, "Be ready Dana."

By Thursday, August 29, our contingency plans were in place. U.S. ships, submarines, aircraft, special operations forces, logistical capabilities, and more were staged and ready. It was amazing to see how quickly CENTCOM and the Pentagon had prepared for action—giving President Obama and the administration a host of military options.

That same day, the British Parliament voted to not take part in any military action against Syria. It was a stunning blow to U.K. Prime Minister David Cameron as the first time in decades that a British prime minister was unable to deliver troops to a joint military operation with the United States. The U.K. Parliament vote was also a blow to the U.S. Still, there were reports that President Obama was prepared to act alone without British help.

That same day as well, General Dempsey briefly visited Jordan again. We met at a joint U.S.-Jordanian air base in north-central Jordan. After the visit, he and I went on the rooftop of the command building so we could speak privately. I had known General Dempsey for years—he'd been one of my mentors.

"Sir, what do you think is really going to happen?" I asked. "Will we go it alone?"

"Just be ready Dana," he replied solemnly. "Depending on the Syrian reaction, this could escalate into something bigger than anticipated."

I got the message.

An Opportunity Lost
Friday, August 30, 2013

As we continued to prepare for all contingencies, we watched on the news as Secretary of State John Kerry made the case to the American people for military action.[6] He detailed a report from the U.S. intelligence community that held the Assad regime as responsible for the August 21 chemical attack in Ghouta.

On Saturday morning, our CF-J chief of staff, Colonel Jay Gallivan, and my deputy, Brigadier General Joe Harrington, had ensured that our entire headquarters in Jordan was ready for action. We checked and rechecked our procedures and took part in exhaustive final planning briefings via video-teleconference with CENTCOM. The mission to strike was all but a go, and we were just a few hours away from the start of the first U.S. attack against the Syrian regime.

By that evening, most of the staff at the CF-J headquarters were glued to the television monitors as President Obama spoke from the White House Rose Garden. We all gasped when President Obama announced that he would seek congressional approval for U.S. military action in Syria.[7]

To us on the front lines, his announcement did not seem very decisive. Even worse, he opted not to call Congress back into session immediately which delayed any potential action on our part considerably. Over the next ten days, congressional support was weak.

By September 9, Vladimir Putin and the Russians had diplomatically outmaneuvered the Obama administration and enacted a plan for

---

6   Washington Post Staff, "FULL TRANSCRIPT: Secretary of State John Kerry's Remarks on Syria on Aug. 30," *The Washington Post*, August 30, 2013, accessed April 24, 2018, https://www.washingtonpost.com/world/national-security/running-transcript-secretary-of-state-john-kerrys-remarks-on-syria-on-aug-30/2013/08/30/f3a63a1a-1193-11e3-85b6-d27422650fd5_story.html?utm_term=.35a161ee6b42.

7   Peter Baker and Jonathan Weisman, "Obama Seeks Approval by Congress for Strike in Syria," *The New York Times*, August 31, 2013, accessed April 24, 2018, https://www.nytimes.com/2013/09/01/world/middleeast/syria.html.

Syria to hand over its chemical weapons to Russia and the international community. Assad agreed to the Russian plan.

Over the next seventy-two hours, CENTCOM and our U.S. military forces in the region underwent a massive stand down. An opportunity to strike Syria—and subsequently add known targets such as the al-Qaeda-linked al-Nusra Front and the first units of ISIS—had been lost. The only consolation was that the majority of Syria's chemical munitions were ultimately destroyed under the international plan brokered by Russia.

CHAPTER 4

As Vultures Nest

WES BRYANT

In 2013, as a special operations JTAC, I could not have cared less what was happening in Iraq or Syria. We'd already pulled out of Iraq, and we weren't even in Syria. Our world was Afghanistan—especially after the full withdrawal of conventional forces and the war becoming sole ownership of special operations.[1]

As for Syria with its internal conflict, it was a world away. I easily dismissed it as just another Middle Eastern country imploding, the norm in that part of the world. It didn't necessarily mean people like me were going to be employed to do anything about it. My mind was on the mission at hand.

Later that year, representatives in Washington and senior military leaders like Major General Pittard would wrestle with the world-altering strategic decision of whether or not to launch military strikes on the Syrian regime. But as such events unfolded, men like me trudged away on the relentless Afghanistan front with few people back home even realizing we were still waging war there.

---

1   Rick Hampson, "Drawn-out Afghanistan War Drains Post-9/11 Fervor," *USA Today*, September 5, 2013, accessed April 24, 2018, https://www.usatoday.com/story/news/nation/2013/09/05/911 -anniversary-afghanistan-war-syria/2771437/.

Small wonder I was at the peak of frustration. It was nearly twelve years since U.S. forces had pushed into Afghanistan to take vengeance for 9/11. We'd fully invaded and uprooted the Taliban government, yet failed to prevent the development of a formidable insurgency against pro-U.S. Afghan forces and the government that we'd helped emplace. In Afghanistan we were constantly taking ground, losing it, and then taking it again—an endless cycle to nowhere.

The ongoing failure in Afghanistan was a result of inconsistent and wavering strategies. Over the years we'd endured ongoing shifts in operational and tactical focus, ever-changing rules of engagement based on the political flavor of the day, and the fears and criticisms of public perception. Topping it off, we'd gone through countless changes in troop numbers, culminating in an ineffective and unnecessary troop surge that only preceded a monumental withdrawal. It all added to one big mess that was the war in Afghanistan.

Somewhere along the way, leadership came up with a name for the implementation of the new U.S. strategy against terrorism: "counterinsurgency" or *COIN*. "COIN" became a phrase vastly popular among military leaders once a doctrinal and operational manual was published on the subject. *Joint Publication 3-24, Counterinsurgency*, became the Department of Defense doctrinal manual for COIN. It defined insurgency as "the organized use of subversion and violence to seize, nullify, or challenge political control of a region," and counterinsurgency as "a comprehensive civilian and military effort designed to simultaneously defeat and contain insurgency and address its root causes."[2]

In over two hundred pages, the excellent manual detailed guidance for the implementation of COIN operations. In reality, though, COIN ended up amounting to little more than a fancy catchphrase because, to be successful in Afghanistan, we needed more than a doctrinal manual. We needed clear intent from Washington and the Pentagon via a well-coordinated and well-communicated strategy and precisely defined operational guidance. Down at the warfighter level, that was 100 percent nonexistent.

---

2   "Joint Publication 3-24, Counterinsurgency," Joint Chiefs of Staff, April 25, 2018, accessed January 27, 2019, https://www.jcs.mil/Portals/36/Documents/Doctrine/pubs/jp3_24.pdf?ver=2018-05-11 -102418-000.

The Poppies of Nangarhar
Spring 2013

I was with a Special Forces team in Afghanistan's eastern Nangarhar Province securing a district named Khogyani—a historical hotbed of Taliban activity and sanctuary to the most "named objectives" in the region.

When the military or other agencies gained ample intelligence on a key enemy leader, coordinator, or facilitator, he would be put onto a classified kill/capture list. He'd then become an "objective." That objective would be given a codename, and a primary mission of special operations was to hunt and capture or, in many cases, kill such named objectives.

Our camp sat atop a small hill just north of a modest village, with brilliant multi-colored fields of opium poppies surrounding us for miles. The village was the district center. A "district" in Afghanistan was similar to a U.S. county, its center typically the largest city in the district, containing the seat of local governance for the area. The district center was comprised mainly of *qalat* (mud hut) residences, with a smattering of masonry buildings that were mostly local government offices and police and military compounds.

A few kilometers south of the district center stood the snow-capped Spin Ghar mountain range, with rich white peaks reaching up to more than 15,000 feet. A range that divided Pakistan and Afghanistan, Spin Ghar was a stunningly beautiful backdrop to one of the most dangerous places in the world. To me, the mountains were noble and benevolent giants sitting majestically still—ever-reminding us that the human war we waged below was of little consequence in the large scope of things.

Those giants were not wholly untouched by our wars, though. The mountain range contained a region otherwise known as *Tora Bora*, the location of the first major fight of the Afghanistan War in winter of 2001 when our special operations units had tried to capture Osama bin Laden there and he escaped into Pakistan. I'd soon spend days freezing in its hills when my team responded to an Apache helicopter shot down and destroyed while on reconnaissance through the remote Taliban village havens.

My Special Forces team was busy. They'd taken two casualties in an ambush just weeks before I'd come in. The team wasn't in any mood to pussyfoot around. We went on regular clearing operations to root out

Taliban leadership and fighting networks in the region. We orchestrated "hits" against named objectives—pushing out at a moment's notice on precision raids when we received real-time intelligence on their locations. We met with local leaders to elicit information and ensure the economic, political, and financial needs of the populace were met.

In war, offense truly is the best defense. Despite the American political climate at the time, we did whatever was necessary to secure our mission and stay safe in our small camp on the hill surrounded by Taliban. We executed night raids to keep pressure on local Taliban networks, while guidance from higher was that no forces were to conduct night raids without special approval. We held and interrogated captured fighters and facilitators to pull vital information from them, while senior leadership instructed our forces to turn prisoners over to Afghan officials. (All too often, prisoners would be released within weeks, even *days*, through connections within the Afghan government or because of undermanned and underfunded governmental structures—only to be right back out fighting us again.)

In exchange for safe haven of their opium poppy fields, we constantly elicited information from locals about Taliban locations and activity, while elsewhere in the country other U.S. special operations teams were facilitating massive poppy eradication efforts by the Afghan government. Opium poppies were the financial foundation for many of the locals, helping them feed their families, but most of the revenue made its way into the hands of the Taliban and eventually funded their operations against the Afghan government—and us. Letting the locals keep their poppies was a delicate balance, but we were keeping them on our side. Since there was a heavy presence of "shadow" governance in the region— the Taliban "government" working behind the scenes—keeping the locals on our side was key to uprooting it.

Our mission was constantly encumbered by the strangling policies instated by higher leadership. Even when teams like ours sidestepped the impeding guidance—as much as we could get away with—we were still dangerously handcuffed. We were regularly told our primary goal was to "win the hearts and minds of the people." Although we all knew that was an important facet of the mission, it was only one small part—and yet it seemed to dominate the operational environment. The cautious mindset among senior military leadership led to restrictions on approval for certain types of missions, strict limits on the use of air-to-ground ordnances for close air support, and severe restrictions on approval criteria for airstrikes.

While we understood that the welfare and well-being of the Afghan people were extremely important, our policies in Afghanistan crossed a line that often led to the needless endangerment of troops on the ground. As a military, year after year we continued taking casualties from both direct fire and improvised bombs. Many of those enemy attacks were successful because most U.S. forces had been reduced to routine and predictable security and assistance patrols on the same routes to the same places, time and again. To top it off, U.S. personnel were constantly vulnerable to attacks by Taliban infiltrators within the very Afghan forces they embedded with. Referred to as *green-on-blue* attacks, they caused casualty after casualty within our ranks.

Because of all that, there was a strong belief among warfighters that higher leadership placed *not just* the lives—but the *perceptions* of the Afghan people above the welfare of U.S. warfighters. At the tactical and operational level, the morale was so bad it was a regular mantra pushed down from higher leadership to just "put the politics aside" and "concentrate on the mission."

To many of us, we were no closer to handing over a stable country to the Afghan people in 2013 than we had been ten years prior. Needless to say, it was extremely difficult to put personal feelings aside when most of us felt like we were sacrificing everything for absolutely nothing.

Years later, in the summer of 2017, I would infill into Afghanistan as the senior Special Tactics JTAC for the Special Operations Task Force-Afghanistan on my final combat deployment. I quickly found that, since I'd last been there, the U.S. had kept an oft non-committal footprint— concentrating more on the heavy fight against ISIS in Iraq and Syria. Because of that, ISIS had crept its way into the very rugged terrain of eastern Afghanistan where I'd trudged four-years previous. They'd gained a strong foothold in a short amount of time and in the process reinvigorated a Taliban network that we'd spent a fruitless decade-plus waging war against. Now, we had to deal with the Taliban *and* ISIS.

Imagine my frustration.

CHAPTER 5

An Enemy Apart

DANA PITTARD

ISIS formed from the remnants of al-Qaeda in Iraq after the U.S. invasion in 2003, its members coming from the more violent and experienced fighters that split off and later fought against al-Qaeda.

The leader of the offshoot was a Jordanian thug turned Islamic extremist whose *nom du guerre* was Abu Musab al-Zarqawi.[1] After fighting the Soviets in Afghanistan, he had moved into Iraq with the insurgency to fight against the United States and its allies after they brought down the government of Saddam Hussein in 2003.[2]

Zarqawi's extremists were strengthened by veteran Sunni fighters who joined the insurgency after the U.S. disbanded Saddam's army. Their numbers grew as the insurgency spread into the Sunni-dominated provinces of western, central, and northern Iraq. Zarqawi's extremists opposed and fought against Iraq's majority population of Shia Muslims.

From 2004 through 2005, I was a brigade commander with the U.S. Army's First Infantry Division known as *The Big Red One* in Diyala Province, Iraq. The leaders and soldiers of my brigade fought several battles

---

1 Jason M. Breslow, "Who Was the Founder of ISIS?" *Frontline*, May 17, 2016, accessed April 24, 2018, http://www.pbs.org/ wgbh/frontline/article/who-was-the-founder-of-isis/.
2 History.com Editors, "Saddam Hussein Captured," *History*, July 21, 2010, accessed April 24, 2018, http://www.history.com/this-day-in-history/saddam-hussein-captured.

against Zarqawi and his fighters. In June 2004, we reportedly slightly wounded Zarqawi in a battle outside of Baqubah, the capital of Diyala Province. Zarqawi was later killed in 2006 by a U.S. airstrike near the town of Hibhib in Diyala Province.

I deployed to Iraq again from 2006 through 2007 as the commanding general of the Iraq Assistance Group. I was responsible for the coalition's hundreds of advisory teams that were assisting Iraqi Security Forces. It was a tough time to be in Iraq. Saddam Hussein's former *Baath Party* had been a part of the ruling Sunni minority. Once Saddam was defeated and removed from power in 2003, the Shia majority had moved to take over Iraq and violence began in earnest.

Following the destruction of the revered Shia holy site in Samarra— the *Golden Dome*—by Zarqawi's Sunni insurgents in February of 2006, Iraq moved to the brink of open civil war between the Sunnis and Shias. Violence peaked during the period from 2006 into 2007 and was marked by the highest number of Americans killed in Iraq.

U.S. and Iraqi security forces defeated Zarqawi's organization— al-Qaeda in Iraq, known as *AQI*—during the surge of U.S. troops between 2007 and 2009. Unfortunately, some of the AQI survivors later escaped to Syria. By 2011 they'd helped form what came to be known as the Islamic State of Iraq and Syria, or ISIS.

ISIS was led by extremist Abu Bakr al-Baghdadi, an Iraqi who'd once been a serious religious scholar and had, in fact, been in U.S. custody in 2006—believed to have been imprisoned at Camp Bucca, Iraq. Under al-Baghdadi's leadership, ISIS established a foothold in Syria, recruiting veteran fighters from more than 1,100 opposition groups fighting to depose Syrian President Bashar al-Assad.

By early 2012, ISIS emerged as a distinct and powerful entity in the Middle East, formed from fighters drawn from the shattered remnants of Zarqawi's AQI and others recruited from hundreds of smaller groups opposed to the oppressive and murderous regime of Bashar al-Assad. Eventually, a third source of manpower emerged in the form of aggressive recruiting throughout the Middle East and the West.

In the summer of 2013, I quickly saw what set ISIS apart. Aside from their fanaticism—marked by the slaughter of innocents and public beheadings—ISIS distinguished itself as an impressive fighting force, one with ambitious plans and a disciplined army to carry them out. They were determined to move into Iraq from Syria and establish an Islamic *caliphate* across the region. Their plan was to rule under ancient *Sharia Law* based on Islamic rule in the 8th century. They intended to establish, essentially, a throwback religious dictatorship in which non-believers were slaughtered and women were regarded as property and sex slaves.

ISIS was sophisticated—not just in its military ability but in its recruitment techniques and use of social media for propaganda purposes. The terrorist group had consolidated its base of support in eastern Syria and prepared to spread its influence to Sunni areas in both Syria and Iraq.

ISIS Captures Fallujah
January 2014

ISIS made its first major regional statement when it launched an attack into western Iraq's Anbar Province and seized the large Sunni city of Fallujah, just sixty-nine kilometers west of Baghdad.[3] That first attack didn't attract much attention in the worldwide media. Unfortunately, it was only the beginning.

I'd had several deployments to the Middle East by then, and I had seen quite a few radical Islamic terrorist groups. None of them, however, were as well financed, highly disciplined, and competently led as ISIS. When ISIS seized Fallujah, Lieutenant General Terry and I expected ARCENT would be called to serve as the initial headquarters to reinforce and support the Iraqi military and/or assist in the evacuation of American citizens out of Baghdad.

The call never came.

Although it was clear that General Austin, as the commander of CENTCOM, took the ISIS threat very seriously, it was not clear whether the Obama administration did. That same month in a profile interview in

---

3   Liz Sly, "Al-Qaeda force captures Fallujah amid rise in violence in Iraq," *The Washington Post*, January 3, 2014, accessed April 24, 2018, https://www.washingtonpost.com/world/al-qaeda-force -captures-fallujah-amid-rise-in-violence-in-iraq/2014/01/03/8abaeb2a-74aa-11e3-8def- a33011492df2_story.html?utm_term=.ec59c5f85778.

The New Yorker magazine, President Obama described the ISIS fighters in Iraq and Syria dismissively as the "JV team."[4]

The statement couldn't have been further from the truth. More decisive action earlier on by the Obama administration in the form of supporting Iraqi Security Forces (ISF) might have stopped ISIS from taking over nearly a third of Iraq by the summer of 2014.

The main reason ISIS gained a foothold in Sunni western Iraq was because of the oppressive policies and harsh treatment of the Iraqi Sunni population by Prime Minister Nouri al-Maliki and his Shia-led government. Al-Maliki had once been supported by the U.S. and had been Prime Minister of Iraq since 2006. But he and his government were heavily influenced and supported by Shia Iran.[5]

Admittedly, the Obama administration was caught between a "rock and a hard place." Supporting al-Maliki against the primarily Sunni ISIS could give the appearance that the administration was anti-Sunni and pro-Iran. Most of the nearly one billion Muslims throughout the world were Sunni—that included our Middle Eastern allies such as Saudi Arabia, Jordan, Kuwait, UAE, and Turkey.

In May 2014, as the situation in Iraq worsened, General Austin ordered us to send a small group of senior U.S. Army and Marine Corps officers to assess and assist the Iraqi Army staff for no more than three to four weeks. As the threat of ISIS in Iraq increased, we decided to keep the assessment group there into mid-June.

ISIS Captures Mosul

By early June we were seeing indicators that ISIS was trying to infiltrate fighters into the Sunni provinces of Ninewa and Salah ad-Din in northern and north-central Iraq. However, it seemed like the Iraqi military had things under control. Four Iraqi Army divisions and one Federal Police

---

4 Shreeya Sinha, "Obama's Evolution on ISIS," *The New Yorker*, June 9, 2015, accessed October 17, 2018, https://www.nytimes.com/interactive/2015/06/09/world/middleeast/obama-isis-strategy.html.
5 Yochi Dreazen, "Maliki Used to Have the Support of Both Iran and the U.S. Now He's Lost Them Both." *Foreign Policy*, August 13, 2014, accessed April 24, 2018, http://foreignpolicy.com/2014/08/13/maliki-used-to-have-the-support-of-both-iran-and-the-u-s-now-hes-lost-them-both/.

division in northern Iraq each had approximately 5,000 personnel, and there were thousands of Iraqi Kurdish Peshmerga troops in the area as well. The Iraqi troops had hundreds of up-armored Humvees, machine guns, mortars, artillery, and even some tanks. The combined forces in the area numbered over 30,000 troops.

On June 4, 2014, Iraqi Security Forces killed the ISIS military chief—Abu Abdul Rahman al-Bilawi—near Mosul. The fact that ISIS' military chief was in Iraq and near Mosul caused alarm bells to go off in both the military and intelligence circles throughout the Middle East. The conventional wisdom at the time was that, whatever ISIS had been planning, the death of their military chief would set them back by weeks or months.

Boy, was that wrong! Bilawi's death so enraged the senior ISIS leadership that they *accelerated* their attack plans. They called their new operation *Bilawi Vengeance* to honor their slain military chief. On June 6, hundreds of pickup trucks carrying ISIS fighters entered Mosul—shooting and suppressing the city's checkpoints and overrunning the Iraqi Army's outer defenses. The ISIS fighters brutally hanged, burned, and crucified Iraqi soldiers during the attack.

Within four days, the ISIS force of 3,000 fighters along with Sunni sympathizers defeated nearly 25,000 Iraqi and Kurdish troops in Mosul.[6] Five Iraqi divisions were overrun by the hyper-aggressive ISIS juggernaut. Many Iraqi soldiers dropped their weapons, changed into civilian clothes, and fled. Thousands of Iraqi soldiers deserted. ISIS captured over 2,300 American-made Humvees and scores of artillery guns, mortars, and other types of Iraqi military equipment.

ISIS killed over 2,500 Iraqi soldiers in the battle and captured thousands more. They also freed at least 300 Sunni inmates from the federal prison in Mosul—most of them joined ISIS immediately. Later, ISIS brutally executed an estimated 4,000 captured Iraqi soldiers and federal police officers and dumped their bodies in the single largest mass grave

---

6   Liz Sly and Ahmed Ramadan, "Insurgents seize Iraqi city of Mosul as security forces flee," *The Washington Post*, June 10, 2014, accessed April 24, 2018, https://www.washingtonpost.com/world/insurgents-seize-iraqi-city-of-mosul-as-troops-flee/2014/06/10/21061e87-8fcd-4ed3-bc94-0e309af0a674_story.html?utm_term=.5eff6b7eee21.

known to date in Iraq—the *Khafsa Sinkhole*. (The mass grave was uncovered by Iraqi troops in 2017 as they were re-capturing Mosul.)[7]

The fall of Iraq's second largest city was an absolute defeat and a humiliation for Iraq and the Iraqi Security Forces. ISIS wasted no time afterward. They sent fighters south to threaten Iraq's largest city and capital—Baghdad. Later that month, Abu Bakr al-Baghdadi boldly preached at the captured Nouri Mosque in Mosul, declaring the creation of an Islamic State *caliphate* spanning much of Syria and Iraq.[8]

In the 2008 and 2012 U.S. presidential elections, President Obama had campaigned on promises to end the U.S. military involvement in Iraq, Afghanistan, and the Middle East. However, we couldn't ignore the aggressive terrorist army that was taking over Iraq and Syria.

The only question was: How would America respond?

---

7   Bianca Britton, "200 mass graves of thousands of thousands of ISIS victims found," CNN, November 6, 2018, accessed November 13, 2018, https://www.cnn.com/2018/11/06/middleeast/mass-graves-isis-un-intl/index.html.

8   "Isis Rebels Declare 'Islamic State' in Iraq and Syria," BBC News, June 30, 2014, accessed April 24, 2018, http://www.bbc.com/news/world-middle-east-28082962.

PART 2

The Iraq Crisis

CHAPTER 6

Defending Baghdad

DANA PITTARD

June 2014

ISIS quickly gained momentum in the Iraqi provinces with large Sunni populations. Governments in the Middle East and worldwide were stunned by the fall of Mosul—the capital of Ninewa Province—while ISIS continued marching southward capturing towns and villages along the Tigris River Valley. ISIS' fighters were superior to al-Qaeda and nearly any other insurgent force we'd ever seen. In fact, their troops often showed considerable courage on the battlefield.

By June, ISIS forces captured Tikrit, the home of Saddam Hussein and capital of Salah ad-Din Province. Then they took the city of Bayji and isolated and surrounded the Bayji Oil Refinery, the largest oil refinery in all of Iraq. They took control of the Bayji prison and freed all the inmates, most of whom subsequently joined ISIS.

In north-central Iraq, Balad Air Base was threatened. In Al Anbar Province in western Iraq, ISIS fighters pressed forward along the Euphrates River Valley threatening the cities of Hit and the provincial capital of Ramadi. They isolated the strategically vital Haditha Dam in Al Anbar in western Iraq, and were looming over the Diyala provincial capital of Baqubah—northeast of Baghdad and not far from the Iranian border. Closer to Baghdad, ISIS captured the towns of Jurf Al Sakhur and Abu Ghraib.

Buoyed by victory after victory, ISIS seemed unstoppable. Their fighters, infiltrators, and sympathizers edged closer and closer to Baghdad—a thriving city of over seven million people. The sounds of violent explosions from roadside bombs, car bombs, and rocket attacks could be heard daily. Thousands of U.S. and western contractors—responsible for assisting the Iraqi military with maintenance, logistics, training, and essential services for tanks, helicopters, aircraft, artillery, and other military equipment—began fleeing in anticipation of ISIS seizing Baghdad. The loss of these contractors soon had a crippling effect on the Iraqi Security Forces' ability to re-constitute their equipment and units. As well, the U.S.-sponsored Iraqi F-16 fighter-bomber training program had to be moved from Balad Air Base in Iraq to the United States for fear ISIS would soon capture Balad.

The U.S. Embassy in Baghdad felt the pressure too. The embassy compound was the largest U.S. diplomatic post in the world, self-sustaining with its own power generation and water source. As the threat grew, the embassy conducted a partial evacuation of its personnel. Roughly one-third of the personnel evacuated to other posts within Iraq—either Erbil in Kurdistan, Basra in Shia-dominated southern Iraq, elsewhere in the Middle East, or back to the United States.

The State Department and the Obama administration debated whether to evacuate the embassy entirely. America's recent experience evacuating the U.S. Embassy in Libya due to the intense militia violence in Tripoli,[1] and the lingering memory of the brutal killing of Ambassador J. Christopher Stevens and others at the U.S. Consulate in Benghazi in 2012[2] were central factors in those discussions.

Pressure increased on the Obama administration from regional allies, the American people, and Congress to do something about ISIS

1   Barbara Starr, Joe Sterling, and Azadeh Ansari, "U.S. Embassy in Libya evacuates personnel," CNN, July 26, 2014, accessed October 24, 2018, https://www.cnn.com/2014/07/26/world/africa/libya-us-embassy-evacuation/index.html.

2   Erica Ryan, "Chronology: The Benghazi Attack And The Fallout," *NPR*, December 19, 2012, accessed October 24, 2018, https://www.npr.org/2012/11/30/166243318/chronology-the-benghazi-attack-and-the-fallout.

and see to the security of the thousands of Americans in Iraq. On June 15, Congressman Mike Rogers—chairman of the House Intelligence Committee—said the situation in Iraq was "as dangerous as it gets," and called for the Obama administration to reunite with Arab nation partners to stop the ISIS surge.[3]

To that, President Obama publicly reiterated that he wouldn't send troops to Iraq, but left open the possibility of military action. In anticipation, the U.S. moved the Navy aircraft carrier USS *George H. W. Bush* into the Arabian Gulf.

The U.S. Sends a Response Force

Within a week of the fall of Mosul, the CENTCOM commander, General Austin, in coordination with the U.S. ambassador in Iraq Steven Beecroft, deployed the Navy's fifty-man FAST platoon and the CENTCOM Crisis Response Force (CRF, pronounced *"kriff"*).[4] Composed of Navy, Army, and Air Force special operations forces, the CRF was led by an extremely competent Navy SEAL officer named Commander Black (name changed for security). The capabilities brought to Baghdad by the response force would prove very useful to our efforts over the next several months.

As the deputy commander of operations for ARCENT, in June 2014 I'd been visiting some of our troops in Egypt's Sinai Desert. Due to the unfolding of the ISIS threat in Iraq, ARCENT was quickly placed in a heightened state of readiness and I soon found I'd been chosen to lead the initial effort into Iraq to protect the U.S. Embassy and assess the ISIS situation. With three previous extended combat command tours to Iraq and as a former Army division commander, I was told I was the choice general to lead the effort.

I arrived back in Kuwait from Egypt and went to Lieutenant General James Terry's forward headquarters right away. James Terry was a serious,

3 Steve Contorno, "Are thousands of Westerners and Americans fighting with extremists in Iraq and Syria?" *Politifact*, June 18, 2014, accessed April 24, 2018, https://www.politifact.com/truth-o-meter/statements/2014/jun/18/mike-rogers/are-thousands-westerners-and-americans-fighting-ex/.

4 David Jackson et al., "Obama is sending 275 U.S. forces to Iraq for embassy security," *USA Today*, June 16, 2014, accessed April 24, 2018, https://www.usatoday.com/story/news/world/2014/06/16/iraq-insurgency/10569133/.

reserved-but-intense north Georgia native with extensive combat leadership experience including three extended combat tours in Afghanistan. He was probably one of the most experienced senior warfighters in the U.S. Army at that time.

His *aide-de-camp*, Major Brian Ducote, opened the door. Brian was an old friend I'd known since he was a young lieutenant. He shook my hand as I stepped into LTG Terry's office. Terry motioned for me to have a seat.

"Dana, we have an interesting mission," he said. "Within the next forty-eight to seventy-two hours, you will take no more than one hundred personnel to the U.S. Embassy in Baghdad and set up a command and control headquarters to assess the situation on the ground."

I nodded, listening raptly as he continued.

"Be prepared to protect American citizens, American property, and—if necessary—evacuate the embassy," he said. "The overall situation is somewhat ambiguous…we know that the numbers we're sending are way too few for the task, but we have to try to stay within our limited guidance."

"What about fighting ISIS, sir?"

Terry looked at me. "That's not our mission, but the situation is still pretty fluid."

General Terry gave me more guidance as we discussed the mission a little further. I relished going into an ambiguous situation, it seemed to be hardwired into my DNA.

"Sir, thank you for your confidence in us," I told him. "We won't let you down."

"I know, Dana," he replied. "That's why you're the one to lead us back into Iraq."

Guests of the State Department

Splitting a rear headquarters to establish a forward headquarters element was not an easy task. Most U.S. Army division and corps headquarters did it routinely in deployments to the Middle East; however, it was not something that ARCENT normally carried out.

Still, we moved quickly. Our headquarters was already split between Kuwait and Shaw Air Force Base in South Carolina, so—with a herculean effort by the forward-deployed ARCENT staff in Kuwait, the main ARCENT staff in South Carolina, and assistance from other U.S. CENTCOM service component commands throughout the Middle East—we formed a joint team made up of Army, Air Force, Marine, and Navy personnel to deploy to Iraq.

Our noncommissioned officer in charge (NCOIC), Operations Sergeant Major Glen Robinson, got the new staff prepared to deploy and operate in Baghdad. Sergeant Major Robinson would stay with me as our senior enlisted advisor during the entire deployment. I knew we also needed a competent and experienced deputy commander. The new Marine Corps Forces Central (MARCENT) commander—Lieutenant General Kenneth McKenzie—jumped at the opportunity to help out. The Marine Corps came through in a big way and sent Brigadier General Robert "Cas" Castellvi—the commanding general of the 45,000 Marines at Camp Lejeune, North Carolina—to be my deputy. Cas Castellvi was extremely talented and would make a huge difference in our future operations in Iraq.

To make it a little easier on our staff in Kuwait, and to take advantage of their experience, I requested that the Iraq Assessment Team we'd sent to Baghdad in early May remain there to temporarily form the core of our new joint command headquarters. The assessment team, led by Army Colonel Eric Timmerman, had already been extended in Iraq beyond their initial three-week mandate. Eric Timmerman would become my new chief of staff, Marine Colonel Ed Abisellan the J3/Operations officer, Marine Lieutenant Colonel John Barnett the J2/Intelligence officer, and Army Colonel Andy Danwin the J4/Logistics officer. Other members of the assessment team filled other vital positions on the staff.

The assessment team became our *advance party* in Iraq. Since they'd already established excellent relations with both the embassy staff and the Iraqi Army staff, they proved to be a godsend for establishing our new headquarters.

Our advance team arrived in Iraq on June 22, less than two weeks after ISIS had invaded the country and seized Mosul. The bulk of the hundred staff officers and NCOs from every branch in the U.S. military arrived the next day. They would form the nucleus of our new command—the Joint Forces Land Component Command-Iraq (JFLCC-I).

I took an Army transport plane with my personal staff and security to the U.S. State Department compound at the Baghdad International Airport (BIAP). As we walked onto the tarmac, I turned to my executive officer, Major "B.J." Pauley.

"We're back!" I told him cheekily. B.J. and I had served in Iraq in the 1st Infantry Division together back in 2004 to 2005.

I received a briefing on the defenses at BIAP, then took a tour of the U.S. compound before hopping on a State Department helicopter for the short flight from BIAP to the U.S. Embassy compound in the *Green Zone*—the secured governance area of Baghdad. As we flew over Baghdad, a bustling city of seven million people, I wondered out loud what the people were thinking about ISIS. We passed over the moat-surrounded Al Faw Palace—once the center of Camp Victory and Camp Liberty where the former U.S. Forces headquarters in Iraq had been located. The massive compound of camps once housed over 60,000 U.S. and coalition troops and was a hub of activity during my last Iraq combat tour in 2006 to 2007. Now it was deserted—the structure and infrastructure mostly gone.

Reluctantly, I wondered if maybe we had left Iraq too soon back in 2011. Would it have changed the current situation? Three years later there we were, back in Iraq. I thought of the former U.S. commanders I'd served under during multiple tours—Lieutenant General Ricardo Sanchez, General George Casey, General David Petraeus, General Ray Odierno, and General Lloyd Austin. I wondered what advice they would give now.

I thought of the tremendous sacrifices of our troops and their families, especially those that died or were wounded between 2003 and 2011. I thought of our fallen comrades, those I had personally known and served with during multiple combat tours. They were all great soldiers and Americans—Colonel Tom Felts, Captain Sean Sims, Command Sergeant Major Steve Falkenburg, Captain Humayun Khan, Sergeant Michael "Shrek" Carlson, Specialist Martin Kondor, Private First Class Lyndon Marcus, and thousands more like them.

Had it all been worth it?

I knew the answer was a somber "yes."

We'd sacrificed so much to give Iraq a chance to be a free country that could determine its own destiny. ISIS had since invaded the struggling sovereign democracy and then occupied a third of Iraq's territory. They assaulted a sovereign democracy that we, as Americans, had helped to create.

Why wasn't there more outrage in America at the ISIS invasion?

In 1990, after Iraqi dictator Saddam Hussein invaded the monarchy of Kuwait, President George H.W. Bush had drawn "a line in the sand" and said, "This will not stand, this aggression against Kuwait."[5] Yet, we seemed to lack the same resolve to help the government and people of Iraq.

After nearly thirteen years of war in Afghanistan and Iraq, most Americans were justifiably war-weary and certainly did not want to get involved in Iraq again. Many blamed Iraq's problems on Iraqi Prime Minister Nouri al-Malaki's unfair policies toward the Sunni minority. Prime Minister al-Malaki's lack of inclusion, and his Shia-dominated regime's overall persecution of the Sunni minority, was despicable to be sure. However, Iraq still deserved a chance to become a sovereign nation—a democracy. ISIS had to be stopped. America had invested too much blood and treasure to *not* assist the struggling young Iraqi democracy we had helped to create. ISIS was an existential threat to Iraq, the region, and even the American homeland. Orders or no orders, we needed to defeat them.

As our State Department helicopter landed in the Baghdad Green Zone heliport, we were absolutely determined to do all that we could to protect the U.S. Embassy and help the Iraqi Security Forces defeat ISIS and get their country back. We believed we could accomplish the task with a relatively small U.S. footprint. It was time for the Iraqis to step up and take their country back—with *assistance* from us.

The key question was: Were *they* up to the task?

When I arrived at the U.S. Embassy, the situation was tense. Many thought that our small group of advisors and staff were there initially to evacuate the embassy. I quickly dispelled that notion, letting everyone know that we were there to conduct multiple missions as orders came

5   "Remarks by President Bush," *Margaret Thatcher Foundation*, August 5, 1990, accessed October 24, 2018, https://www.margaretthatcher.org/document/110704.

down. The ambassador and his staff were just happy we were there to prevent ISIS from overrunning the embassy.

Ambassador Beecroft was fluent in Arabic and had spent decades in the Middle East. He gave me a frank assessment and his overall perspective of the situation. Then I met with Brett McGurk, the White House's man on the ground in Iraq. Brett was very competent, an interesting personality, and had a direct line to the White House staff.

I also met with the Office of Security Cooperation-Iraq (OSC-I), led by U.S. Army Lieutenant General Mick Bednarek. I'd known Mick Bednarek for years and I respected his judgment and perspective. He outranked me, but I did not work for him and we needed his cooperation because he was well respected by all the Iraqi senior military leaders. As it stood, all the conventional operational forces in Iraq under both ARCENT and CENTCOM came under my command. Lieutenant General Bednarek had the mission of supporting the Iraqi military forces with resources and equipment. So, to avoid confusion I would later tell the Iraqis that if they needed beans, bullets, and vehicles to see Mick Bednarek. If they wanted to kill ISIS, they were to talk to me.

Our mission in Baghdad was a unique situation. The military was not completely in charge—we were more like "guests" of the State Department and the U.S. Embassy. There was no Status of Forces Agreement (SOFA) with Iraq at that point, so our legal status there as U.S. military personnel was in question. We were only legally protected under a *diplomatic note*. At first there were a few growing pains with the State Department's rules and procedures, but we were all able to work through the friction.

It wasn't an easy task setting up our headquarters and joint operations center in such a condensed time period. To get us ready as quickly as possible, Colonel Eric Timmerman, Sergeant Major Glenn Robinson, and the team worked around the clock. I'm not even sure if our communications team slept within the first seventy-two hours of arrival.

Within a few short days, we had the JFLCC-I headquarters set up in the embassy's compound. We were now prepared for a possible ISIS attack on Baghdad. We were poised to protect American infrastructure and citizens at both the U.S. Embassy and the Baghdad Airport compound. And, we were ready to assist with the evacuation of U.S. citizens.

CHAPTER 7

The Crisis Response Force

WES BRYANT

June 2014

Throughout the first half of 2014, the operational demand in America's ongoing war on terror was still focused mainly on the special operations mission in Afghanistan. There, as we continued to weed out remaining Taliban and al-Qaeda networks, special operations JTACs were at the forefront of the mission as most of the hunting and killing was done by way of the very airstrikes we controlled.

Earlier that summer I was getting ready for my unit's standard deployment cycle—another infil back to Afghanistan. I was set to attach to a Special Forces team in the ongoing Foreign Internal Defense (FID) mission assisting and accompanying the Afghan National Security Forces (ANSF) against the insurgency in Afghanistan. But in the weeks leading up to the deployment, the threat of ISIS in Iraq seemed to explode overnight. We began receiving constant intelligence updates about the alarming activity of this new, offshoot terrorist cell.

Still, it didn't seem as if anything was going to come of it, not as far as U.S. military action was concerned. As far as we saw it, the intel updates were simply to keep us aware of a developing situation in a country we'd long pulled out of. We kept our focus on the upcoming mission to Afghanistan.

I always tried to relax the last few days before a deployment. I'd strive in earnest to put aside the anxiety of the impending time away and all that could go wrong, and just try to be in the moment with my family. But that wasn't going to happen. A couple of days before we were set to head out, I got a call from my operations chief.

"The mission's changed for a few of you guys, Wes," he started. "You're not going to Afghanistan...that's all I can say here. Show tomorrow morning same time as briefed and you'll get all the info." Before hanging up he quickly added, "Oh, and make sure you pack plenty of civilian clothes instead."

I was enticed. It was the very thing I'd become a special operator for—a last minute tasking to some exotic locale for a mission vital to national security.

The next morning I got the brief. The locale wasn't quite as "exotic" as I'd hoped, but it was definitely a high-profile mission. We were to push into Baghdad to reinforce the special operations CRF tasked by President Obama to respond to the ISIS threat.

The CRF would comprise the first combat troops to hit Iraq since the withdrawal in 2011. Its mission: to defend the Baghdad International Airport and U.S. Embassy from ISIS assault.[1] One of our Combat Control JTACs was already on his way into the Iraqi capital attached to the advance forces of the CRF. As we received our new orders, a handful more of us were soon to follow.

We were told that the CRF's primary mission was strictly to safeguard the airport and the embassy. President Obama maintained he had no plan for re-initiation of combat operations in Iraq, and he'd authorized only a small force for the mission. He emplaced a "boots on the ground" (*BOG*) cap of 300.[2] That meant a maximum of 300 U.S. military personnel were authorized to enter Iraq, to include any support elements. The CRF would make up the bulk of that number.

---

1   Nash Jenkins, "The First U.S. Special Forces Have Arrived in Baghdad," *Time*, June 25, 2014, accessed April 24, 2018, http://time.com/2920342/first-us-special-forces-arrive-iraq-baghdad/.

2   Barbara Starr and Tom Cohen, "Obama says 'small number' of military advisers going to Iraq," CNN, June 19, 2014, accessed April 24, 2018, https://www.cnn.com/2014/06/19/politics/us-iraq/index.html.

We all wondered why the arbitrary number of 300 was picked. The going joke was that someone in the administration had been inspired by the contemporary movie *300*—depicting a small force of 300 Spartans battling the huge Persian army in the *Battle of Thermopylae*. Even so, we knew it would never turn out the same for us. We were the American military, after all—unstoppable.

The initial manning of the CRF was comprised of a couple of Special Forces teams with one of our CCT JTACs attached. Soon, a couple of SEAL Task Units infilled and along with them a Navy F/A-18 pilot as the task force fires officer. "Vern" was a JTAC-qualified fighter pilot with a lot of experience killing the enemy from the cockpit at the behest of ground JTACs like me. The two of us would become good friends.

Six more Special Forces teams later inserted as reinforcements with our SOF TACP and Combat Control JTACs attached. A host of personnel specializing in intelligence, targeting, communications, and other aspects necessary to enable a special operations task force were also dispatched. On the conventional force side, a small contingent of Marines was sent to reinforce the embassy while a handful of conventional Army soldiers went to BIAP to assist with ground security so that the Special Forces ODAs (Operational Detachment Alphas) could concentrate solely on their mission.

Soon after, even more special operations teams along with a larger contingent of conventional forces would mass in Kuwait in anticipation of a lift of the BOG cap and initiation of full ground combat operations in Iraq. (An anticipation that would never quite materialize as hoped.)

As for me, I soon found that I'd been tasked with a different mission entirely—one that did not initially involve going into Baghdad. I was to make my way to the Kingdom of Bahrain and integrate into the Joint Special Operations Task Force-Gulf Cooperation Council (JSOTF-GCC) as the senior JTAC and joint firepower expert for the command overseeing the CRF.

Two of my good friends at the unit and fellow SOF TACPs, Jeremy and Adam, were simultaneously dispatched as JTAC liaisons to the Special Operations Command Central (SOCCENT) headquarters in Tampa, Florida. I'd be at the conduit between SOCCENT and the task force in Baghdad.

The JSOTF-GCC was a Naval Special Warfare (NSW) task force—NSW being the command element of the Navy SEALS. Historically, the task force's mission was largely diplomatic in nature. It had the main objective of nourishing friendly cooperation among a "council" of Arabian Gulf nations that were willing to assist in the mutually-agreed-upon goal to bring more stability to the region.

The NSW task force in Bahrain found itself thrust out of the shadows and into the military limelight as the lead operational command element in charge of the special operations response force sent to secure Baghdad. I was given the daunting task of embedding with and leveraging the task force to establish the command, control, and communication infrastructure needed to enable close air support to our special operations forces on the ground.

While the other JTACs on my team made their way to Baghdad, I went my own way to Bahrain. A tiny island nation nestled in the Arabian Gulf, east of Saudi Arabia and north of Qatar, Bahrain was about the most humid place I'd ever been. That was saying a lot since I'd spent half my career in the south and southwestern United States and had tramped through the deserts of Iraq and Afghanistan. Bahrain's hot desert temperatures combined with the extreme moisture brought by encircling Arabian Gulf waters made the climate that time of year *besieging*. I could literally drink the air.

On hitting the ground, a Navy lieutenant from the task force picked me up and drove me through the capital of Manama as we made our way to the task force headquarters. My first impression of Bahrain was of an intriguing blend of West and Middle East. I took in a bustling, modern city—one full of people who looked so much like those I'd long painted in my mind as the enemy.

The task force was in an unassuming compound on a port at the far end of a secured but run-down Bahraini Navy annex. The entrance to the annex was nearly hidden among city blocks packed with slums and industrial businesses. U.S. Navy patrol ships docked off the port near the compound.

I was escorted into the task force building for a meet-and-greet of the chain of command. The secured operations center was manned by a skeleton crew, mostly of Navy and Marine special operators and support.

At the time, the task force's staff had no air support or indirect firepower experts—mostly because their mission didn't typically necessitate the use of that arm of the military. I was to be that expert, to build relationships and advocate at the command level for exactly what our guys would need in Baghdad.

In the following days I was welcomed with open arms by the staff. The "Skipper" (the task force commander and an O-6 in the Navy) was a jovial and kind-spoken SEAL commander. He was a prior SEAL Team officer and a highly experienced leader who I'd come to find hawkishly perceptive. He and I got along really well from the start. The captain gave me full latitude to bring whatever I had to the table in order to help our new mission in Baghdad.

My mission soon proved difficult for many reasons. For one, I was used to the Army Special Forces world and was comfortable in it. The SEALs—and the Navy in general—were a different animal altogether. They talked, thought, planned, and executed entirely differently than I was used to. For two, although the commander was extremely competent and much of the staff had previous experience in Afghanistan and Iraq, the task force was truly ill-equipped to run the CRF mission in Baghdad.

They'd been given responsibility for oversight of too many missions throughout the Arabian Gulf. For example, while the Iraq crisis was occurring, the *Houthi uprising* in Yemen was also stirring[3]—and so the small task force headquarters was scrambling to simultaneously gin up contingency plans for military efforts in Yemen while still trying to command and support our budding mission against ISIS in Iraq. From my perspective, that often left the command and control of the mission in Baghdad lacking.

Compounding the difficulty was the state of the mission in Iraq during the first weeks of U.S. boots on the ground. Iraq was no longer a combat zone as it had been through the first decade of the century. Gone were the days of dozens of combat aircraft "stacked" overhead at any given time waiting for a call from a JTAC on the ground to drop ordnance onto enemy positions. Iraq was then a diplomatic mission, fully turned

---

3   "Yemen profile – Timeline," BBC, November 5, 2018, accessed January 27, 2019, https://www.bbc. com/news/world-middle-east-14704951.

over to the State Department since the U.S. withdrawal back in 2011. Any semblance of military tactical infrastructure had since been lost.

Really, I had never been handed such a challenging mission. As a JTAC, I was used to being farmed out and on my own figuring out how best to accomplish a given mission with a given team. Still, my objective with the task force in Bahrain was a tall order. I had no idea what I would end up doing to help the effort—or how I would end up doing it.

I set my mind to figuring out exactly how I could most effectively support our guys in Iraq. I had to ensure they had everything they needed from a fires and close air support standpoint. Identifying the main problem sets was easy—getting to the solutions, on the other hand, was the challenging part.

CHAPTER 8

The Ground Truth

DANA PITTARD

June 2014

It was within twenty-four hours of our arrival in Baghdad and I was chomping at the bit to get to the Iraqi Combined Joint Operations Center (CJOC) so I could get an update from the Iraqis themselves. Though I was scheduled to meet with the senior Iraqi military leadership in three days, I decided to go to the CJOC immediately.

The U.S. Embassy security personnel drove us to the Ministry of Defense (MoD). Three large, black, armored SUVs made their way on the five-minute drive from the U.S. Embassy to the Ministry of Defense compound all within the secured Green Zone. We stopped at the MoD checkpoint. An Iraqi guard asked us in Arabic if we had an appointment.

My interpreter responded back to him in Arabic, "This is American General Pittard. He is here to help Iraq!" he told him promptly. The guard's eyes got big and he quickly waved us through.

As we drove up toward the front of the main MoD building, another vehicle stopped in front of us. An Iraqi general got out. There were a lot of salutes exchanged and quite a commotion. When our three SUVs pulled up in front of the grand entrance to the MoD, with its red carpet and large outdoor stairway leading up, the commotion stopped.

I slowly stepped out of my SUV. The embassy security personnel quickly stepped in front of me for my protection. I waved them off and boldly walked up the steps toward the large outdoor entrance. Two very tall Iraqi guards wearing dress uniforms and holding long ceremonial pikes stood staring at me—their jaws gaping.

We walked down a long, red-carpeted hallway. Lots of people milled around. No one had been expecting us. When they saw our party dressed in U.S.-camouflage combat uniforms, there were many shocked looks and audible gasps. For the last three years prior, American military personnel visiting the MoD from the Office of Security Cooperation-Iraq would normally go in civilian business suits at the urging of the State Department (given the then-diplomatic nature of the mission in Iraq). Our arrival was one of the few times in the three years since American forces had left Iraq that the Iraqis saw Americans in combat uniforms walk into the MoD.

They knew what it meant. The gasps quickly turned into smiles and even some clapping. The Iraqis were glad to see us. They knew we were there to help them protect Baghdad and fight ISIS. We were soon treated like old friends.

Not everyone was clapping. I exchanged quick glances with two bearded gentlemen wearing suits. I could tell they were not Arabs, but Persians—Iranians, to be more precise. The men had sour looks on their faces and were clearly not happy to see us. One of the Iranians put his hand up to someone unseen from our vantage point who was obviously about to walk in through a side door, but instead quickly departed. (Months later, I found out the unseen person was more than likely Major General Qasem Soleimani—commander of the special forces unit of Iran's Revolutionary Guard, the *Quds Forces*, which the U.S. had designated a sponsor of terrorism. I could never quite confirm the close encounter, but we never saw another Iranian at the Ministry of Defense for the rest of 2014.)

We were soon escorted into the Iraqi Combined Joint Operations Center. The large, smoke-filled room had tactical maps on all the walls with red and blue pins to track the numerous ongoing fights with ISIS. The maps depicted just how close ISIS fighters had gotten to the outskirts Baghdad. Things were more chaotic than I'd expected within the Iraqi

CJOC—with a lot of shouting, pointing, and phone conversations buzzing. I was welcomed then briefed on the current situation by Iraqi Lieutenant General Hassan, the Army's chief of operations.

He told us the city of Tikrit had fallen to ISIS and that both the strategic Bayji Oil Refinery in central Iraq and Haditha Dam along the Euphrates River in western Iraq were under siege. As well, ISIS had made huge gains in Diyala Province just northeast of Baghdad. The Kurdish Peshmerga were filling the vacuum created by the fleeing Iraqi Army and had secured the Mosul Dam along the Tigris River, the city of Kirkuk, and the oil fields in north-central Iraq in order to prevent ISIS from seizing them.

After the brief I met with the prominent members of the senior Iraqi military leadership. They seemed to be lacking in confidence. Most of the Iraqi generals could not even look me in the eye. Worse, Iraqi senior military leadership was focused mostly on tactical engagements and responding to constant inquiries from Iraqi Prime Minster Maliki's office rather than the strategic or operational aspects they should have been concentrating on.

ISIS seemed unstoppable to them. Only one Iraqi general seemed to have confidence. That key exception was General Talib al-Kenani. General Kenani commanded the elite U.S. Special Forces-trained Counter Terrorism Service (CTS).[1] The CTS was one of the few Iraqi Security Forces units that did not retreat from ISIS—they stood and fought. General Kenani had just been appointed the overall Iraqi Joint Forces Commander only a couple of days earlier after the former commander was fired.

Kenani looked me in the eye and quietly said, "With your help, we are going to beat *Daesh*!" (*Daesh* was a derogatory term for the Islamic State—a term that was growing in popularity.) I could tell immediately that General Kenani and I were going to work well together. He laid out what he thought needed to be done against ISIS. Almost no one except General Kenani was focused on the operational or strategic-level fight.

---

1   David Witty, "The Iraqi Counter Terrorism Service," *Brookings*, June 1, 2016, accessed April 24, 2018, https://www.brookings.edu/wp-content/uploads/2016/06/David-Witty-Paper_Final_Web.pdf.

Despite their obvious shortcomings and humiliating defeats over the previous couple of weeks, I detected a glimmer of hope amongst the Iraqi military leadership—primarily due to General Kenani's confidence and competence. There seemed to be a quiet, but firm determination to prevent ISIS from taking Baghdad. I slowly began to feel their resolve. I departed my first visit to the Iraqi Ministry of Defense cautiously hopeful about the Iraqi military's desire to fight ISIS.

The Situation

Within forty-eight hours of hitting the ground, we concluded that Baghdad could be held by the Iraqi military and *there was no need to further evacuate the U.S. Embassy*. Based on the belief that the Iraqi Army would fold against ISIS—a belief held by much of the senior American military and civilian leadership back in the U.S.—our conclusion seemed pretty bold. Even some of the military personnel at the American embassy in Baghdad, who had been in Iraq for over a year, disagreed with our assessment. Many believed ISIS would overrun the Iraqi Army and seize Baghdad.

I briefed our assessment to Lieutenant General Terry and General Austin: ISIS maintained a clear momentum at the tactical level. In fact, in individual tactical engagements ISIS fighters showed a greater ability to conduct maneuver and mass firepower than the Iraqi Security Forces. And, it was clear that ISIS was militarily stronger than what we had anticipated; however, I did not believe ISIS was strong enough to seize the Iraqi capital.

ISIS' manpower shortages and recruiting problems were slightly more complex. ISIS would have to either send more fighters from Syria or convince more Sunni tribes in Iraq to fight with them. ISIS could potentially capture more Iraqi prisons and coerce the freed inmates to join their ranks—which they'd already done in places in Syria as well as in Mosul and Tikrit. Those manpower difficulties slowed ISIS' offensive operations, and that gave the Iraqis—and our forces—a potential window of opportunity to strike.

We believed the Iraqi Security Forces had more than enough manpower around Baghdad to stop ISIS from seizing the capital. This included Iraqi Shia volunteers and militia. On June 13, the much-revered Shia religious leader Grand Ayatollah Sistani decreed that all Shias had a duty to defend Iraq and defeat ISIS. After the decree, Shia men from all over Iraq arrived into the Baghdad area volunteering to fight. Thanks to Grand Ayatollah Sistani, there was no shortage of Iraqi manpower.

It would be extremely difficult for ISIS to sustain a massive offensive against Baghdad. As ISIS forces moved forward and expanded, their logistical problems would increase. In the meantime, any Iraqi forces that fell back closer to Baghdad would consolidate and have a far easier time logistically supporting themselves. In military terms, the Iraqi military would be taking advantage of their "interior lines." The Iraqi military clearly had the force structure necessary to stop ISIS. But did they have the *will* to fight?

Since U.S. forces were not allowed to take part directly in ground combat operations, we were left to observe from afar how ISIS fought against the Iraqi troops we would be supporting. We spoke to and grilled any Iraqi military leaders we could find who had commanded troops against ISIS, and we watched ISIS fighters maneuver through the lens of our aerial drones via live feeds into our joint operations center in the U.S. Embassy compound. In July, the Iraqi Army conducted a counterattack to re-take the city of Tikrit from ISIS. We watched a portion of the Iraqi counterattack from our operations center.

The initial combined arms assault was pretty effective, and the Iraqi Army made gains against ISIS on the southern side of Tikrit. Unfortunately, the assault broke down when ISIS was able to separate the Iraqi infantry from their tanks and infantry support vehicles through the skilled use of IED (improvised explosive device) ambushes combined with direct fire. Though the Iraqis had helicopter gunship support, they had no fixed-wing air support. And we were still prohibited by our government from supporting the Iraqi Army with airstrikes.

The counterattack failed, and the Iraqi Army was forced to retreat from Tikrit. But we believed the Iraqis could have succeeded if we had been authorized to support them with airstrikes from U.S. and coalition aircraft.

In the battle for Tikrit and on other battlefields, we observed that ISIS senior leaders typically rushed to the front lines when their troops were challenged. Even the ISIS supreme leader himself—Abu Bakr al-Baghdadi—was reported to have visited battlefronts earlier in the summer to motivate his fighters.

Their cause may have been a warped and extremist brand of Islam, but there was no denying that ISIS leaders appeared to be very courageous. We quickly learned (to our dismay) that ISIS often fought harder and more disciplined than either U.S.-trained Iraqi Security Forces or the Syrian Army forces. Months later, we would turn that brave ISIS trait into a liability as we hunted ISIS leadership.

I knew that General Austin took ISIS seriously from the very beginning. He realized they were a threat to Iraq and Syria. Even so, he was slightly surprised at the recommendation I made within just a few days of my arrival to Baghdad: ISIS was a real threat. They were better equipped, more competently led, and could tactically outfight the Iraqis. We needed to assist the Iraqi Security Forces.

Barbaric Acts

It was around that same time that a U.S. television network correspondent suddenly asked to meet with me personally. Initially I declined to meet, but the journalist assured me it would not be an interview so I agreed. I had known the journalist since 2004 when we were both in Iraq's Diyala Province.

The correspondent came to me with an unusual request well outside the typical military command's interaction with the media. The journalist had a friend and colleague—Peter Kassig—who'd been taken hostage by ISIS.[2] A former Army Ranger, Kassig was an Indiana native in his mid-twenties. After the military and college, he'd joined a humanitarian effort in Lebanon to aid refugees of the civil war in Syria. He was captured while delivering medical aid to refugees.

A trained emergency medical technician, Kassig had told his parents that he felt called to use his medical skills to help the refugees. His dedication to the relief project led him from Lebanon across the Syrian border

---

2   Shiv Malik et al., "The Race to save Peter Kassig," *The Guardian*, December 18, 2014, accessed April 24, 2018, https://www.theguardian. com/news/2014/dec/18/-sp-the-race-to-save-peter-kassig.

and into a very dangerous area of western Syria. After being captured by ISIS, Kassig converted from his Methodist faith to Islam and took the name *Abdul-Rahman*. His parents mounted a public campaign to try to win his release, and even held prayer vigils at Islamic centers in Indiana. The Muslim community back home in America as well as a lot of American college students and Syrian refugees took up their cause. Even members of the Islamist al-Qaeda affiliate al-Nusra Front (ANF) supported his release— the ANF respected that Kassig had treated wounded "rebels" as well.

My American journalist colleague asked me to help find and rescue Kassig. I told the journalist that we'd already been looking for him, along with every other hostage held by ISIS at the time, but we hadn't been able to locate Kassig. I said that if we had a location, we might be able to go after him. The correspondent had hundreds of sources throughout the region, and after talking to me tapped into them.

Within a week, Kassig's journalist friend came back to me with a possible location in Syria. Impressed, I relayed the information to our special operations elements. They'd been watching the same area as one of the possible locations for Kassig. They soon identified it as a potential holding area not only for Kassig but three other American hostages— James Foley, Steven Sotloff, and Kayla Mueller.

On July 4, scores of U.S. special operations forces conducted a night raid deep in ISIS territory near the ISIS "capital" of Ar-Raqqah, Syria. They fought their way into an ISIS encampment, killing dozens of ISIS fighters. However, unfortunately there were no American hostages—only a makeshift prison with some half-eaten meals and a wisp of hair.[3]

The hostages had been there but were gone by the time the rescue element showed up. To our horror—Peter Kassig, James Foley, and Steven Sotloff were later beheaded. Kayla Mueller was also declared dead by ISIS (they claimed she was killed by a Jordanian airstrike).[4]

---

3 Karen DeYoung, "The Anatomy of a Failed Hostage Rescue Deep in Islamic State Territory," *The Washington Post*, February 14, 2015, accessed April 24, 2018, https://www.washingtonpost.com/world/national-security/the-anatomy-of-a-failed-hostage-rescue-deep-into-islamic-state-territory/2015/02/14/09a5d9a0-b2fc-11e4-827f-93f454140e2b_story.html?utm_term=.b914258bb1a1.

4 Karen Yourish, "The Fates of 23 ISIS Hostages in Syria," *The New York Times*, February 10, 2015, accessed April 24, 2018, https://www.nytimes.com/interactive/2014/10/24/world/middleeast/the-fate-of-23-hostages-in-syria.html.

Once it was made public, the rescue mission became quite controversial back home. President Obama acknowledged during interviews that the special operations team had "probably missed [the hostages] by a day or two." Senior officials said it was one of the most complex and dangerous rescue missions ever undertaken and had moved through planning, approval, and execution at "warp speed."[5]

The torture and killing of the hostages had a profound impact on all of us. The publicly recorded beheadings served as grim reminders that we were in a high-stakes war. But they also furthered our resolve. We could not—and *would not*—allow a barbaric entity like ISIS to terrorize the world.

---

5   Karen DeYoung, "The Anatomy of a Failed Hostage Rescue Deep in Islamic State Territory," *The Washington Post*, February 14, 2015, accessed April 24, 2018, https://www.washingtonpost. com/world/national-security/the-anatomy-of-a-failed-hostage-rescue-deep-into-islamic- state-territory/2015/02/14/09a5d9a0-b2fc-11e4-827f-93f454140e2b_story.html?utm_term=. b914258bb1a1.

CHAPTER 9

Quick-Look Teams

DANA PITTARD

July 2014

We'd been on the ground in Iraq less than a week when we received an additional mission tasking from President Obama and the National Security Council. They wanted CENTCOM to conduct a formal assessment of the fighting capability of the Iraqi Security Forces.

Of course, I felt that we already knew that answer. But I also knew that taking time to conduct formal assessments would help buy time for the Obama administration to figure out what to do to thwart ISIS without giving the impression that the United States was supporting the abusive Shia government of Prime Minister Maliki.

The formal assessments, called "Quick Looks," would build on the foundation already established by the work of our ten-person assessment team led by Colonel Eric Timmerman back in May, and would be accomplished primarily around the greater Baghdad area.[1] That made sense because over 70 percent of the Iraqi Security Forces were in the area to safeguard the capital city.

---

1 Cheryl Pellerin, "Hagel: All Assessments Needed for Full Picture in Iraq," *U.S. Department of Defense*, July 10, 2014, accessed April 24, 2018, https://www.defense.gov/News/Article/Article/602849/hagel-all-assessments-needed-for-full-picture-in-iraq/.

Special Forces teams dispatched under the Special Operations Command Central (SOCCENT) would visit individual Iraqi battalions, brigades, and divisions in the area. Simultaneously, my U.S. Joint Operations Center leadership would assess Iraqi senior commands.

We worked closely with the Special Forces teams from Navy SEAL Commander Black's task force to support their ground movements throughout the Baghdad area as they assessed the Iraqi units. Major General Mike Nagata, the SOCCENT commander, had been able to bring in senior special operations officers—Army lieutenant colonels and Navy commanders—and senior NCOs to augment the CRF. That helped with the assessment effort. Wes Bryant's JTACs from the special operations task force were attached to the teams for added firepower in case ISIS got bold and the teams ran into trouble.

The "Quick Look" teams were escorted throughout the greater Baghdad area by an elite Iraqi Counter Terrorism Service patrol. A U.S. quick reaction force (QRF) was also on standby. We did not want to take any unnecessary chances since the situation in the Baghdad area was still very precarious.

In the end, there were no major roadblocks to the assessments and no firefights with ISIS ensued. However, the assessments were not without their hiccups. On a mission to the Iraqi 25th Brigade, 17th Division, one of our Special Forces teams encountered hostile Shia militias and there was a brief standoff. Luckily, it was deescalated with the help of the accompanying Iraqi CTS forces as well as a show of presence (SoP) by one of our F-16 fighter jets—a fly-over controlled by the JTAC to warn the Shia militias that we weren't to be trifled with.

For another assessment to an Iraqi military base near Taji, one of our Special Forces teams was forced to cancel the mission last minute because they observed suspected Shia militias while *soaking* the area with drone coverage prior to pushing out. We had to avoid some of the militias because we knew that teams of Iranian Quds Forces were in Iraq embedded with and enabling Shia militias with arms.[2] Interaction with the Quds Forces could have created an even more convoluted situation.

2   Janine Di Giovanni, "Nemesis: The Shadowy Iranian Training Shia Militias in Iraq," *Newsweek*, November 27, 2016, accessed April 24, 2018, http://www.newsweek.com/2014/12/05/nemesis-shadowy-iranian-training-shia-militias-iraq-287610.html.

The contact with the Shia militias had caused alarm bells to go off throughout ARCENT in Kuwait and at the CENTCOM and SOCCENT headquarters back in Florida. But I wondered if we were slightly over-blowing the potential consequences of any contact with Shia militias. Suddenly, it seemed that we were saying all Shia militias were bad. Having worked successfully with some in Diyala Province ten years earlier—primarily the Badr Corps—I knew that all Shia militias were not the same. I concurred that groups like Asaib Ahl al-Haq (AAH) and Hezbollah (KH) absolutely hated us and we could probably never trust or work with them. However, I felt like the largest Shia militia—the Badr Corps—could actually find common cause with us against ISIS.

The Combined Joint Task Force (CJTF) staff in Kuwait turned all the "Quick Look" reports into a coherent, formal assessment for LTG Terry to present to General Austin. The final assessment went to the highest levels of the Pentagon and the White House. Overall, we concluded the Iraqi Security Forces could, and would, fight to defend Baghdad.

As expected, one of the most important outcomes of the report was that it gave President Obama and his advisors much needed time to figure out what they wanted to do about ISIS, and how to encourage a change in Iraqi civilian national leadership. But those decisions didn't come right away.

In lieu of further orders, we began working in parallel with the staffs of CJTF in Kuwait and CENTCOM and SOCCENT in Florida. We needed to have a campaign plan against ISIS ready to go—one that we could launch as soon as we got a thumbs-up from Washington.

CHAPTER 10

Dangerous Rules of Engagement

WES BRYANT

When our special operators hit the ground in Baghdad, all intelligence pointed to an impending large-scale attack on BIAP by ISIS, with the embassy not far behind. Even in that environment, our guys were faced with a huge legal hurdle: if ISIS mounted an attack against them, they were to hold in-place with zero authority to call in close air support.

The U.S. military did not then have the authorizations to utilize combat airpower over Baghdad—even though our small CRF element had been taking rocket attacks from ISIS forces northwest of their small base on BIAP on a regular basis. Early on in the crisis, Vern along with our team of SEAL, SOF TACP, and CCT JTACs took shifts on top of the stone compound that served as the CRF's commandeered headquarters. They endured the 120-degree Iraqi summer heat to control an extremely limited amount of "noncombat" aircraft sent in from the USS *George H.W. Bush* in the Northern Arabian Gulf and provide the task force at least some sort of overwatch against nearby ISIS forces.

The CRF was operating under what was called *Title 22*—a non-combat authorization under the political umbrella of the State Department. Title 22 did not grant authorization for the military to conduct combat operations in Iraq. Of course, the use of close air support fell well within that realm. It was shocking to all of us when we grasped the reality for our guys on the ground in Baghdad: We were the first military forces tasked by the president himself to the "Iraq crisis" to quell a reportedly extremely dangerous terrorist threat—yet we didn't actually have the authorization to do anything about it.

In no small way, our guys were on their own in Baghdad; handcuffed by politics and bureaucrats in Washington. None of us considered that we would ever be placed in such a precarious situation by our government and military leadership. We had to change that.

At the special operations task force in Bahrain I was to establish a fires infrastructure for a fight that we didn't even have the authorization to wage. My priority quickly became ensuring that combat airpower would be there for our guys in the event they took effective contact from the very hardened, capable enemy force that lurked right outside their gates. Luckily, within a couple of weeks, the operation in Baghdad transitioned under *Title 10*, putting us back within military combat jurisdiction and authorization. That change coincided with the kickoff of our "Quick Look" assessment missions.

Once we were legally authorized to utilize close air support in self-defense against an ISIS attack, combat air assets flooded into theatre. AH-64 Apache attack helicopters based out of the Baghdad airport were tasked as primary security for BIAP and the embassy. Navy F/A-18 Hornets and AV-8 Harriers based from carriers in the Arabian Gulf were on-call for close air support. Air Force fighter jets, strike aircraft, bombers, and drones were staged elsewhere throughout the Middle East—all ready to support the flowering mission in Iraq.

Still—none of it was as good as it sounds. The rules of engagement (ROE) for the utilization of close air support emplaced by Washington and the Pentagon were incredibly stringent. So much, in fact, that we may as well have not even had the airpower at hand. If one of our teams were to take fire from ISIS, they still wouldn't be legally allowed to use close air support until they received approval directly from the commander of Iraq—Major General Pittard himself.

There were big problems with that mandate. The communications chain from a Special Forces team in a fight all the way to the commander of Iraq would be quite lengthy. And there was not a guarantee that the general—as busy as he was—would be anywhere near his staff when they received the request to utilize close air support. Even if he was, he'd still have to be briefed on the situation, deliberate, then provide his decision that would have to be filtered through at least three entities before it got back down to the Special Forces team leader on the ground.

In the heat of a "near ambush"—the most likely course of action ISIS would take—our teams would be hammered while waiting for approval from the general. The ROE, to put it simply, were dangerous. I had no idea who General Pittard was at that point from my position at the JSOTF-GCC in Bahrain, but I cursed his name daily.

"Who is this damn general who thinks we should get his approval to strike if our guys are taking fire?!"

I was a senior noncommissioned officer, admittedly proud to a fault, who by then had years of experience that served largely to jade me against both the officer corps and our civilian political leadership. To me, the situation in Iraq was yet another case of senior military officers and politicians in Washington risking the lives of those on the ground for the sake of political perception. I was angry—as were a lot of my peers and pretty much everyone directly involved in the special operations mission in Iraq.

At the JSOTF-GCC in Bahrain, my most important mission became a push to change the rules of engagement. We needed to gain authorities to allow our forward ground commanders the ability to rely on close air support in defense of their teams without the need to wait on some special approval from a general. American lives were at stake—the lives of my brothers and SOF brethren.

I worked exhaustively with two different command staff judge advocates—military lawyers assigned to the joint task force. Alongside and with the help of those very smart lawyers, I drafted several proposals for ROE change. We sent them up through the wickets with the intent that they'd eventually get to the U.S. Central Command for review and, hopefully, approval.

We didn't quite know at what level past CENTCOM our proposal would need to reach in order to be approved. What we did know was that political and public visibility on the operation in Iraq was so high—and sensitivity toward not involving the U.S. in any repeat combat operations so great—that the level of approval we had to seek for the ROE change was beyond the norm. We suspected it would have to be blessed off by Secretary of Defense Chuck Hagel, but we couldn't be certain.

Immediately, we encountered almost nothing but push-back from senior headquarters elements. The timid political climate in Washington extended well into the senior military levels, to the point that there wasn't even an appetite for the proposal in the senior staff channels. The overarching sentiment was that we "shouldn't even bother trying" because no one in Washington wanted U.S. bombs dropping in Iraq again, regardless of the reason, based on the potential perception that we'd be initiating another Iraq War. To us it was a figurative "to hell with our guys on the ground."

I elicited the help of my Air Force chain of command back at Al Udeid Air Base in the tiny nation of Qatar. Major Matt Psilos, a prior Army infantry officer, was an intelligent and driven Special Tactics Officer (STO). He knew I'd been having trouble getting the ROE change proposal past the task force in Bahrain. He was able to gather forces with a few key officers from various other agencies. Eventually, he even managed to get the commander of Iraq himself behind the proposal. (I would later find out that General Pittard was never behind the restrictive ROE in the first place—he was obligated to enforce it by his superiors and Washington. I'd finally stop cursing his name once I learned that.)

Major Psilos visited me in Bahrain in order to help with our final ROE change proposal. After a full day of planning and briefing at the task force, we made our way to an ocean-side restaurant in the wealthy section of Manama for a gourmet steak dinner. That was my idea, of course—I always believed in taking time to enjoy the finer things when given the chance.

After a nothing short of amazing dinner that went *way* over our allotted government per diem, we made our way to a poolside courtyard patio with an unbridled view of the ocean. Palm leaves wisped in the cool breeze of a Bahraini dusk as we chatted over glasses of single malt scotch and high-end cigars.

"Ya know, sir…I really never would have thought I'd be sitting here with you in the lap of luxury in Bahrain, nursing a scotch and planning how we're gonna take out ISIS in Iraq," I said with a grin as I leaned back and took a long puff on my cigar.

"Me either, Wes...me either," Major Psilos returned, in his signature soft but commanding voice that sounded like a character out of a James Bond movie. He smiled at me as he puffed from his own cigar, and we both looked toward the ocean, taking a few moments to enjoy the picturesque Bahraini evening.

There were so many questions with the mission, and so many frustrations with the politically-based restrictions in the effort against ISIS. But, over the coming weeks, we persisted with the ROE change proposal and it paid off. Once the concerns we highlighted were fully understood by senior U.S. military and civilian leadership, the proposal gained traction.

It would take time still, but the ROE were finally changed. From that point on, when our teams went forward, the on-scene commander—the Special Forces team leader on the ground—would have full authorization to direct his JTAC to use close air support without the need to ask a general miles away. Since our Special Forces ODAs and Navy SEAL teams would be dispersed throughout Iraq within the coming weeks for various mission taskings, that meant they'd have the firepower at hand needed to safeguard their teams and crush ISIS if need be.

In my years as a JTAC up to that point, I'd done a fair amount toward the war on terror. I'd hunted the enemy from the remote mountains of Afghanistan to the urban sprawls of Baghdad attached to infantry units and Special Forces teams. But I never felt more professionally accomplished than when I got the word that our ROE change proposal had finally gone through. As the fight against ISIS would surely evolve over the coming months, I knew the ROE change would be vital in safeguarding American lives—and I was damn proud.

CHAPTER 11

Eyewitness to a Massacre

DANA PITTARD

August 2014

As the senior commander of U.S. forces in Iraq, part of my job was to oversee the surveillance and reconnaissance of ISIS and to gather intelligence on them. Later our operations center would serve a far more lethal role—but not on this day.

On August 3, I watched our Predator drone feed display a gut-wrenching live video that haunts me to this day. The Predator was flying over the village of Qiniyeh near Sinjar, southwest of Mosul in Iraq. We'd been checking out the village of Qiniyeh by drone only by chance because we had intelligence reports that top ISIS leader Abu Bakr might be there with some of his fighters. The village was home to an Iraqi religious minority group known as the *Yazidi*.

The Yazidi, who had once numbered around half a million in northern Iraq, had long been persecuted for following an ancient faith that had elements of Islam, Zoroastrianism, and Christianity. They believed that God created a world ruled by seven angels. Some Muslims considered it to be a form of devil worship. We'd heard scattered reports of the ISIS terrorist army slaughtering thousands of Yazidi civilians, but hadn't yet confirmed any of them.

We watched the drone feed as ISIS fighters armed with machine guns, rifles, and handguns rounded up several hundred residents in the center of the village. The terrorist fighters marched the civilians to the outskirts of town. (As we later learned, ISIS had demanded all residents convert to Islam—their typical ploy.)

The ISIS fighters separated the Yazidi men from the women and children. They escorted the women and children to a group of vehicles and separated them before loading them up and driving off. We suspected that the women and girls would be forced into sex slavery or marriage, and that the boys would be forced into slavery or made to join the ISIS army.[1] If they refused either, they would be killed.

After the women and children were driven off from the village, the ISIS fighters handed out shovels to the group of about eighty Yazidi men. They ordered the group, at gunpoint, to dig a long trench at the edge of town. I asked my staff if they thought it might be some sort of defensive trench that ISIS was forcing the Yazidi men to dig in order to shore up their defenses. I knew deep down, though, that the ditch was probably meant for a far more nefarious purpose. Our intelligence officer, Lieutenant Colonel John Barnett, confirmed my worst fears. He said the Yazidi men were likely being forced to dig their own graves.

Our mission in Iraq was solely to "advise and assist" our coalition allies consisting primarily of the Iraqi Security Forces and Kurdish Peshmerga troops. We were prohibited from engaging ISIS on the ground or from the air unless in direct self-defense of U.S. forces. Still, holding on to the faint hope that I could get permission to go against our limited rules of engagement if it meant stopping a slaughter, I asked my JTACs if we had any fighter aircraft overhead near the area.

The answer was no.

Once the men finished their trench, we watched grimly as the ISIS fighters lined them up near it. They took aim with their machine guns and opened fire. Once the smoke and dust settled, we could see clearly that ISIS had executed all eighty men.[2]

1   Cathy Otten, "Slaves of Isis: the long walk of the Yazidi women," *The Guardian*, July 25, 2017, accessed April 24, 2018, https://www.theguardian.com/world/2017/jul/25/slaves-of-isis-the-long-walk-of-the-yazidi-women.

2   "Iraq Crisis: Yazidi villagers 'massacred' by IS," BBC News, August 16, 2014, accessed April 24, 2018, http://www.bbc.com/news/world-middle-east-28814633.

Those of us watching were all combat veterans. Most had seen a lot of combat, yet we were all sickened by what we saw. It was pure religious fanaticism—not an act of war. The unarmed Yazidi were no threat to the ISIS fighters. It was genocide, clear and simple.

After slaughtering the Yazidi villagers, the ISIS murderers kicked and dragged their bodies into the trench. It was a horrific scene of brutality. It made me even more frustrated and angry about our severely limited rules of engagement. Despite all the military might at my control, I stood helpless and unable to stop the barbaric acts that unfolded before our eyes.

Angry and disgusted by our inability to act, I called my commander in Kuwait, Lieutenant General James Terry, and let him know my feelings.

"Sir, did you just see the mass execution of the Yazidi men on your drone feeds there?"

Terry replied solemnly. He had not yet seen the slaughter, but he'd heard about it.

"We cannot stand by and allow this to happen again," I said. "Sir, we have to get permission to intervene."

He agreed and told me that he would speak with "the boss" at CENTCOM—our commander General Austin. A few hours later, LTG Terry called me back to pass word that we were authorized to intervene with airpower to prevent future mass killings.

Unfortunately, we never saw another opportunity to stop a mass execution—even though the slaughter we witnessed that day marked the beginning of an ISIS rampage that would leave tens of thousands of Yazidi dead and force more than 200,000 to flee to Sinjar Mountain in northern Iraq.[3]

We would soon be able to stop ISIS in other ways, though.

---

3   Martin Chulov, "40,000 Iraqis stranded on mountain as Isis jihadists threaten death," *The Guardian*, August 6, 2014, accessed April 24, 2018, https://www.theguardian.com/world/2014/aug/07/40000-iraqis-stranded-mountain-isis-death-threat.

PART 3

The First Strikes on ISIS

CHAPTER 12

A Mission Unknown

WES BRYANT

August 2014

I'd had a few short weeks in Bahrain, weeks that felt a lot longer with the frustration that came with a career ground warfighter suddenly being forced to battle political bureaucracy and senior military staffers in order to advocate for our guys on the ground in Baghdad.

While I was in Bahrain, my close friend and teammate Dennis had been working alongside Vern as the senior enlisted JTAC at the CRF. Since hitting the ground in Baghdad, Dennis had gotten our JTACs tasked out with their assigned Special Forces teams spread throughout Baghdad and Erbil, he'd established relationships with the CRF chain of command, and he'd been managing our JTACs in Iraq and their missions. He was also vital in helping me field the ROE change proposals to the staffs in Baghdad both at the CRF and at General Pittard's JOC at the embassy.

My work at the JSOTF-GCC in Bahrain was done. I'd helped set the stage for close air support operations in Iraq, helped establish the command and control infrastructure necessary to utilize it, and gotten the change in the ROE for close air support pushed through. It was time for me to move on. My chain of command thought I'd be far better utilized on the ground in Baghdad versus continuing with the senior staff

91

in Bahrain, and I wholeheartedly agreed. Even with the good things I'd done from Bahrain, I was growing a bit stir crazy.

Dennis was tasked back to the States to help prep our home station JTACs for what we thought might turn out to be a full-on special operations ground mission in Iraq, and I was slated to replace him at the newly designated *SOTF-I.* (The CRF became re-designated the Special Operations Task Force-Iraq once CENTCOM and Washington realized that the mission in Iraq was no longer merely a "crisis response" but was turning into a sustained operation.)

I hoped I could hold a candle to the work Dennis had done, he was one of the best and most experienced JTACs in our career field. Soon I caught a "grey tail," a small civilian plane reserved specifically for transporting special operations personnel—we always had our perks—from Bahrain to Ali Al Salem Air Base in Kuwait. From there I hopped onto a C-130 and infilled into Baghdad.

As soon as I hit the ground, Dennis met me with a man-hug. We caught up in-person in the way you can never really do over the phone. Then we packed my gear into a black, up-armored SUV and he drove us around the base complex to give me the lay of the land as I soaked in sites that I hadn't seen in half a decade.

BIAP was a shell of what it had been years back when thousands of U.S. troops lived on the then-giant military base complex. In the years since, the only people who'd remained were employees and contractors of the U.S. State Department. The State Department held a large headquarters on the former base known as the Baghdad Diplomatic Support Center, or BDSC (pronounced "*bed-sey*").

The place felt like a ghost town in comparison to the memories I'd had of traveling through and working there years back during Operations *Iraqi Freedom* and *New Dawn.* Still, the State Department had maintained the bare necessity infrastructure. There was a decent chow hall and a small exchange where we could get hygiene items, snacks and the like. To my delight, even the old Green Beans coffee shop was still operating—a staple of American bases during the height of the wars in Iraq and Afghanistan. Although, it was only open certain hours and was in pretty bad disrepair compared to its "glory days" with all the U.S. dollars flowing through.

The SOTF-I (formerly known as the CRF) had commandeered some old troop barracks—single-room CHUs or "containerized housing units" strewn about the base—most of which had remained empty since the withdrawal. The entire complex was a bit post-apocalyptic looking. Dennis had managed to make his CHU at least comfortable by rummaging through some long-abandoned rooms to find a desk, chair, wall lockers, and the cleanest, newest mattress he could scavenge. As soon as I got the chance, I'd do the same and get lucky in finding a working mini-fridge.

I was relieved to be on the ground in Baghdad and in the fight—whatever that fight was going to end up being. I finally felt I was exactly back where I should be. Dennis and I grabbed a bite to eat at the State Department chow hall before he took me to the operations center where I'd be taking his place as the lead enlisted JTAC and fires NCO.

The SOTF-I was set up on the west side of BIAP on what had once been known as Sather Air Base back in the days of the Iraq war. It was named after Combat Control JTAC Scott Sather, the first enlisted Airman of the Iraq War to be killed-in-action. Sather was killed by direct enemy fire in the first weeks of the war while on a high-profile special operations mission to oust Saddam Hussein's military regime. [1] Later I would find it fitting that our airstrike campaign against ISIS in central Iraq was born out of that place.

The SOTF-I headquarters was established in a single-story half-concrete/half-glass building situated right off the airfield known as the *Glass House*. It was a stately grey building topped with a blue-green dome with intricate glass mosaics, and with glass-encased walls that were surrounded by huge concrete barriers to protect from ISIS rocket and mortar attacks.

Before the U.S. had invaded Iraq in 2003, the Glass House had been Saddam's personal military airport terminal and VIP lounge. Ironically, it was there in 2011 that Defense Secretary Leon E. Panetta gave a grandiose speech for the ceremony that marked the formal end to the Iraq

---

1   "Scott D. Sather," *Veteran Tributes*, accessed April 24, 2018, http://www.veterantributes.org/TributeDetail.php?recordID=2308.

War and full withdrawal of American combat troops.[2] There we were again in the summer of 2014—all but starting over and with an entirely new enemy.

As far as our mission went, apart from the earlier combat assessments of the Iraqi military, there was a whole lot of waiting around for orders and gearing-up for operations that never materialized. From Tampa, the Special Operations Command Central constantly directed our teams to prep for missions based on proposals they had submitted to Washington and were anticipating approval on but that were shot down time and again. On countless occasions, our Special Forces teams sat on the BIAP airfield for hours fully kitted-up, armed, and ready to push out for a planned mission only to eventually be stood down.

There just was no palate in Washington for combat operations in Iraq. Despite that, Major General Mike Nagata, the SOCCENT commander, continued to work adamantly to gain the authorization to execute his proposed "advise, assist, and accompany" mission. The plan—known as "Triple-A"—would enable our special operations teams to *advise* the Iraqis in the planning of their combat operations against ISIS, *assist* them during operations, and *accompany* them in the fight on the ground. In short: it would enable our teams to fight alongside the Iraqis and the Kurds against ISIS.

Major General Nagata and his staff deemed Triple-A as the most effective method by which the U.S. could quickly quell the threat of ISIS. They briefed the merits of the mission in Washington several times. In fact, during one of our daily SOCCENT video teleconferences, General Nagata directed his staff to reduce the Triple-A mission briefing slides down to "one slide, with no acronyms and a lot of pictures." He clarified that the people he'd be briefing were mostly younger congressional staffers with absolutely no military experience or operational understanding. With such disconnect between those of us carrying out the mission and those back in Washington guiding it, small wonder we had such frustrations.

2   Thom Shanker, Michael S. Schmidt, and Robert F. Worth, "In Baghdad, Panetta Leads Uneasy Moment of Closure," *The New York Times*, December 15, 2011, accessed April 24, 2018, http://www.nytimes.com/2011/12/16/world/middleeast/panetta-in-baghdad-for-iraq-military-handover-ceremony.html.

Despite all Nagata's efforts, Washington and the president wouldn't have any of it. The mission in Iraq remained solely to advise and assist— we were not to accompany ground forces in offensive operations against ISIS nor to conduct any airstrikes in support of the Iraqis.

We were also tasked to create plans for *NEO* (noncombatant evacuation operations) to evacuate all State Department personnel and American citizens from BIAP and the U.S. Embassy.[3] Our Special Tactics assault zone reconnaissance team surveyed Iraq's airfields for the best options, while we worked on the details of the evacuation plan at the task force. NEO was "Plan B" to be triggered if ISIS mounted an attack on the Baghdad region. U.S. military forces would evacuate last. It definitely wasn't in our nature to run away from a fight—so we all hoped NEO wasn't going to be the intent from Washington.

All of us knee-deep on the ground in the Iraq crisis were standing by for some kind of clear intent from the Obama administration and our senior military leadership. But, day after day, we didn't know whether we were going to continue in some semblance of a war effort, evacuate the embassy, or just pack it up and go home. We were incredibly confused, angry, and frustrated.

What exactly are we doing here?

What is the mission? The desired end-state?

No one seemed to know the answers to those questions.[4] All we knew, for sure, was that we were to hold in-place and take absolutely no part in forward combat operations. Sure, we had a tasking to advise and assist the Iraqi forces in their counterassault operations against ISIS. But the scope of that mission was loosely defined, really. And the Iraqis, quite honestly, seemed to have little motivation to fight.[5]

Dennis and I took a few short days to finish our handover of responsibilities—days during which we spent a lot of time venting about our

3   Ibrahim Khalil, "URGENT – U.S. Embassy prepares evacuation plans," *Iraq News*, June 12, 2014, accessed April 24, 2018, https://www.iraqinews.com/iraq-war/urgent-u-s-embassy-prepares-evacuation-plans/.

4   Julie Pace and Lara Jakes, "U.S. troops move into position for Iraq security mission," PBS, June 17, 2014, accessed April 24, 2018, https://www.pbs.org/newshour/world/u-s-troops-take-position-iraq-security-mission.

5   Kenneth Katzman et al., "Iraq Crisis and U.S. Policy," *Homeland Security Digital Library*, July 3, 2014, accessed April 24, 2018, https://www.hsdl.org/?view&did=755842.

frustrations with the mission. We both felt that our special operations task force was just not doing enough. One afternoon, as we waited in the task force operations center for the C-130 that would start Dennis on his journey back to the States, we spent our last few minutes talking about our ideas on the way ahead for the mission.

I turned to Dennis, and with matter-of-fact determination said, "Mark my words, man…I'll be controlling strikes against ISIS within a couple weeks."

If my closest friends knew one thing about me it was that, for better or worse, I always had a way of doing *exactly* what I thought should happen despite what anyone—especially my superiors—said.

Dennis returned a sly, knowing smile that broke into a laugh as he patted me on the shoulder. "I have no doubt about that, Wes…no doubt."

CHAPTER 13

Herding Cats

DANA PITTARD

August 2014

Working with the anti-ISIS coalition was like herding cats—wildly cunning feral cats that clawed at each other even as they fought a mutual enemy. Our anti-ISIS forces consisted of a growing coalition of U.S. allies as well as a contentious coalition of Iraqi Security Forces, Kurdish Peshmerga, Shia militias, Syrian Kurds, Iraqi Sunni tribes, and even Syrian Army troops. On top of that, other anti-ISIS forces included our foes Iran and Russia.

If that wasn't enough of a challenge, we were only allowed to talk to certain members of the anti-ISIS coalition through certain other members of the coalition. And our hands were tied as we saw one opportunity after another to destroy key enemy forces.

Mounting a fight against ISIS was one of the most frustrating experiences I'd yet had in the military. Our commander in chief in Washington certainly had legitimate reasons for wanting to keep U.S. troops out of harm's way as much as possible. Yet, despite the good intentions of the emerging strategy against ISIS, it forced us to rely on a contentious coalition that was basically at war with itself. My job, and that of my superiors such as Lieutenant General Terry, was to somehow mount a fight against a vicious, aggressive, and disciplined enemy using a pack of petty, squabbling, and warring Kurds, Sunni Iraqis, and Shia Iraqis.

Many of the anti-ISIS coalition members were sometimes more interested in fighting each other than fighting ISIS. The Kurds, especially, drove us crazy because they had adopted a "live and let live" relationship with ISIS since the fall of Mosul two months earlier in June 2014. We wanted the Kurds to help fight ISIS, but they had refused, maintaining an uneasy peace along their unofficial "border" with ISIS. The Kurds hoped to keep their border with ISIS as calm as possible. They didn't think ISIS would dare attack their territories—but that seemed an inevitability to most U.S. military leaders, myself included.

Sure enough, ISIS began to enter Kurdish territory in early August when its forces attacked the respected Kurdish Peshmerga troops at Sinjar then moved on to the strategically important Mosul Dam. I'd first heard about the ISIS attacks near Mosul Dam and Sinjar—about sixty-five miles southwest of the dam—on August 1 during a meeting at the Ministry of Defense with the Iraqi Joint Forces commander, General Kenani, and the other senior leadership of the Iraqi Security Forces.

Mosul Dam, situated on the ancient Tigris River, was the largest dam in Iraq. Once ISIS controlled it they would have the power to flood Mosul, about thirty miles downriver, and possibly even Baghdad—290 miles south of the dam. An ISIS victory at the Mosul Dam would also pose a serious threat to the Kurdish capital of Erbil, just eighty-two miles southeast of the dam.

Considered a highly effective fighting force, the *Peshmerga*—whose name translates to "Those Who Face Death"—had become legendary during their many years of fighting Saddam Hussein's troops.[1] However, the vaunted Peshmerga forces had pushed back the initial ISIS attack, but were eventually overrun by the sheer numbers, superior equipment, and aggressive offensive tactics of ISIS. The defeat of the fierce Peshmerga fighters was alarming to the Kurds—and to us. When word came down of their defeat, I made my way to the combined joint operations center in the Iraqi MoD that by then we'd manned with both U.S. and Iraqi personnel.

---

1   "Profile: Who are the Peshmerga?" BBC, August 12, 2014, accessed April 24, 2018, https://www.bbc.com/news/world-middle-east-28738975.

I saw the worry on the faces of the Iraqi generals. They feared that ISIS would take over all northern Iraq and then Baghdad. The upside was that the aggressive move by ISIS provided us with a huge strategic opportunity to get the Kurds involved in the fight. I was concerned for those in the path of ISIS, certainly, but I saw their move into Kurdish territory as a strategic blunder that we could use to our advantage. I knew the Kurds could no longer stay out of the fight. ISIS threatened their homeland, and they had to defend Kurdistan and their capital of Erbil. I also suspected the Obama administration would not stand by and allow our close allies, the Kurds, to be overrun. My hope was that this event would finally convince President Obama to allow us to unleash U.S. airpower.

I was certain the Kurds and their European allies would ask the U.S. to intervene with airstrikes. And, if we were given the green light to conduct strikes, I anticipated our severely limited rules of engagement would be lifted.

While ISIS forces were making headway at the Mosul Dam and Sinjar, they were simultaneously conducting small-scale attacks in the greater Baghdad area. It was a tactic that was keeping the Iraqi military and their political leadership focused on Baghdad and not the broader and more significant ISIS attacks throughout Iraq.

I met with General Kenani and the senior leadership at the Iraqi Ministry of Defense. I needed to get them more focused on the ISIS attacks to the north, near Mosul and the dam. I made the point that the attacks around the greater Baghdad area were only diversions. It was not an easy sell—the Iraqis became enraged, indignant, and were overly focused on even the smallest of threats against the capital regardless of what was going on elsewhere in their country.

The increase of ISIS attacks on the Kurdistan territory in northern Iraq provided the push we needed to get the attention of the Kurdish military and their political leadership. On August 6, General Babikir Zebari—a Kurd and Iraq's chairman of the Joint Chiefs of Staff—asked to meet with me in his office. There he pleaded for me to call the White House and ask for airstrikes.

I thought the request was an amazing occurrence since the Kurdish general hadn't previously been at all inclined to engage his forces with ISIS, even after ISIS had so easily overrun other areas of Iraq. Now that his beloved Kurdistan was being attacked, he was ready to call out the dogs of hell. The irony of that was not missed by any of the other senior Iraqi military leadership.

I couldn't resist asking General Zebari if the Kurds would now get serious about fighting ISIS. He said the Kurds would fight for their homeland. I pressed him and made the point that it would have been much better if the Kurds had been fighting all along. The general didn't bother to offer a defense. Instead he gave me a sad, hurtful sort of look.

To me, all the pettiness and squabbling between the Kurds, Sunni Iraqis, and Shia Iraqis always seemed like such a huge waste of energy. We were supposed to be fighting a common enemy, not each other—but such were the traditions and sordid history that tormented the region.

We had all been surprised at how quickly the Peshmerga had folded and begun retreating east toward Erbil. I told General Austin that we could hardly stand by and watch as ISIS took over another major city, especially the Kurdish capital. He agreed with me, but he needed to get the authorization for airstrikes from President Obama. He said he'd get back to me.

Within hours, President Obama authorized us to protect Erbil. However, his administration issued very restrictive guidance: we could conduct airstrikes to protect Erbil but nowhere else in Iraq. [2] It was not quite the green light I'd wanted, but it was at least a step in the right direction. We finally had the opportunity we'd been waiting for—the chance to lethally strike ISIS. We got the gears of war in motion to do just that, and for whatever came next.

2   Helene Cooper, Mark Landler, and Alissa J. Rubin, "Obama Allows Limited Airstrikes on ISIS," *The New York Times*, August 7, 2014, accessed April 24, 2018, https://www.nytimes.com/2014/08/08/world/middleeast/obama-weighs-military-strikes-to-aid-trapped-iraqis-officials-say.html.

CHAPTER 14

The Abisellan Line

DANA PITTARD

August 2014

My team huddled at the joint operations command center at the U.S. Embassy to finalize what we would and wouldn't do under the newly issued rules of engagement. The meeting included our team of intelligence experts, logisticians, communications specialists, JTACs, and many others as we laid the groundwork for morphing our operations center into an *ad hoc* strike cell.

We weren't alone. Accelerated planning and coordination was also taking place at CENTCOM headquarters in Tampa, Florida, at ARCENT's forward headquarters in Kuwait, as well as at the Air Force's Combined Air Operations Center in Qatar. In Qatar, the commander of all Air Forces in CENTCOM, Lieutenant General John "Kid" Hesterman, and his deputy, Major General Jeff "Butkus" Longren, had been chomping at the bit. (As a confession, I was always a little jealous that the Air Force officers got to use their nicknames officially—we didn't have that option in the Army! If given the chance, I would have probably been called "Cool Hand Luke" or "Pistachio.")

I wanted us to do our best to push the envelope on what was considered "authorized" to give us maximum flexibility to target ISIS fighters. I directed our J3 operations officer Marine Colonel Eduardo Abisellan, our chief of staff Colonel Eric Timmerman, and our operations planner Major John Holstad to draw a red "no penetration line" on our operational maps. To protect Erbil and Kurdistan, we would attack any ISIS fighters that crossed that red line.

I told our guys to push the line out as far west of Erbil as we possibly could while still trying to stay within the spirit of our commander in chief's guidance. I called the demarcation the *Abisellan Line*, after the excellent Marine officer who physically drew it on the map.

It was swiftly approved. As our campaign went on, the Abisellan Line would become commonly referenced as it defined where we could and could not prosecute our airstrikes on ISIS in the early days of the campaign.

ISIS had gained momentum in early August by seizing the Mosul Dam, moving into the Kurdish Erbil Province, and sending the Kurds' once feared Peshmerga troops into retreat. The terrorist army seemed unstoppable. We received frantic calls from the senior Kurdish leadership pleading for American airstrikes on ISIS. I could hear the anxiety in their voices. They feared ISIS would take over Erbil. Still, we couldn't yet strike until ISIS crossed the Abisellan Line—even though it was a line we'd arbitrarily drawn on the map just to meet President Obama's restrictive rules of engagement.

On August 8, one of our F/A-18 pilots reported a group of ISIS fighters on the east side of the Abisellan Line in four U.S. Humvees that were likely captured from the Iraqi Army. We sent a drone over the area. We watched what appeared to be an ISIS reconnaissance patrol as it moved within sixty kilometers of the Kurdish capital.

The small ISIS patrol soon ran into a Peshmerga force of about 100 soldiers. Much to our surprise, the ISIS fighters unleashed a barrage of machine gun fire from their Humvees that sent the Peshmerga force into retreat. The ISIS patrol's aggressiveness and skills were impressive. The Peshmerga fled to some half-finished defensive positions they'd been frantically preparing before the attack; and appeared to be in shock from the ISIS onslaught.

The ISIS fighters returned to their vehicles and continued traveling steadily east. Our intelligence officer, Lieutenant Colonel John Barnett, along with our targeting staff and Air Force TACP JTACs, all recommended we hit the patrol with an airstrike.

I approved the strike after getting blanket permission from my superiors.

The plan was to knock out the lead and rear vehicles first so the rest of the convoy couldn't escape, then finish off the middle two. As our JTACs coordinated the strike with the pair of F/A-18 Hornets, we watched on our drone feeds as the ISIS patrol continued toward Erbil. They were bold, but they had no idea of the hell we were about to unleash.

Within minutes, the Hornets dropped two 500-pound bombs on the ISIS convoy, hitting the first and last vehicles. The ISIS fighters must have heard the whistling sound of the bombs coming down because about five seconds before they impacted the fighters started scrambling out of their trucks. But they didn't scramble fast enough. We saw only one survivor, and he was severely wounded.

Cheers went up in our operations center at the U.S. Embassy. Colonel Timmerman gave me a thumbs-up. Later that same day we engaged another larger ISIS convoy on the east side of the Abisellan Line.

It appeared that we'd stopped ISIS from entering Iraq's northern region, but we couldn't be sure. The strikes that day marked the initiation of strike cell operations against ISIS—and they were the first of thousands of future airstrikes against the caliphate.[1]

---

1   Dan Roberts and Spencer Ackerman, "US begins air strikes against Isis targets in Iraq, Pentagon says," *The Guardian*, August 8, 2014, accessed April 24, 2018, https://www.theguardian.com/world/2014/aug/08/us-begins-air-strikes-iraq-isis.

CHAPTER 15

A New War's Fog

DANA PITTARD

August 2014

On the day we kicked off the first strikes of the campaign, everyone was ecstatic to finally be killing ISIS. But we would quickly be humbled by—and somberly reminded of—the potential pitfalls in strike cell operations and the huge responsibility that came with each and every authorization to strike.

We received an alarming spotter report from one of our F-16 fighter pilots as he patrolled the skies of northern Iraq. He described a very large ISIS force of at least 500 fighters rapidly moving from the west toward Erbil.

Our newly initiated Embassy Strike Cell went on full alert, but I knew extreme caution was required. In the war against ISIS, conducting airstrikes was more complicated than we were used to. We couldn't use our best resources for identifying targets and directing strikes—JTACs embedded with ground troops on the battlefield. Our JTACs were in the strike cell and they had the difficult job of overcoming language, cultural, and technical obstacles to communicate with our Iraqi and Kurdish partners on the ground and control strikes onto the right targets while themselves far removed.

When we received our pilot's report, we kicked into high gear. Our targeting team recommended we attack the suspected ISIS force with everything we had. I called Lieutenant General Terry, who gave me the authority to strike pending CENTCOM approval. I called General Austin at CENTCOM to apprise him of the situation. He gave me authorization to strike once we confirmed the target as ISIS. Still, we both thought it would be prudent to get a second set of eyes on the ISIS fighters before engaging.

I requested a Predator drone be pushed to the area. I was all for pulling the trigger, but a nagging thought made me hold up: we'd been tracking ISIS forces for seventy-two hours straight since getting authorization to protect Erbil, and then this tantalizing target just appeared out of nowhere.

How did they get so far east of the Abisellan Line without detection? Wouldn't we have seen them earlier?

It was hard to believe that the huge ISIS force had gotten so far without being spotted up to that point, but our drone coverage in northern Iraq was limited due to a shortage of drones throughout the CENTCOM Middle East theater of operations. We knew we had some surveillance gaps that left us unable to monitor all road networks and approaches to Erbil. Still, I wanted a good look at the force before I ordered a strike, and the only way to do that was with a Predator drone.

Our fighter pilots were often great resources for identifying friend from foe. Yet even with those eyes it was tough for them to distinguish ISIS fighters from other troops or groups of refugees and civilians. You had to understand how they moved, what sort of equipment and weaponry they carried, and ideally you had to have communication with partner forces on the ground to gain ground intelligence. I respected our Air Force pilots, but it was difficult for them to discern one group of fighters from another. Despite all the training they received, their observations of ground troops were affected by high speeds and altitude.

I asked the JTACs to pull up the video feed of the Predator drone we'd tasked to the target area so we could take a closer look, but it was another thirty minutes before it could be overhead. Our eager F-16 pilot was itching to strike. He requested authorization to engage the large force. The pilot was trigger happy, for sure—but I was in charge of making that call, and my JTAC would be the one to deliver the message.

Every set of eyes in the strike cell was on me awaiting the decision. The operations center was hot and humid. We were already tense and sweating. The easy and popular decision would have been to grant the request and call out the dogs of war, but my gut told me to hold off. I'd had experiences in the past with battlefield pilot reports that were not totally accurate. On the other hand, I'd been one of the strongest voices against our extremely limited rules of engagement up to that point, so I hoped my gut wasn't working against me.

I had received the go-ahead from my superiors, and on the surface it seemed to be a chance to use our vast firepower on a despicable enemy that we'd observed slaughtering civilians without qualms. Still, as much as I wanted to order the pilot to drop his bombs, I directed our JTACs to hold off.

"I need a drone on the scene. I gotta make this call knowing full well those are ISIS fighters," I told everyone.

A collective groan emerged. We were all fighting fatigue and stress. We'd been so frustrated from the time we'd hit the ground in Baghdad, and we all wanted to take down ISIS whenever we got the chance. The suspected ISIS force was still an hour out from Erbil, though. If I could get the drone overhead within thirty minutes, we could determine the situation definitively with plenty of time.

"We'll still have time to act once we've confirmed this is ISIS," I said.

I called Lieutenant General Terry in Kuwait and ran my decision by him. He supported me, and that helped, yet I still felt like the least popular guy in the command center. It took exactly twenty-seven minutes for the Predator drone to reach the target area—but it seemed like twenty-seven *hours*.

The Predator drone's video feed finally came up on our screen. One of my young staff officers blurted out, "See, they're ISIS fighters moving east...what an awesome target!"

It didn't look so awesome to me, though. The image was obscured due to cloud cover. I asked our JTACs to deliver guidance to the drone pilot—more than 7,000 miles away at an Air Force base in the Nevada desert.

"Tell him to move the Predator closer to the target area so we can see it more clearly."

The Predator moved in and I directed our JTACs to have it zero in on the vehicles and fighters who had stopped along the route. Slowly, an image came into focus, revealing sand-colored vehicles and uniformed men, some wearing scarves over their heads. Some soldiers were directing traffic and others appeared to be aiding what looked like refugees walking along the road. Some of the soldiers were pointing their weapons west, away from Erbil and in the direction of ISIS forces.

I stared at the video feed for five or six minutes, trying to make sense of what I was seeing. In the meantime, I could feel all the eyes in the operations center on me. I had to go with what my own eyes were telling me.

This was *not* an ISIS fighting force.

They were most probably Kurdish Peshmerga fighters. It was a force of more than 500 friendlies! I realized my gut had tapped into my experiences working with the Kurdish Peshmerga and traveling throughout Erbil in the past. Only a few other people in the operations center had similar experiences. Most had been deployed to either the Baghdad area or Al Anbar Province in western Iraq. They hadn't served in the northern Iraqi provinces of Ninewa or Erbil where they might have worked with the Kurdish Peshmerga. I was then one of only a few American military officers in Iraq at that time who'd been in every province and interacted in-depth with the Kurdish Peshmerga, Iraqi Army, Iraqi Police, Border Guards, Shia Militias, and other Iraqi Security Forces.

When I pointed out everything I observed based on my experience, most in the room agreed with my assessment. I told the JTACs to stand-down the F-16s. Still, one staff officer adamantly protested, insisting it was an ISIS force. Before I could respond to the young officer, Colonel Abisellan took him for a "walk" (probably a wise move).

We sent a message to the Kurdish military leadership and promptly received confirmation that the forces were Kurdish troops and not ISIS. When that word came down, the operations center went silent. A sigh of relief went up—and it wasn't just from me.

The old saying "it's lonely at the top" is often quite true, but I did receive a few thumbs-up, several smiles of congratulations, and one hand-shake. I thanked them all and went back to my small office and shut the door. I allowed myself a smile and a few deep breaths to release the stress.

No one had to point out that if I had authorized the airstrike it would have been the largest fratricide of a U.S. ally since the war on terror began back in 2001. My name would have gone down in infamy.

Whew.

I gladly took the scattered "attaboys" instead.

CHAPTER 16

Is This Any Way to Run a War?

DANA PITTARD

August 2014

We finally had a real mission against ISIS. We began receiving constant reports of ISIS activity and clashes throughout Iraq, which stirred plenty of excitement in our Embassy Strike Cell. Unfortunately, we were still only allowed to conduct airstrikes in defense of Erbil and only when ISIS crossed the Abisellan Line.

On August 9, we received a report of a large group of ISIS fighters approaching Erbil from the south. There was some skepticism about the report because of the similar circumstance just the day before that had proven false. This time, I wasn't among the skeptics—and neither was Colonel Abisellan. We agreed that it was a very likely approach strategy for ISIS to attack the Kurdish capital.

Our intelligence analysts confirmed that as many as 600 ISIS fighters were at the reported location. The force was just outside the Abisellan Line, approaching the Kurdish town of Makhmur and traveling in over fifty U.S.-made armored Humvees and other military and civilian vehicles.

It was truly the largest concentration of ISIS fighters we had seen up to that point. We believed it to be the same strike force that was the initial spearhead for all of ISIS' offensive operations in the Mosul area earlier that summer.

110   *Hunting the Caliphate*

Watching their movements on our drone feed was quite instructive. The ISIS force appeared to be a well-trained and disciplined unit. It was divided into three major columns: one on the road and two others about one-to-two kilometers bracketing either side. It was a well-coordinated movement.

We watched the initial few minutes of their attack on the city of Makhmur. The ISIS fighters fired their weapons deliberately and accurately, and they used hand and arm signals as they cleared buildings and streets in a disciplined and tactical offensive maneuver. As much as I admired their tactics, I had no problem ordering their destruction. I directed our JTACs to target the entire force.

As one of our JTACS began coordinating the attack with a set of U.S. fighter pilots, Colonel Timmerman took me aside saying we had a "slight problem." The ISIS strike force was five kilometers *outside* the Abisellan Line, to the west. Based on the restrictions of the presidential authorization, we could not strike until the ISIS forces moved east inside the line.

I laughed. It seemed so silly to me because we'd arbitrarily drawn the line on the map in the last forty-eight hours just to give Washington what they wanted. In asymmetric warfare against an insurgency force, there was never an actual "line in the sand."

My inclination was to simply bring out the red pen, hand it to Colonel Abisellan and have him re-draw the line to include the town of Makhmur so we could bomb the ISIS force. Colonel Timmerman nodded and we prepared to strike the targets. Then the lawyers stepped in. They wouldn't budge, and neither would their legal counterparts at CENTCOM. They refused to legally certify our striking the target.

We were shocked. Everyone in the operations center (minus the lawyers) was up in arms. To keep from inflaming the situation visibly, I went to my office and called Lieutenant General Terry. He was one tough cookie and a combat veteran of vast experience. When I frustratingly explained that the lawyers had shut down our plan to strike the major ISIS force, he stood by the lawyers. He noted that we didn't want to risk losing our newly-won airstrike authorization by going beyond the president's orders.

My response was not the most thoughtful I'd ever come up with. "Sir, that's bullshit! We just drew that damn line within the last forty-eight hours. We can re-draw it. We need to strike now!"

His north Georgia drawl came back with an even harder edge. "We have to follow orders, Dana."

I thought our lawyers were insane. We would never get another opportunity like this one. At that point ISIS had not yet been hit by a massive-scale airstrike. I was so pissed off that I went up the ladder to four-star General Austin at CENTCOM. I made the case that we had a rare and fleeting opportunity.

He listened, and then told me to stand by the president's guidelines. "No targets beyond the approved red line."

I felt as though the top of my head would blow off. "*Approved* red line? Sir, we just drew that freakin' line two days ago. Let me re-draw it five more kilometers west! I'll tell President Obama myself."

I had met the president on three different occasions. I would have had no qualms telling him I'd taken a fat red felt marker and extended the line five more damn kilometers.

That brought a light chuckle from General Austin, along with a stern reminder that we had to stay within the guidance of the man in the Oval Office. It seemed crazy to me. My only consolation was that, sooner or later, the fanatical terrorists would have to cross our *approved* red line. I was just afraid we'd never be able to hit them this effectively ever again.

I returned to the operations center to await that opportunity. We waited...and waited some more. To our collective consternation, most of the ISIS force stayed near Makhmur. They did not move east into our killing zone. In fact, they parked nearly fifty vehicles just outside of town and staged what looked like an Islamic extremist pep rally, raising their weapons in the air and cheering. A man jumped on top of one of the vehicles and spoke to the amassed ISIS fighters—he was obviously one of their leaders, which made me all the more frustrated.

I held my head in my hands. The whole scene made me sick. A pall of disbelief overtook the operations center as we watched the terrorists party on.

The ISIS fighters never crossed our arbitrary Abisselan Line. It was as if someone had shown it to them on a map and said, "Hey, don't cross here!" We later learned that as many as three top ISIS leaders were in Makhmur that day. We never got another shot at such a lucrative target.

The image of the ISIS strike force partying with impunity just outside our authorized killing zone still haunts me. Ever since that moment, I thought that if we had only been able to show the scene to President Obama to let him see what we were seeing, he would have told us to strike.

As I'd feared, it was quickly disseminated throughout the ISIS ranks that we were authorized to conduct airstrikes and they soon began adjusting their tactics. Shortly after we initiated our airstrike campaign *en masse*, we rarely saw ISIS move with more than three military vehicles in a convoy. They began using civilian cars to move their fighters, which made it far more difficult to identify them. They started using "human shields" from the civilian population knowing we wouldn't strike.

In addition to those increasing challenges, we dealt with a severe drone shortage. We relied on drones to corroborate intelligence and gain eyes on ISIS positions. The shortage was a significant limiting factor. I had some tense phone conversations with my superiors on the topic.

General Austin was in a tough position. From his command he had to allocate a limited number of Predator and Reaper aerial drones for the entire twenty-nation CENTCOM region. That included Afghanistan—where we were still heavily involved in a ground and air campaign. Afghanistan was allocated *fifteen times* the number of drone "lines" that we had in Iraq. I understood why Afghanistan was the priority—we still had troops on the ground there in need of support—but I was frustrated and amazed that we were not being allocated more drones to fight ISIS.

The lack of drone allocations to our operations in Iraq, coupled with the restrictive rules of engagement, really limited our effectiveness during that critical time. Due to the drone shortage we were often forced to race against time. We had to fly the drones from their base in Kuwait southeast of Iraq all the way up to northern Iraq. By the time they flew into our coverage areas in northern Iraq, they had limited loitering time to support operations. Since our operating area included at least three potential ISIS avenues of approach to Erbil—from the north, center, and south—it was a lot of area to cover with very few drones.

We thought that flying drones out of southern Turkey would be better, but getting clearance to do that became an issue. I contacted the CENTCOM deputy commander of air forces, Major General Jeff "Butkus" Lofgren, and the CENTCOM operations officer, Major General Ken

"Cruiser" Wilsbach. They understood the urgency of the situation around Erbil—that we could not allow Erbil to fall to ISIS—and they helped us get two additional drone allocations for the region.

We were finally able to see more, and what we saw wasn't pretty.

It was chaos on the ground as ISIS poured into Iraq on several fronts. They were moving more fighters from Syria to Iraq to fight the Kurds in their territories while also conducting operations in western Al Anbar Province, threatening the strategic Haditha Dam and Baghdad. ISIS forces were also attacking in eastern Diyala Province and putting pressure on the Iraqi Security Forces guarding the economic and strategically important Bayji Oil Refinery in central Iraq.

In northern Iraq, the Kurdish Peshmerga attempted to put up a fight along each of the three major routes to Erbil, but they were outgunned and outflanked by the experienced and more aggressive ISIS fighters. In the meantime, thousands of Kurdish, Iraqi, and Yazidi civilian refugees were fleeing an ISIS invasion and jamming the roads as they escaped east toward Erbil.

Because of the limited authorizations for airstrikes we'd been given, we couldn't do anything about a lot of what we saw. We even had ISIS rocket and mortar attacks aimed at the U.S. Embassy and our joint operations center, as well as our special operations forces on BIAP, but we were unable to retaliate. It seemed insanely timid to sit on our hands while Iraq was attacked in multiple locations from ISIS forces. I had to wonder what the Pentagon and White House staffers were thinking.

I understood President Obama did not want to get dragged into another war, but I felt the United States had invested too much in trying to create a democracy in Iraq to just let it fall away. We'd taken out the dictator Saddam Hussein in 2003, and now we were standing by, eleven years later, while ISIS seized the country in their vision to create a throwback empire where women become sex slaves, beheadings are a daily occurrence, and extremist Muslims slaughter anyone who doesn't share their beliefs.

Our response to the ISIS threat was truly underwhelming. It was no way for the world's last remaining true superpower to lead. The reluctance of our president and Congress to take on ISIS with a full-on military response was embarrassing. The Kurds and the Iraqis were fighting for their very existence, and they were incredulous that we offered such limited assistance.

Compounding that, our joint operations center was constantly under siege and yanked in all directions. We were bombarded with anxious calls from the Combined Joint Task Force staff, U.S. Central Command, U.S. Embassy, State Department, Defense Department, various intelligence agencies, Iraqi senior military staffs, Kurds, and a host of others.

Everyone had a stake in the game. Half of them wanted ISIS wiped off the map immediately regardless of any collateral damage, while the other half wanted a gentler approach. They *all* wanted constant updates and reassurances that we were playing by their rules, as varied as those rules were.

As the U.S. military leader in Iraq, I did the best I could given the handcuffs placed upon us. Our goal was to keep ISIS from overrunning the Middle East and turning the region into a primitive Islamic caliphate and terrorist breeding ground. But the question that kept popping into my mind was: "*Is this any way to run a war?*"

PART 4

The Campaign Expands

CHAPTER 17

The True Enemy

WES BRYANT

I was finally on the ground in Baghdad to make my own fight against ISIS a little more up close and personal. Perhaps a bit serendipitously, before I had left Bahrain I'd found myself in another kind of battle altogether—one that would prepare me to mount an even more intelligent campaign against ISIS once I pushed into Iraq.

Manama, the capital of Bahrain, was well known for its grand and lavish shopping malls. There were several large malls in the downtown region, all considerably upscale, which turned out to be the best bet for a westerner like me to get food more palatable to my taste (I'd never been a fan of Middle Eastern cuisine).

There was one smaller and quieter than the others, and I preferred that. I still felt uncomfortable in the Muslim kingdom full of people that looked exactly like those I'd grown a deep distrust and hatred toward over the years. It didn't matter that I'd never fought against any Bahrainis and that they were, in fact, our allies in the war on terror. My experiences in Iraq and Afghanistan had given me a deep suspicion of all Arabs and Middle Easterners—all Muslims, really—even if I knew deep down that it was irrational to feel that way.

I found a gourmet chocolate café fitting with my cardinal rule of never missing an opportunity to enjoy the finer things. I ended up having time to go a couple times before I left for Baghdad. There I enjoyed a favorite dish, simple, but decadent—a flavorful dollop of vanilla bean ice cream paired with a small ceramic full of freshly melted house-made milk chocolate. I coupled it with a rich, smooth espresso. I felt like I was in a scene from the Pixar film *Ratatouille* as I took bites of the ice cream-dipped warm chocolate. That was some of the best dessert I've ever had.

One evening, in my last few days before heading out for Baghdad, I hit the café after dinner. I looked out into the common area below from my table in the second-story café, and casually people-watched. Couples strode by in no hurry. Moms and dads whisked through on one-minded shopping missions. Children played and ran around while their parents took solace from an exhausting day out. Periodically, a miniature train chugged by full of joyous kids as it winded its regular route through the mall. Truly, it could have been a scene from a mall in America, minus a few slight differences.

Most of the men were dressed in modern style clothing, with the occasional wearing traditional Muslim garb. Saudi Arabian men, known to frequent Bahrain on vacation or business, were the easiest to pick out with their pristine white robes and red and white headdresses. Most of the women were dressed in wholly modern clothing with the sole exception of a *hijab*—a large scarf covering the neck and back of the head—and were typically well made with hair and make-up. Women in full *burkhas*—robes and headdresses covering all but their eyes—could be seen here and there but were not quite as commonplace. Pretty much all the children wore modern, western clothes.

I nursed my coffee and dessert at a small, two-seat table. Thoughts raced through my mind, alternating between missing my family back home and the mission in Baghdad, when a group of about eight young teenage girls came into the café and sat at a long table next to mine. They were hard not to notice because they were so giddy—giggling with one another just like any group of young girls might do in the States.

I smiled to myself. It was a bit of joy to see that happiness, especially with my mind so immersed in the gravity of the mission in Iraq. But the girls had one stark difference from a group of American teens: they all wore traditional black *burkhas* with just their faces showing. The *burkhas* were made of high-end material, and their faces were extravagantly made-up as if they had just come from some sort of formal event.

A thought flashed through my mind. Maybe the contrast of their well made-up faces with the rest of them being completely covered exemplified some sort of internal struggle with their religious mandate to wear the *burkhas*? Was it possible that making up their faces as glamorous as possible was the one method of self-expression they had within the confines of the subjugating dogma of their religion? I was probably projecting my own cultural and religious biases onto the situation, but the thought flashed through my mind nonetheless.

The group gathered at the end of their table. One of them raised a selfie-stick with an iPhone on the end of it. They posed and made funny faces, laughing together as they snapped pictures. In their youthful innocence they seemed not to have a care in the world for anything other than the fun they were having at that very moment.

Maybe it took that blend of West and Middle East that Bahrain seemed to embody to allow me to see our similarities in that moment, but a torrent of emotion suddenly overcame me. I glanced at the black-clad group of young women next to me and then looked around at all the other people going about their day. Somehow, I suddenly recognized what I had been carrying inside me for years.

How can I hate these people simply because of what they wear, how they look, or the religion they follow?

I realized within the span of a few moments how much hate I had been harboring—the prejudices I'd developed and how unjustified those prejudices had been. Admittedly, my combat experiences had made me hate Middle Easterners, the Arab world, and all of Islam. I'd harbored contempt toward such people for years. But as I sat in that café I had the sudden awareness that they were not really any different from the rest of us.

These people are not my enemy. They are not our enemy.

My wife and I had named our daughters, London and Berlynn, after key cities of World War II. We loved the names, but we also did it as a sort of homage to our lives together consumed with war. We wanted their names to also be a lesson for them when they got old enough to understand. I had always found myself in a dichotomic struggle of at once recognizing the need for war while at the same time wishing none of us had to do it. But that just wasn't my reality, and it wasn't the world's reality. My wife and I had resolved that our daughters would be taught to appreciate the reasons, implications, and costs of our nation's wars.

Strangely, it was in that epiphanic moment in the chocolate café in Bahrain that I realized I probably wasn't on my way to becoming the example for my daughters that I'd always wanted to be—the example that I had set out to be from the moment we'd named them. I knew I harbored a lot of hate, anger, and bitterness inside. I had only seen the bad in that part of the world, and it had shaped me accordingly.

I didn't want my girls to grow up harboring the prejudices I'd developed over the years. I wanted to raise them to know that even though we may look different from one another, speak different languages, follow different religions, and hold different perspectives toward the world— most of us are fundamentally the same. Our enemies cannot be defined by a single ethnicity, race, religion, or part of the world.

I noticed a shelf in the café laden with gifts. One of them was a small, white teddy bear cloaked in an elaborately decorated black and gold *burkha*. I bought it for my girls back home with the thought that, when they got older, I could tell them the story of this illuminating day in the chocolate café in Bahrain right before I pushed into Baghdad to wage the war against ISIS.

As time went on, and long beyond my tour in Iraq hunting ISIS, I would work on letting go of the blind hate that I realized since that moment had dwelt in me for so long and was creeping through the depths of my being like a demon. It was a personal battle that I would share with almost no one. In time I would prevail—and I would become a better husband, more loving father, and far less angry person. And in the fight against ISIS, I would be a more even-tempered warfighter.

As I sat in that café I knew that, only a few hundred miles to the northwest, ISIS was terrorizing innocent people across the Middle East— Muslims, Christians, Yazidis, and anyone who didn't bow down to them and their extremist ideologies.

As the warrior learns to do, I compartmentalized my dramatic sentiment and emotions—I had to keep my mind on the mission against ISIS. The Bahrainis hadn't yet been affected directly, but I knew that if they ever were, the same innocent young people in front of me would quickly become hapless victims of ISIS' reign of terror.

I was on the ground in Baghdad within a few days....

CHAPTER 18

Relief of Sinjar Mountain

DANA PITTARD

WITH REMARKS FROM WES BRYANT

August 2014

The ISIS attacks against Erbil and their offensive momentum in Kurdistan were temporarily thwarted by our Embassy Strike Cell. To reinforce our success in northern Iraq, General Austin requested I send my deputy, Brigadier General Castellvi, to Erbil along with a small command and control team of ten personnel.

The team was to coordinate directly with our U.S. Special Forces who were already embedded up north, along with the senior Kurdish military and political leadership. It was a wise move that would pay huge dividends over the next few months.

ISIS continued to aggressively conduct offensive operations throughout Iraq and Syria. One of their most significant objectives was around Sinjar Mountain in northern Iraq, southwest of Mosul—the same region we'd witnessed the horrible massacre of the eighty Yazidi men. To avoid the brutal and murderous ISIS fighters, Kurdish and Yazidi civilians had since fled to higher ground on Sinjar Mountain. ISIS forces trapped them there, cutting off any escape. The plight of the Kurdish and Yazidi civilians resulted in calls for assistance from around the world.

We closely tracked reports that at least 20,000 civilians were trapped on or around Sinjar Mountain. We were getting hundreds of cell phone calls from Kurds and Yazidis hemmed in by ISIS on the mountain who had numerous American and European contacts. The situation on Sinjar Mountain had the possibility of turning into a full-blown humanitarian crisis. The story was quickly picked up by international media and made global news.

President Obama authorized a special operations team to deploy to Sinjar Mountain in order to ascertain if humanitarian airdrops were necessitated and to assess how many refugees needed to be evacuated. Shortly after that, we worked with the Combined Forces Air Component Commander, Lieutenant General "Kid" Hesterman, and his team to conduct humanitarian parachute airdrops.

The humanitarian airdrops were coordinated and controlled with help from JTACs at the SOTF-I as well as the special operations task force operating in the north. The drops were very successful. The U.S. coalition along with Iraq's small Air Force were able to get aid to thousands of Yazidi and Kurdish villagers who'd fled to Sinjar Mountain under the heavy ISIS assault.[1]

To oversee the relief and evacuation of the refugees, CENTCOM had formed a joint task force led by the MARCENT commander Lieutenant General Ken McKenzie. Unfortunately for them (but fortunately for those thousands surrounded by ISIS), by the time that joint task force was formed we received indications that most of the Kurdish and Yazidi refugees had already been evacuated by the YPG (Syrian Kurds).[2] For the previous ten days, the Syrian Kurds had been evacuating an average of 2,000 refugees every day from Sinjar Mountain and transporting them to safer areas in Syria and far northern Iraq. Most of the refugees had been rescued.

Sinjar Mountain was a strategic mistake by ISIS. It resulted in President Obama finally authorizing airstrikes beyond the Abisellan Line

---

1 Jennifer Hlad, "Breaking the Siege on Sinjar," *Air Force Magazine*, October 2015 Issue: 50-54, accessed April 24, 2018, http://secure.afa.org/joinafa/AFMag2015/AFMag1015/mobile/index.html.
2 Dana Ford and Josh Levs, "'Heroic' mission rescues desperate Yazidis from ISIS," CNN, August 16, 2014, accessed April 24, 2018, http://www.cnn.com/2014/08/11/world/meast/iraq-rescue-mission/index.html.

and it renewed involvement by Kurdish forces that had previously been unwilling to go on the offensive. Once we received the updated authority from the president, the special operations task force near Erbil quickly stood up a small but deadly strike cell manned by their own JTACs as well as some from the SOTF-I. Their barrages of airstrikes combined with counterassaults by Kurdish Peshmerga forces finally helped break ISIS' hold in the Sinjar region.

One thing was becoming increasingly obvious: it was going to be a long and arduous fight against ISIS, and our strike cells in Baghdad and Erbil would be playing a critical role.

Remarks from Wes Bryant

With all the frustration, anger, and confusion we'd felt about our mission since hitting the ground for the Iraq crisis in June, once ISIS began their campaign of inhumanity against the Yazidis and their all-out assault on the Kurds our mission drastically changed.

As soon as President Obama was briefed on the crisis on Sinjar Mountain and the ISIS forces advancing toward the Kurdish capital of Erbil where our special operations forces were embedded with the Peshmerga, his administration sent down a rapid shift in policy. Suddenly, we had the authority to act—and with a vengeance.

Our SOTF-I in Baghdad and the special operations task force in the north pushed teams to assess the refugee situation in the mountains and to assist with humanitarian airdrops and evacuation support. Along with that, America let loose airpower on ISIS in a far bigger way.

To relieve Sinjar Mountain and safeguard Erbil, the small special operations task force near Erbil established an *ad hoc* strike cell. We sent a couple of our SOF TACP JTACs, Marcus and Will, to assist their cell. Soon their coalition airstrikes were destroying ISIS forces in the region—hitting convoy after convoy of armored Humvees and other tactical vehicles that ISIS had captured from Iraqi and Kurdish military forces in their previous victories. They hammered every ISIS position found west of Erbil and around the Sinjar mountain range. The relief of the ISIS siege on Sinjar and the safeguarding of Erbil happened because of the efforts of the special operations strike cell in the north.

Shortly after the liberation of the Yazidis at Sinjar Mountain, President Obama gave a speech on the mission against ISIS in Iraq, where he reminded the world what it means for America to use its might for the good of humanity:

> *When we helped prevent the massacre of civilians trapped on a distant mountain, here's what one of them said. "We owe our American friends our lives. Our children will always remember that there was someone who felt our struggle and made a long journey to protect innocent people."*[3]

ISIS was an insurgency unlike any we had ever faced. They propagated a widespread and systematic method of brutality in their war fighting and displayed tactical abilities and a level of organizational discipline unprecedented for an insurgency force. And they were the most fanatical group we'd ever seen. The fact that we were, at last, hunting and killing such an animalistic enemy on a large scale was satisfying to us all on a primal level.

---

3   "Transcript: President Obama's Speech on Combating ISIS and Terrorism," CNN, September 10, 2014, accessed April 24, 2018, http://www.cnn.com/2014/09/10/politics/transcript-obama-syria-isis-speech/index.html.

CHAPTER 19

Uniting Iraqis and Kurds

DANA PITTARD

Mid-August 2014

Having their offensive against Erbil spoiled in early August was the first time ISIS had been stopped since they'd seized the city of Mosul two months earlier. Temporarily halting the ISIS juggernaut was a landmark event, but it would all be for nothing unless it was followed by vigorous offensive action by the Iraqi Security Forces and Kurds.

General Austin and Lieutenant General Terry supported my outlook, though they were convinced the Iraqis would not be capable of counter-attacking ISIS until at least the spring or summer of 2015. I was on the ground in Iraq, though, and I saw things a little differently. I believed that with U.S. airpower the Iraqis could begin counterattacks immediately—they just needed the will to fight.

General Austin agreed, to an extent. He just wasn't sure the Iraqis were up to the task—will or no will. He was angry about ISIS having captured the Mosul Dam. He felt strongly that ISIS could be planning to blow up the dam and consequently kill thousands of innocent people. He ordered us to get the Kurds to recapture it.

I agreed on the need to quickly recapture the dam. I also felt it could be an opportunity for the Iraqi Army to be part of the operation—a way to get the Kurdish Peshmerga and Iraqi Army to work together. The conventional wisdom of American military leaders at CENTCOM, as well as civilian and military leaders at the U.S. Embassy in Baghdad, was that the Iraqis and Kurds would never work together. They had so many longstanding issues with one another that simply keeping them from fighting *each other* would be the best outcome to hope for, in the eyes of many.

Getting them to work together would be difficult, I knew…but not impossible. I intended to motivate them to join forces and retake the Mosul Dam. I also wanted to push the U.S. government to support the Iraqi military with airstrikes in addition to supporting the Kurds. I was convinced that the only way to get our government to support the Iraqi military was to demonstrate that they were willing to fight ISIS for *all* of Iraq—for the Kurds, the Sunnis, and other minorities—and not just the Shia population. I wanted to show that, with our assistance, the Iraqi military had the will and capability to win against ISIS.

While I was in Baghdad with the Iraqi senior military leadership, Brigadier General "Cas" Castellvi was still in Erbil working with the Kurdish leadership. I called and told him my plan. He didn't think it was possible, but he agreed to do his best to help my efforts to bring the Kurds and Iraqis together.

Cas asked the Kurds if they would *invite* the Iraqi military to participate in the campaign to retake the Mosul Dam. The Kurds' national security advisor, Mansour Barwani—son of the Kurdish President Masoud Barwani—replied with absolutely zero hesitation, "Hell no!"

The Kurds felt strongly that they could not count on the Iraqi forces that had so quickly collapsed and crumbled against ISIS two months earlier. I reminded Cas that the Kurdish Peshmerga had not done very well against ISIS, either. He knowingly sighed and said that it was still going to be difficult to get the two groups to even talk to one another, much less fight side-by-side.

Making the Case

There was no way we would ever be able to defeat ISIS in Iraq unless the Kurdish Peshmerga and Iraqi military somehow worked in concert. I changed my approach and decided to talk to the Iraqi military leadership about cooperating with the Kurds. Around 10 p.m. on August 12, I met with Iraqi General Kenani at the Ministry of Defense.

The Iraqis loved to meet late at night. They would stay up late and sleep in the next morning, sometimes even taking naps in the afternoon. At night was when the Iraqi military leadership at the Ministry of Defense often had their most important meetings, made many of their critical operational decisions, and conducted coordination between major commanders.

I sat with General Kenani and some of his key advisors in his office. He had some operational maps of Iraq on the walls around the large room. One side of the room had a heavy, ornate wooden table with eight chairs around it and a large map of Iraq spread out on top. On the other half of Kenani's office was his own large desk. In front of his desk was a small wooden table with two chairs on each side, facing inward. Those chairs were usually the "seats of honor" for honored guests or close friends. Continuing beyond the seats of honor were two long sofas on each side of the room, with a third sofa across the room facing Kenani's desk to complete a U-shaped configuration.

General Kenani sat behind his desk like a king holding court. I sat in one of the seats of honor. Next to me was my trusted interpreter, Ali—a native Iraqi who later became a U.S. citizen and soldier. We sat across from General Kenani drinking hot, sweetened Chai tea and eating pistachios. A parade of Iraqi generals shuttled in and out with recent battlefield reports for Kenani from the fighting against ISIS throughout Iraq. Each general would stand at attention, stomp his right foot to the ground, and salute General Kenani. He'd return their salutes, take their reports, and send them off after they stomped their right foot again with a final exchange of salutes. (The military custom came from the British Army influence on the Iraqi Army in the 1920s when Iraq was a British Protectorate.[1])

General Kenani was even more powerful in Iraq at the time because Prime Minister al-Maliki was finally leaving office and his successor had

---

1   "British Colonialism and Repression in Iraq," *Global Policy Forum*, accessed April 24, 2018, https://www.globalpolicy.org/iraq-conflict-the-historical-background-/british-colonialism-and-repression-in-iraq.html.

not yet been elected by the Iraqi Parliament. Technically, that meant General Kenani could actually make military decisions with less interference from the outgoing prime minister. I hoped we might take advantage of this unique opportunity to get the Iraqis and Kurds to cooperate.

During a lull in the reporting from the generals, I spoke directly to General Kenani, addressing him with the respectful term "*Sadey*" which roughly translates to "Sir" in Arabic.

I leaned forward. "Sadey, we need you to send forces to help the Kurds retake Mosul Dam."

He chuckled and waved me off with his hand. "General Pittard, Mosul Dam is a Kurdish problem, not my problem."

I remained calm. It was like a high stakes game of poker.

"As you well know, sadey, Mosul Dam belongs to Iraq. You must help retake it. If the Kurds recapture the dam without the Iraqi Army, they might have a legitimate argument and claim Mosul Dam for Kurdistan."

He frowned before responding, and then said that he didn't have enough troops to spare. I decided to break down the real argument. "Sadey, I need you to do this so we can show the world that the Iraqi military cares about *all* of Iraq. It will also give you more *wasta* [power] to ask the U.S. for airstrikes in all of Iraq, not just Kurdistan. You can show the world that the Iraqi Army can still fight!"

Our discussion intensified from there. He said that the Kurds did not want the help of the Iraqis, but I told him the old Western adage "when a man is drowning, he doesn't care who throws him a life raft." Then I fibbed slightly—I said that the Kurds wanted Iraqi help. That seemed to finally open a door. In the end he relented and agreed to send a small brigade of elite Counter Terrorism Service troops. He would have the near-legendary Major General Fadhil—known as the "Black Scorpion"—lead them. After laying out his terms, General Kenani looked into my eyes intensely and said, "General Pittard, I can only afford to send them for seventy-two hours…maybe ninety-six at most. We will need them back to protect Baghdad."

I nodded and smiled. "Yes, sadey. I understand."

It would have to be enough.

Convincing the Kurds

Of course, the truth was the Kurds did not want help from the Iraqis, so our next move was to convince the Kurds to accept it anyway. "Cas" Castellvi had been paving the way by talking with the Kurdish leadership, who were eager for revenge against ISIS. They wanted to make up for faring so poorly in earlier battles.

The Kurds had U.S. Special Forces advisors embedded with them. They were beginning to get their swagger back and were convinced they could retake the Mosul Dam without help from the Iraqi military. They were proud, stubborn, and adamant on the issue. Kurdish leadership categorically refused to allow the Iraqi military to be a part of the operation.

But I was not going to give up on it.

We needed more *firepower* in the argument, so I enlisted General Lloyd Austin who was well respected by both the Kurds and the Iraqis. He called the Kurdish President Masoud Barzani and somehow convinced, cajoled, or threatened Barzani to allow the Iraqi military to participate. It was a monumental achievement, made possible only by the respect and gravitas of General Lloyd Austin.

We were ready to take back the Mosul Dam.

CHAPTER 20

Re-taking Mosul Dam

DANA PITTARD
WITH REMARKS FROM WES BRYANT

Mid-August 2014

It was only days before the Mosul Dam operation was slated to begin. Mansour Barzani, the Kurdish national security advisor, had told Brigadier General "Cas" Castellvi that the Iraqi military could participate but that they would be placed way behind the Kurdish Peshmerga and would play a secondary role in the operation.

The combined operation to retake the Mosul Dam was to kick off on Friday, August 15. Cas and our special operations advisors were able to get the Kurds to agree to delay the operation until Saturday the 16th. That allowed the Iraqi Army units to get up north to Kurdistan to join the operation.

The next big hurdle was how to transport the Iraqi Counter Terrorism Service brigade, with its Humvees and equipment, up to Erbil. Our great logisticians, led by Colonel Andy Danwin, jumped into high gear—flying the Iraqis and their equipment to Kurdistan on U.S. and Iraqi transport planes.

The initial Kurdish maneuver plan called for a complex series of assaults by Kurdish Peshmerga forces from several different directions.

Unfortunately, the Peshmerga really were not trained well enough to execute the plan. It surely would have resulted in *fratricide* (some of the Kurdish forces accidentally shooting each other), and it would have been very difficult to support with airstrikes due to the chaotic maneuver of friendly forces all over the battlefield. Our special operations advisors along with Cas Castellvi talked the Kurds out of the plan. They convinced the Peshmerga to change their scheme of maneuver to a two-directional attack.

The Kurds were anxious to begin. They scheduled a huge outdoor rehearsal and battle group meeting on top of a hill north of Erbil to make final coordination for the operation. At the start of the meeting the Iraqis were no-shows. The senior Kurdish Peshmerga leaders immediately complained that the Iraqi military had not shown up as promised, and they made jokes that the Iraqis were too scared to fight. It was one of the many reasons, they argued, why the Kurdish leadership wanted to keep the Iraqi soldiers in a supporting role. The Kurds believed that the Iraqis just couldn't be counted on.

As if on cue, the ground rumbled with the sound of heavy vehicles coming up the hill. Dirt and dust kicked up as the convoy of Iraqis arrived. The Iraqi Counter Terrorism Service, with their distinctive and daunting black heavily-armored Humvees, appeared out of nowhere like the cavalry in a Hollywood Western ready to save the day.

The convoy stopped, kicking up more dust, and the elite Iraqi troops emerged from their vehicles with unbelievable precision. They were clad in all-black uniforms with black weapons, black body armor, and even black Kevlar helmets. According to our U.S. Special Forces advisors on the scene, the entire Peshmerga leadership was damned impressed.

Major General Fadhil, known as the "Black Scorpion," was an experienced and near-legendary combat leader who inspired love and devotion from his men and fear in his enemies. He and his leaders confidently walked over and met the Kurdish leaders, relaying that they were there to help.

The Kurds were awestruck. They whispered amongst themselves as their leadership strode away into a secluded wooded area. Shouting was overheard, and after a few minutes the Kurdish Peshmerga commander emerged. He told General Fadhil they were so impressed with the elite Iraqi unit that they wanted the CTS to *lead* the attack on Mosul Dam.

What an unbelievable turnaround! We could not have been happier with the decision. The final plan was to conduct one major attack along a single approach led by the Iraqi CTS, with a smaller secondary axis of advance from the Kurds.

The combined Iraqi and Kurdish forces attacked the ISIS fighters defending the Mosul Dam on Saturday, August 16. The special operations strike cell near Erbil supported the offensive with airstrikes. By late Sunday, after some tough fighting, the combined Iraqi-Kurdish force had recaptured the town of Tel Skuf about nine miles east of the Mosul Dam as well as the towns of Sharafiya and Batnaya.

By Monday, August 17, Mosul Dam was recaptured.[1] Both the Iraqi and Kurdish flags flew victoriously over the dam. Iraqi and Kurdish political and military leaders were quick to announce the recapture to the media. Justifiably, they declared a great victory over ISIS.

Upon hearing the news of the recapture of Mosul Dam, President Obama interrupted his family vacation on Martha's Vineyard in Massachusetts to fly to Washington and meet with his national security team at the White House. He then spoke to the nation and the media about the Mosul Dam operation.

President Obama went to great lengths to reassure the American people that the U.S. airstrikes around Mosul Dam were within the same narrow and limited military campaign that he'd authorized to break the siege of the stranded Yazidis and Kurds on Sinjar Mountain and to protect American personnel, citizens, and facilities in Iraq. A senior administration official further reiterated that the United States did not plan to replicate the counteroffensive on Mosul Dam in other parts of Iraq. Unbeknownst to the Obama administration, that was exactly what we planned to do next.

Remarks from Wes Bryant

The Mosul Dam operation was a unique turning point in the evolution of strike cell operations. From the special operations task force in Baghdad,

---

1 Karen DeYoung, Liz Sly, and Loveday Morris, "Obama says Iraqi, Kurdish forces have reclaimed strategic Mosul Dam," *The Washington Post*, August 18, 2014, accessed April 24, 2018, https://www.washingtonpost.com/world/middle_east/iraqi-kurdish-forces-claim-defeat-of-insurgents-at-strategic-mosul-dam/2014/08/18/c869a59a-26d6-11e4-86ca-6f03cbd15c1a_story.html.

we'd tasked one of our Combat Control JTACs, Josh, to embed with the Kurds and the Iraqi Counter Terrorism Service and assist with the operation.

Josh was an especially savvy and innovative JTAC, and among the most experienced in his career field. He came up with the idea to give the Iraqi CTS an app on their smart phones to enable them to send accurate targeting information that he could then pass to the JTACs at the strike cell in Erbil. The Iraqi special operations forces were better trained than many of the regular Iraqi and Kurdish forces. They could be trusted to send accurate targeting information via cell phone after only a brief bit of training and rehearsal.

The CTS soldiers would message targeting information back to Josh, who was embedded at the Iraqi headquarters element. Josh would then quality check and fine-tune the information to send final targeting information to the JTACs in the strike cell so they could coordinate an airstrike.

Josh set up a number of fail-safes in the procedures. First, the Iraqis would snap photos of the readings on their handheld GPS to depict their location. Then they'd take moving map screenshots depicting their own location along with an azimuth and distance to their intended target. If they weren't taking enemy fire bad enough to prevent them from getting their heads up, they'd take a cell phone snap of the target.

Josh went with screenshots as a precaution because his experience with the regular Iraqi troops proved that they would often mix up numbers when passing grids via radio—they'd sometimes say the wrong grid coordinates or even read the numbers in reverse order. A screenshot mitigated any chance of a misread or mistyped coordinate.

Josh also requested that the CTS soldiers pass the "three Ds"—*distance, direction,* and *description* of the target from the vantage point of the friendly position. After getting the snapshots of friendly locations and all targeting information, he'd get a follow up text or phone call translated through one of the Iraqi interpreters. *"We have an ISIS gun truck firing on us! Five hundred meters from our position, azimuth zero-five-two degrees."*

With all of that, Josh and the other JTACs could cross-check the information using their own imagery and drone video feeds and coordinate strikes onto the right targets.

The cellphone texts between Josh and the Iraqi CTS troops were a little different from those sent between most people back home in the States for sure, and they were far more expensive. During the operation to liberate the Mosul Dam, Josh ran up more than $20,000 in data fees on his military-issued global iPhone! But it was a small price to pay to decimate ISIS positions around the Mosul Dam and enable a united Iraqi and Kurdish force to push in and liberate it.

A Hostage Killed—James Foley

James Foley was an American freelance journalist and photographer who'd been reporting on the Syrian Civil War when he was abducted on November 12, 2012. The loss of Mosul Dam and the halting of their attack on Erbil were huge defeats for ISIS. To shift the world's attention from their defeat, ISIS murdered James Foley by beheading him on August 19—forty-eight hours after their defeat in the battle for Mosul Dam.[2] ISIS posted the video online as propaganda.

Foley was the first American to be killed by ISIS executioner "Jihadi John."

James Foley's brutal beheading received condemnation from the United States and throughout the world. His murder began a terrible pattern of beheadings by ISIS that seemed to follow their more spectacular defeats at the hands of the U.S. and its coalition.[3] Unfortunately for ISIS, rather than weaken our morale their murderous beheadings further steeled our resolve and made us even more determined to destroy them.

---

2 Rukmini Callimachi, "The Horror Before the Beheadings," *The New York Times*, October 25, 2014, accessed April 24, 2018, https://www.nytimes.com/2014/10/26/world/middleeast/horror-before-the-beheadings-what-isis-hostages-endured-in-syria.html.
3 Adam Taylor, "From Daniel Pearl to James Foley: The modern tactic of Islamist beheadings," *The Washington Post*, August 20, 2014, accessed April 24, 2018, https://www.washingtonpost.com/news/worldviews/wp/2014/08/20/from-daniel-pearl-to-james-foley-the-modern-tactic-of-islamist-beheadings/?utm_term=.2e21bc5654f1.

PART 5

Unbalancing ISIS

CHAPTER 21

Anticipating ISIS

DANA PITTARD

Re-taking the Mosul Dam with a combined Iraqi and Kurdish force was an amazing achievement. Following the halting of their offensive against Erbil, the relief of the Kurdish and Yazidi refugees on Sinjar Mountain, and their defeat at Mosul Dam, ISIS had lost some momentum in northern Iraq. However, they still retained Iraq's second largest city, Mosul.

At the same time, ISIS was becoming even more aggressive in other areas of Iraq and Syria. Lieutenant General Terry and General Austin wondered where ISIS would strike next. They wanted to know what the Iraqi leaders were thinking. I recommended offensive operations to keep ISIS on its heels, but both Generals Terry and Austin truly believed that the earliest the Iraqis would be capable of conducting coordinated attacks would be in the spring or summer of 2015.

I respectfully disagreed. I thought differently based on what I could see on the ground in Iraq. Colonels Ed Abisellan and Eric Timmerman were of the same mind as me—now was the best time to attack, at a time and a place of our choosing so we could throw ISIS off balance. We developed a tentative plan with Brigadier General Castellvi in Erbil to continue counterattacking ISIS. We just needed to convince the Iraqis and the Kurds to keep up the pressure as well.

At the Iraqi Ministry of Defense, I listened as General Kenani and the senior Iraqi generals argued over where ISIS would attack next. Their discussions all centered on beefing up the defenses of various strategic locations around Iraq. Many said it would be Baghdad, some said Haditha Dam, others said Kirkuk, and still others said the holy Shia city of Karbala or Diyala Province.

Later that evening over hot sweetened chai tea, I met privately with General Kenani and my old friend, Major General Falah—the vice chief of the Iraqi Air Force. General Falah had served as my cultural advisor for an entire year during a previous tour in Iraq (2006-2007). Along with my former aide-de-camp Captain Mike Hastings, we had literally worked together every day for a year and we'd all become good friends. He was now the second in command of the Iraqi Air Force.

"Sadey," I said, "I thought the meeting today was very interesting."

General Kenani replied, "Yes, it is difficult to determine where *Daesh* will attack next, but we must be prepared."

I obviously had a quizzical look on my face. Noticing this, Kenani set down his tea and frowned. "What is it, General Pittard? Do you disagree?"

Here we go, I thought. "Sadey, respectfully, we must place the burden of the dilemma on ISIS. The only way we will continue to stop them is to attack at multiple locations. *We* must choose the time and place to attack. ISIS must be forced to react to *your* actions." I remained silent to let my words settle in.

General Kenani shook his head. "But we are not ready to go on the offense! The Iraqi Army must be rebuilt, re-equipped, and re-trained. You *saw* how we failed in Tikrit two months ago and the disaster in Mosul in early June."

I sipped some hot chai, then gently placed the small glass down on the table. I looked directly at General Kenani. "You don't need much new equipment, and the Iraqi Army is better trained than most ISIS fighters. What you need is the *will* to fight. If you and the other leaders have the *will* to fight and you add the power of our airstrikes—you will be unstoppable! You must take away ISIS' current option to attack wherever they please. We must attack them at multiple locations. ISIS is overextended, now is the time to strike before they are ready again to attack you."

General Kenani sat back in his chair and pondered a moment. "How will we know you will support us with airstrikes? The U.S. only seems to want to support the Kurds and not the rest of Iraq."

"Sadey," I replied, "if the Iraqi Army attacks ISIS we will provide air support. We are in this together."

I knew it was a slight stretch because I didn't then have full authority to support the Iraqis with airstrikes, only the Kurds. But I knew that if the Iraqis aggressively conducted counterattacks against ISIS then I could convince, and practically *shame*, CENTCOM and the Obama administration into supporting them.

Still, it had to be a strategic level objective similar in significance to Mosul Dam. It had to be somewhere like Baghdad, the Haditha Dam, the Bayji Oil Refinery, or some other area of great importance.

"Sadey, I recommend you counterattack ISIS near the Haditha Dam. We've received intelligence they're preparing to seize the dam in three weeks."

Kenani scowled, shaking his head. "Haditha Dam! That is way too far to the west in Al Anbar Province. That will be extremely difficult, if not impossible."

I looked at him, remaining calm but resolute. "Sadey, we are with you. The United States is with you."

The general stroked his chin and thought, holding my stare with his own. After a few seconds he nodded. "I trust *you*, General Pittard. If *you* can ensure we have American air support, we will begin planning for an offensive operation to reinforce Haditha."

I told him I would deliver.

General Kenani stood and walked over to the large map of Iraq on his wall. "Before we go to Haditha, though, I need your help with airstrikes in another area."

I felt a pinch in my gut. I thought, *where the hell is he going with this?*

Kenani continued, "There is a Shia-Turkmen town in the far eastern part of the Salah ad-Din Province called Amerli that has been surrounded by ISIS since June. They cannot hold out much longer. ISIS will slaughter thousands of innocents when they capture the town."[1]

---

1   Michael Higgins, "Amerli – 'Iraq's other humanitarian crisis': A few hundred fighters fighting to protect town from ISIS jihadists," *National Post*, August 15, 2014, accessed April 24, 2018, http://nationalpost.com/news/amerli-iraqs-other-humanitarian-crisis-a-few-hundred-fighters-fighting-to-protect-town-from-isis-jihadists.

I gazed at the map before answering. "Amerli is where ISIS may expect you to go because it's a Shia town. ISIS will not be expecting you to attack them at Haditha Dam since it's a Sunni tribal area. We will possibly lose the element of surprise in Amerli."

Kenani was adamant. "The political and military ramifications of losing Amerli are too great to ignore, General Pittard. I need your help."

My old friend, Major General Falah—who had been sitting quietly through our exchange—finally chimed in. "My dear brother, General Pittard, the Americans and the coalition helped the Kurdish and Yazidi people in northern Iraq when they were surrounded on Sinjar Mountain. What about the Shia-Turkmen people surrounded in Amerli? If you are able to help us lift the ISIS siege of Amerli, it would allow us to get more political support from our civilian leaders, who are mainly Shia, for the offensive at Haditha Dam."

General Kenani nodded in agreement. Deep down I knew that what they said made sense. I thought about it for a moment, then told them that I would do what I could to help with Amerli, but no promises.

CHAPTER 22

Liberating Amerli

DANA PITTARD

Late August 2014

I knew it would be difficult to get approval from CENTCOM and the Obama administration to support an offensive operation to relieve the Shia-Turkmen town of Amerli. The area was of no real strategic importance and was over a hundred miles northeast of Baghdad. It was literally on none of our operational "radar screens." However, it was quickly becoming a moral litmus test with the Shia-dominated Iraqi government and military leaders.

To get approval for airstrikes I consciously avoided referring to any U.S. effort in Amerli as an "offensive operation" during briefings. Instead we called it a "potential humanitarian relief." I spoke to Lieutenant General Terry on the phone about the possibility of conducting the operation, and he was lukewarm at best even though he didn't actually say no.

Luckily, we received inadvertent help from an unexpected source—the United Nations. On August 23, the UN expressed worldwide concern over the situation in Amerli.[1] The UN warned about the possibility of ISIS committing a massacre or genocide in the town. At that point,

---

1   Jomana Karadsheh, Laura Smith-Spark, and Chelsea J. Carter, "U.N.: 'Unspeakable' suffering in Iraqi town besieged by ISIS fighters," CNN, August 23, 2014, accessed April 24, 2018, http://www.cnn.com/2014/08/23/world/meast/iraq-violence/index.html.

General Austin and Lieutenant General Terry quickly came around to the idea of a humanitarian mission at Amerli, and we soon received approval from both CENTCOM and the administration to provide relief. I silently thanked the UN!

Ed Abisellan, Eric Timmerman, and the JFLCC-I staff—with timely help from ARCENT and Combined Joint Forces Air Component Command (CJFACC)—were able to develop a credible plan with the Iraqi military similar to the one we'd carried out at Sinjar Mountain. It centered on providing humanitarian airdrops, protecting the civilian population, and facilitating a ground force to lift the ISIS siege.

Generals Terry and Austin supported the concept. General Austin sold the plan to the Pentagon and the White House, but I was given quite a few restrictions on the operation—including ensuring not to support any pro-Shia Iranian forces. The entire operation would be complex and sensitive. Anything involving the Iranians or giving the appearance of our working with the Iranians was very politically delicate.

For the operation to relieve Amerli, three major ground forces would form the anti-ISIS coalition: The Iraqi Army units that we were advising and assisting from Baghdad would approach Amerli from the south. The Kurdish Peshmerga that Brigadier General Castellvi and our U.S. Special Forces were advising from Erbil would approach from the north. And various groups of Shia militias supported by Iranian Quds Force advisors would approach from the east. (Ironically, they and their Iranian advisors were generally hostile to the U.S.)

Our Iraqi Army contacts would coordinate the necessary de-con-fliction with the Shia militias and Iranians—even despite major issues at first with the de-confliction of Iraqi, Kurdish, and Iranian artillery fires as well as our humanitarian airdrops and airstrikes. We certainly did not want to hit any of our friendly partners nor our reluctant anti-ISIS "allies." Luckily, we managed to work out most of our de-confliction issues before the operation began.

We briefed the operational and fire support plans via video telecon-ference to General Austin in Tampa and Lieutenant General Terry in Kuwait on Wednesday, August 27. General Austin had a lot of questions and plenty of guidance, but ultimately approved the plan. They both reit-erated the need to carefully de-conflict and control our airstrikes and the artillery from Iraqi and Kurdish forces so that we did not inadvertently kill any friendly forces, civilians, Shia militias, or Iranians.

Because of the sensitivity of the mission, Lieutenant General Terry would provide clearance of fires authority. I chaffed at having our clearance authority all the way back in Kuwait. In the end, though, I was just happy we were supporting the operation in Amerli. I knew how important it was to our Iraqi allies.

Most of the ground forces moved to their initial staging areas by Friday, August 29. We quickly found that the roads leading into Amerli were laced with ISIS-emplaced IEDs. This forced both the Kurdish Peshmerga in the north and the Shia militias in the east to maneuver off-road due to their lack of route-clearing engineers and equipment necessary to clear IEDs.

The Iraqi Army force—a brigade-sized element—moved at a slower pace. They approached from the south, clearing nearly every IED on the road. They had the additional mission of opening the highway between Baghdad and Amerli to facilitate the safe passage of humanitarian relief trucks in their wake.

On Saturday, August 30, our anti-ISIS coalition attacked ISIS forces and secured the towns surrounding Amerli to the north, east, and south. The fighting was heaviest in the east between ISIS fighters that had teamed up with local Sunnis and the Iranian-backed Shia militias.

Late that night we carried out selected airstrikes against ISIS targets outside of Amerli. We still had growing pains within our small strike cell in the U.S. Embassy, and we had a very restrictive and time-consuming process to gain airstrike approval.

On Sunday, August 31, the Iraqi Air Force airdropped humanitarian supplies to the outskirts of Amerli. That relief was followed by massive humanitarian airdrops from coalition transport aircraft from the U.S., France, U.K., and Australia.[2] The live video of hundreds of parachuted supplies sailing down through the air was indeed an amazing sight to see on our Predator drone feed! It felt good to witness the event.

---

2   AFP, "US drops humanitarian aid in besieged Iraq town Amerli," *The Telegraph*, August 31, 2014, accessed April 24, 2018, http://www.telegraph.co.uk/news/worldnews/middleeast/iraq/11066175 /US-drops-humanitarian-aid-in-besieged-Iraq-town-Amerli.html.

As the anti-ISIS coalition on the ground attacked to break the siege, we continued to control airstrikes against ISIS forces throughout the greater Amerli area. The Iraqis and Kurds allowed some of the ISIS fighters to escape to the desert in the west with the plan that the city would be easier to take back if it wasn't full of fighters willing to fight to the death. As they escaped, those ISIS fighters became lucrative targets for our airstrikes as well as strikes from Iraqi helicopter gunships. None of us were interested in leaving ISIS survivors.

By the early evening of August 31, Amerli had been liberated.[3] Still, we relentlessly pursued and eliminated groups of ISIS fighters escaping to the west, directing airstrikes well into the night and the next morning. Around 11 p.m. on the night of the liberation, I went to the Iraqi Ministry of Defense to confer with General Kenani. On the way I stopped by the Iraqi-American combined joint operations center to check on our U.S. personnel.

I walked in to the sound of cheers from the Iraqi generals as soon as they saw me. Some came up to me with tears in their eyes, vigorously shaking my hand and kissing me on the cheeks to thank me for the U.S. role in liberating Amerli. I was surprised and impressed by the outpouring of happiness over the liberation of the Shia-Turkmen people of Amerli, and I was truly touched by their gratitude.

General Kenani's office was heavily guarded by large men in the sharp, all-black uniforms that signified they were members of the elite CTS. As I approached the imposing guards, they were also emotional about Amerli and were happy to see me—smiling and nodding their heads in gestures of appreciation. When I walked into Kenani's office, several other Iraqi generals were there celebrating the liberation.

General Kenani raised his hands and yelled out, "General Pittard!" He got up and rushed to shake my hand, kissed me on both cheeks and gushed about how Amerli was a great success for Iraq. He raised his fists victoriously in the air. "The people of Iraq are so grateful for the liberation of Amerli. It could not have been done without your support, General!"

---

3   Peter Kenyon, "Islamic State Suffers Rare Defeat In Amerli," NPR, August 31, 2014, accessed April 24, 2018, http://www.npr.org/2014/08/31/344809411/islamic-state-suffers-rare-defeat-in-amerli.

I thanked him for his kind words and calmly but firmly told him that Amerli was just the beginning. The operation in Amerli showed how the Iraqi armed forces with the *will* to fight, an *offensive* focus, and *determined* leadership, along with American airpower and intelligence, could defeat ISIS every time.

Kenani nodded with approval. "Yes, we are ready to fight ISIS. Now, let's talk about the offensive operation around Haditha!"

I smiled and rolled out a map of western Iraq and the Haditha Dam area.

The Impact of Amerli
September 1, 2014

The Shia militias and the Iranians shamelessly took complete credit for liberating Amerli. They downplayed the U.S.-led coalition and the Iraqi Army and Kurdish Peshmerga's role in helping to lift the siege. Major General Qasem Soleimani, the Iranian Quds Force commander, even went to Amerli that day to be greeted as a liberator.

Even so, one thing that the liberation of Amerli proved was that a common enemy could help bring together strange bedfellows. We showed that we could coordinate with the Shia militias and the Iranian military for a positive outcome against ISIS. I wasn't sure if my superiors ever fully understood just what an immense impact our support had on the psyche of the Iraqi military and Iraq's political leadership.

In the eyes of the Iraqis, we had become full partners as we'd helped both Shias and Kurds. That gave us the additional leverage I was determined to take full advantage of. We were going to get the Iraqis to go on the offense against ISIS.

A Hostage Killed—Steven Sotloff

Steven Sotloff was an Israeli-American journalist working for *Time Magazine* and the *Jerusalem Post* when he was kidnapped in 2013 in Aleppo, Syria. Within twenty-four hours of the liberation of Amerli—another major defeat of ISIS at the hands of the anti-ISIS coalition—Sotloff was beheaded by ISIS murderers on September 2, 2014.[4]

After Sotloff's murder we came to expect a similar response to ISIS defeats in the future. That consequence weighed heavily on us, but we couldn't let their tactics of terror, no matter how cruel, sway us from victory. We would make ISIS pay in blood and defeat for every murder and every barbaric act one hundred-fold.

---

4   Chelsea J. Carter and Ashley Fantz, "ISIS video shows beheading of Steven Sotloff," CNN, September 9, 2014, accessed April 24, 2018, https://www.cnn.com/2014/09/02/world/meast/isis-american-journalist-sotloff/index.html.

CHAPTER 23

The Battle for Haditha Dam

DANA PITTARD
WITH REMARKS FROM WES BRYANT

Early September 2014

We'd had a lot of indicators that ISIS was planning to seize the strategically important Haditha Dam in the western Iraq province of Al Anbar.[1] Al Anbar was a Sunni province that included the ISIS-held city of Fallujah as well as the contested provincial capital city of Ramadi.

In the north, Brigadier General Castellvi had been doing an excellent job convincing the Kurds to go on the offense. The Kurdish leadership from President Masoud Barzani on down was embarrassed at how poorly the Kurdish Peshmerga had fought against ISIS back in early August. The successful Mosul Dam operation had helped them regain some of their prestige, but they were intent on seeking revenge against ISIS and recovering all the lost Kurdish territory in northern Iraq's Ninewa Province.

Cas and I needed to de-conflict the various offensive opportunities we saw in northern, central, and western Iraq. It was a nice problem to have. Both the Kurds and Iraqis finally wanted to attack ISIS. We developed an

---

1   Rebecca Collard, "Iraq's Battleground Dams Are Key to Saving the Country from ISIS," *Time*, September 8, 2014, accessed April 24, 2018, http://time.com/3303403/strikes-against-isis-in-iraq-dams/.

aggressive timetable for operations to continue to keep ISIS off balance, one that considered the operations being conducted by the Syrian Army, the YPG (Syrian Kurds), and other groups fighting ISIS in Syria supported by our special operations forces in northern Iraq.

The first operation under our new timetable would be the Kurdish Peshmerga's attack to seize Mount Zerkel. From Mount Zerkel, the Kurds would be able to observe movements in and around Mosul. That operation was quick and successful—the Kurds seized Mount Zerkel from ISIS on September 5.

Pushing the Iraqi military leadership into conducting an offensive operation over 175 miles west of Baghdad, however—and within a Sunni province—was not an easy task. The remnants of the Iraqi 7th Division were barely holding on to the Haditha Dam, the large town of Hit, and nearby Al Asad Air Base.[2] The rest of the Euphrates River Valley was dominated by ISIS, and they maneuvered freely from the Syrian border at Al Qaim all the way east down to Fallujah, about seventy kilometers from Baghdad.

Colonel Ed Abisellan and our operational planner, Major John Holsted, worked closely with the Iraqi military staff to develop an operational plan that would integrate air support from the U.S. and Iraqi Air Force as well as Iraqi helicopters temporarily based out of Al Asad Air Base. The plan called for the movement of a battalion of the elite CTS—something around 400 men—to reinforce a brigade of the 7th Iraqi Division and conduct the attack at Haditha. Additionally, hundreds of friendly Sunni fighters from the Al-Jaghaifa and Alba Mahal tribes, as well as a contingent of Shia militiamen, were willing to fight.

The operation would be a two-pronged attack from both sides of the Euphrates River, moving south-to-north to free the town of Barwana first and clear all ISIS fighters on both sides of the river between the dam and Barwana.

We'd briefed General Austin and Lieutenant General Terry on September 4. I let them know that I strongly expected seizing positions around Haditha would cause a violent reaction from ISIS, and

---

2   Alissa J. Rubin and Rod Nordland, "Sunni Militants Advance Toward Large Iraqi Dam," *The New York Times*, June 25, 2014, accessed April 24, 2018, https://www.nytimes.com/2014/06/26/world/middleeast/isis-iraq.html.

that we were preparing for a fierce counterattack after the initial battle. We suspected ISIS would attempt to reinforce with fighters from Syria through the ISIS-owned Iraqi border post at Al Qaim, fifty kilometers west of Haditha Dam. We also expected to see some ISIS senior leaders visit the battlefield to rally their fighters.

On Saturday, September 6, we kicked off our airstrike campaign day and night against ISIS positions in the area.[3] We hit ISIS hard, even though the airstrike approval process was still long and laborious since approval authority continued to remain with Lieutenant General Terry in Kuwait. (It was becoming clearer by then that airstrike authority had to be delegated to my command in Iraq.)

The Iraqi Army's ground attack began on Sunday morning, September 7. ISIS put up a staunch resistance near the railroad station outside of Barwana, with quite a bit of ISIS crossfire coming from both sides of the Euphrates River toward our ground forces. We supported with airstrikes while the Iraqis laid down very effective fire with their helicopter gunships—modified Russian-made Mi-17s and Mi-35s—as well as a contingent of Russian-made Su-25 fighter-bombers led by my old friend, Major General Falah.

By the middle of the first day of fighting, it had become clear that the Iraqis would win. Even before the fighting was completely over, the Iraqi military flew their very polished spokesperson, Lieutenant General Qassan Atta, along with a lot of Iraqi media and press personnel into the Haditha area to show the Iraqi people that ISIS could be beaten. Other Iraqi politicians such as the Governor of Al Anbar, tribal leaders, and local town mayors also came to see the great victory.

Our JFLCC-I staff was very wary of the Iraqi politicians' visits since the battle was not yet over. We told the Iraqi Army leaders that winning the initial fight would only be the first step, and to expect a violent ISIS response to our success. We warned them that ISIS was wounded in Haditha, but not dead. Unfortunately, as we'd feared would happen, an ISIS mortar round hit near the assemblage of Iraqi politicians and media. Some were killed and many injured, including the governor of Al Anbar province.

---

3   "US strikes Islamic State militants at Iraq's Haditha dam," BBC News, September 7, 2014, accessed April 24, 2018, http://www.bbc.com/news/world-middle-east-29098791.

That evening at the Iraqi Ministry of Defense headquarters, General Kenani and his staff were nonetheless jubilant over the day's successful battle. I told him to make sure Major General Wahab and the other Iraqi Army commanders in Haditha were preparing for an ISIS counterattack. Accordingly, the Iraqi Army and their Sunni tribal allies consolidated their forces in the Haditha area and hastily set up defensive positions. Once nightfall descended, we were amazed at the ISIS activity near the Iraqi Army positions around Haditha. As expected, ISIS attempted multiple counterattacks that evening—but the Iraqi Army was ready at every turn.

Remarks from Wes Bryant

ISIS was incredibly bold. So much that we couldn't quite believe it when we witnessed them on the battlefield. Even so, when we initiated our airstrike campaign, ISIS really didn't know what hit them. Even up to the Haditha Dam operation it was obvious that ISIS was reeling from such a large-scale military response from the United States.

Because of that element of surprise, many of our targets in the first weeks of the airstrike campaign were lucrative and unlike any we'd ever seen as JTACs. ISIS forces were often so easily discovered by our drones and fighter pilots that they may as well have had red targets painted on them. ISIS had previously been so used to moving unchecked and unafraid throughout the territories they controlled that we'd routinely come across large units of maneuvering ISIS fighters, huge convoys of gun trucks and armored vehicles, and embedded fighting positions that showed little attempt at overhead concealment. The new campaign against ISIS was truly a JTAC's dream come true.

Still, even with all our successes up to that point, the reality was that the U.S. had launched a military campaign against ISIS later than we ideally should have. By the time we'd finally acted with any substantial military response, ISIS was well-embedded throughout Iraq. That created an operational environment where, by the time we planned and launched a counteroffensive against ISIS in one region, they'd already taken ground elsewhere. So, early on, we were flowing from counteroffensive to counteroffensive in a game of catch-up to get the strategic edge.

A Hostage Killed—David Haines

David Haines was a British social worker who'd been abducted by ISIS in Syria in 2013. Following the Iraqi military's triumph at Haditha combined with the successful operation by the YPG to take the Syrian town of Kobani around the same time, Haines was beheaded by ISIS.[4] The gruesome video was released on September 13, 2014, as more ISIS terror propaganda.

We came to expect that a western hostage would likely be executed after every ISIS military defeat or setback. If ISIS thought it was doing any good, it still only strengthened our resolve to destroy them.

4   Greg Botelho, "ISIS executes British aid worker David Haines; Cameron vows justice," CNN, September 14, 2014, accessed April 24, 2018, http://www.cnn.com/2014/09/13/world/meast/isis-haines-family-message/index.html.

CHAPTER 24

Rebirth of the Iraqi Air Force

DANA PITTARD

Some of the most courageous air support for the Haditha Dam operation came from Major General Falah and his squadron of fighter-bombers. During the fighting, I watched as one of the Iraqi strike aircraft scored a direct hit on an ISIS air defense gun—a Russian-made *ZSU-23* hidden under a carport next to a building. Later I found out that the mission had been flown by Major General Falah himself!

I was impressed with the skill and grit of my friend Major General Falah and his eleven Iraqi pilots. Granted, they should have been flying American-made F-16s and not the older Russian Su-25s, but ISIS' invasion had changed everything for the Iraqi Air Force. Back in 2012, Iraq had made the decision to buy a fleet of modern F-16 fighter aircraft from the United States. When ISIS seized Mosul in June 2014, the Iraqi Air Force was then running a transition pilot training course for the F-16s at Balad Air Base in north-central Iraq. Since Balad was in the Sunni-majority province of Salah ad-Din, the former home of Saddam Hussein, there was great fear that the air base would be overrun and taken by ISIS. For that reason, the F-16 training program was hastily moved to the United States.

ISIS was never actually able to seize Balad Air Base, but we didn't know that then. The change in training venue and all the logistical and administrative delays that came along with it meant that the new Iraqi F-16s would not be ready to be fielded until late 2015. The Iraqi military needed indigenous Iraqi air support immediately to fight ISIS.

As a temporary stopgap measure, Iraq bought five older Russian-made Su-25 fighter-bombers from Iran. The fighter-bombers had 1970s and 1980s technology on board, but they could still do the job. Iraq then bought five more in July at a higher price—from Russia.[1]

The Iraqi's now had aircraft to use, but there was one big problem: almost no one in the Iraqi Air Force knew how to fly the antiquated Su-25s. All the young, promising Iraqi pilots had been sent to America to learn how to fly the F-16s—a decision set in place back in 2012.

In an ironic twist, Major General Falah decided to search for any current or former Iraqi pilots who were veterans of the Gulf War (*Desert Storm*) against the U.S.-led coalition twenty-three years earlier. Falah was able to find ten pilots in addition to himself who were at least minimally qualified and had some experience flying the old Su-25s. All of his prospective pilots were between the ages of forty-five and sixty years old, and all were above the rank of major in the Iraqi Air Force.

General Falah and his pilots went through a breakneck, two-week Su-25 refresher course in Iran.[2] The Iranians warmly greeted them as fellow Shia brothers. General Falah relayed an interesting conversation to me that he'd had early on when they got to Iran. An Iranian Air Force general asked him how he could stomach working with the Americans.

Falah laughed, "Some of my best friends are Americans!"

The Iranian general gave Falah a look of horror and incredulity. "But the Americans are so dirty and unclean. How can you stand the stench?"

Falah smiled. "That is not true. Americans are at least as clean as we are, I promise you."

The Iranian general's eyes got big, then narrowed. "Still, I would not be able to stand being around the disciples of the Great Satan!"

---

1   Rod Nordland, "Russian Jets and Experts Sent to Iraq to Aid Army," *The New York Times*, June 29, 2014, accessed April 24, 2018, https://www.nytimes.com/2014/06/30/world/middleeast/iraq .html?mtrref=www.google.com&gwh=BEA5779696050294B9D16AF38D6E7D39&gwt =pay&assetType=nyt _now.

2   Loveday Morris, "Iraq cobbling together makeshift Air Force to fight ISIS," *The Washington Post*, June 27, 2014, accessed April 24, 2018, https://www.washingtonpost.com/world/2014/06/27/ be172f43-cf98-4677-8e6d-4d64a5ae5e1d_story.html?utm_term=.442c76f00422.

"Hmm. It really is okay, my friend," Falah maintained. "Much is misleading," he continued calmly. "My daughter and her family live in America, in the state of Arizona."

The Iranian general was so disgusted by the positive comments about America from General Falah that he waved Falah off and walked out of the room. The rest of their training continued without a hitch. Following the two-week Su-25 refresher in Iran, Falah and his pilots returned to Iraq by mid-July, 2014.

Maintaining the Su-25s and getting spare parts to keep them flying was another hurdle. To properly maintain the ten fighter jets, the Iraqis had to keep at least three in maintenance at any one time. With only seven possible planes available for combat missions, the Iraqi Air Force simply could not fulfill all the airstrike requests called on by nervous Iraqi ground commanders throughout Iraq.

The introduction of U.S. airpower against ISIS in August was certainly welcomed by the tiny Iraqi Air Force. Unfortunately, there was a period of cat-and-mouse between the modern U.S. fighter aircraft and the antiquated Iraqi fighter-bombers. This was based largely on issues with the IFF—identification, friend or foe—equipment on the Iraqi aircraft.

During one of our multiple daily video teleconferences with CENTCOM, the air component commander, Lieutenant General John "Kid" Hesterman, warned about us not knowing if the Iraqi aircraft were friendly or enemy. He said that "most of them were being piloted by Iranians," and it was "just a matter of time" before the U.S. accidentally shot down one of the Iraqi aircraft.

I chuckled before replying. "The Iraqi Su-25s are definitely friendly, and none of them are piloted by Iranians."

Lieutenant General Hesterman seemed taken aback. "Our intelligence has reported that at least half of the pilots of the Iraqi Su-25s are Iranians."

"Your intelligence is either incorrect or old," I confidently answered. "There were some Iranian instructor pilots who flew the jets during their two-week refresher course in Iran. A few of them assisted in getting the aircraft back into Iraq, but the Iranian pilots have returned to Iran and now only Iraqis are piloting the Su-25s."

"How do you know that for sure?"

"Sir, my good friend, Major General Falah, is the Iraqi Air Force vice chief of staff. He was my cultural advisor during my last deployment to Iraq from 2006 to 2007. General Falah himself told me. I'm sorry...but I thought you knew all of this."

Lieutenant General Hesterman paused briefly before responding thoughtfully, "Can you arrange a meeting with General Falah so we can meet him and work out coordination and other aircraft protocols?"

"Of course, sir."

Within days Hesterman's deputy, Major General Jeff "Butkus" Lofgren, flew to Baghdad where I introduced him to Major General Falah. They worked out all the necessary coordination and details so the Iraqi Air Force could become true partners with the coalition air forces. The Iraqis agreed to put their fighter aircraft sorties on the daily "air tasking order" (ATO), which helped immensely to de-conflict sortie times and locations throughout Iraq.

The Haditha Dam operation marked the first time U.S. and Iraqi fighter aircraft formally coordinated in battle. It was a monumental achievement.

The airspace in and around Haditha Dam was incredibly crowded during the operation. Airspace had to be cleared and de-conflicted between Iraqi fighter-bombers and helicopters and our coalition aircraft and drones—in addition to Iraqi artillery rounds and mortars from Shia militia and tribal fighters—all with very little pre-coordination having taken place among the various elements. It was very complex and admittedly quite dangerous for our pilots. I was appreciative of the hard work and coordination done by our air staff, Lieutenant General Hesterman's staff, and Major General Falah's staff to make sure our air operations were coordinated and de-conflicted as we continued in the campaign against ISIS.

As time went on and the campaign developed, we did our best to provide intelligence-driven target packets for Major General Falah and his pilots. If we gave Falah an ISIS target, he and his fellow pilots would hit it. It was almost never "pretty," but more than 70 percent of the time they killed the target.

Still, we had to be careful. On one occasion we handed Falah a suspected location of a senior ISIS leader in Fallujah. It was a difficult target because of the heavy saturation of buildings around the location; it had high potential for collateral damage. The Iraqi Air Force ended up going after the ISIS target and killing the leader—but they destroyed nearly an entire city block in the process.

In those cases, ultimately we only provided the intelligence on their targets. It was up to the Iraqi leadership how they would action them. Unfortunately, the fight against ISIS was not a black-and-white contest; it was truly a hundred shades of gray. ISIS was a brutal enemy and one that did not play by the rules. They'd seized nearly one-third of Iraq's territory and the Iraqis were fighting for their survival as a nation. The Iraqi military—especially the Air Force—understood that truth loud and clear.

General Falah led by example. He flew many combat missions against ISIS personally and his pilots went after the enemy like bloodhounds. The Iraqi people truly owed a debt of gratitude to General Falah and his brave Su-25 pilots.

CHAPTER 25

Virtual Mutiny

WES BRYANT

Shortly after the liberation of Amerli, rumors had come down that questions were being posed at the senior military and State Department levels regarding legalities of running an airstrike campaign from the U.S. Embassy. To avoid any drama, General Pittard ordered immediate transition of the strike cell off the embassy compound.

He ordered a new strike cell set up across Baghdad, at my neck of the woods near the SOTF-I at the Baghdad International Airport. The operation to take back the Haditha Dam would constitute the last strikes controlled from the Embassy Strike Cell, and Vern and I would be taking over the new cell at BIAP and using our special operations JTACs to man it.

While the Haditha operation played out at the Embassy Strike Cell, Vern and I worked day and night to set up the new cell on BIAP. He and I got along quite well even if we'd incessantly, albeit affectionately, argue over which of us knew close air support doctrine the best. (Of course, I always won that argument.) That was a good thing, because we had a lot of work to do.

We coordinated with General Pittard's lead air liaison officer (ALO) and senior TACP JTAC who'd been running the strike cell from the embassy. The two had spearheaded the Embassy Strike Cell and we leaned on them to get the new cell up and running. We made the trek across

Baghdad to the joint operations center to observe the inner workings of their strike cell during the Haditha operation and begin planning for the first operations from our own.

General Pittard's ALO, Major Joel Poche, was a keen and spirited Air Force TACP officer who proved to be of vital assistance. His lead JTAC was an experienced, veteran TACP who helped us immensely with the technicalities and details of the new strike cell operations.

Over the next couple of weeks we assisted the Embassy Strike Cell in the planning and execution of the Haditha Dam operation. After Haditha, Major Poche and his senior TACP followed us back to BIAP to help guide the first operations from our new cell. They soon handed us all the jewels of experience they'd gained in running the Embassy Strike Cell.

The BIAP Strike Cell was to be manned by an unprecedented team of conventional and special operations members from three different services. While "joint" operations between military services were common in the operating environment of the day, the particular mix of multiservice special operators and conventional forces all working together as one was unique to our team.

The cell was to be owned by the commander of Iraq himself—Major General Pittard. General Pittard directed Army Colonel Tim Kehoe to stand up the new strike cell and serve as the director. A swarthy artillery commander of the 17th Field Artillery Brigade with extensive joint fires background, Kehoe commanded a truly professional and capable brigade staff. After setting up all the communications, targeting equipment, and overall infrastructure for the cell in record speed, their skills and equipment became ours for the molding.

The JTACs in the cell would hail from three different services—my Air Force Special Tactics JTACS, Vern's JTAC-qualified Navy SEALs, and a couple of JTAC-qualified Green Berets we'd borrow from the Special Forces teams within the task force. Later we'd incorporate a couple of conventional TACP JTACs who would infill to BIAP attached to the infantry company dispatched to assist with base security operations.

All the JTACs in the strike cell fell under my and Vern's tactical and operational guidance as the fires officer and NCO for the task force. In turn, we fell under the tactical and operational guidance of Colonel Kehoe and General Pittard.

As special operators we had a unique command relationship with General Pittard. By that I mean technically we did not fall under his command even though he was the ground commander for the U.S. mission in Iraq. Instead, we fell under the operational control of Commander Black at the special operations task force in Baghdad, above that the commander of the JSOTF-GCC in Bahrain where I'd been tasked in the first weeks of the crisis, and ultimately under Major General Mike Nagata at SOCCENT back in Tampa. And actually, our special operations task force wasn't even formally tasked by SOCCENT to support the new strike cell operation on BIAP, so there was no formal precedent for me, Vern, or any of the task force JTACs to man it.

Really, our support to General Pittard's strike cell ended up being more of an "informal lateral support agreement" between Major General Nagata and Major General Pittard. That is to say, it would have been if Vern or I had ever really *asked* our chain of command for permission—which we did not.

We both felt that our special operations task force had been flailing along in the fight against ISIS up to that point. The task force was concentrating on standing up a *targeting* mission—to kill and capture high value targets in the Baghdad region—but that was gaining little traction and moving way too slowly. Our Special Forces teams and JTACs had done some amazing work assisting in the relief at Sinjar, the safeguarding of Erbil, the liberation of the Mosul Dam, and the protection of Amerli—but the main task force had little play in those operations and there was no real forward vision to get truly aggressive toward fighting ISIS on part of the task force itself.

Vern and I saw the SOTF-I as missing the boat in the opportunity to make a real difference in the campaign against ISIS, while other entities had been doing just that—specifically the special operations strike cell in Erbil and the Embassy Strike Cell in Baghdad. So, to us it was almost serendipitous that the Embassy Strike Cell was suddenly mandated to move to our location on BIAP.

Vern and I saw an opportunity to make a real difference in the fight against ISIS, so the decision to volunteer our services as JTACs to the ground commander of Iraq was entirely our own. In special operations, when you see a "gap" you fill it; and that's exactly what we did.

Outside the immediate honor and privilege of hunting ISIS, we had another specific purpose in mind when taking the new strike cell: it was our special operations teams running the *advise* and *assist* mission with the Iraqis forces, and it was our Special Forces teams embedded with the Iraqis and assisting General Pittard's staff by doing much of the tactical-level planning, coordinating, and advising for the Iraqi counteroffensives. We believed it should be our special operations JTACs controlling the airstrikes that supported those offensives.

Major Poche was completely on board. He was already struggling with running strike cell operations from the embassy. He admittedly had a small air staff that hadn't come into Iraq under the assumption they'd be initiating the airstrike campaign against ISIS. They had other mission priorities and they were already overtasked from the operations they'd been conducting so far.

As far as our chain of command at the SOTF-I, Commander Black was definitely not keen on losing his fires officer and NCO to the new strike cell. Understandably, he wanted us to be on hand for him 24/7. But we were fortunate enough to have the support of a like-minded operations officer who reported directly to Commander Black and was our immediate "boss" at the task force. He insisted to Commander Black that we were in dire need at the new strike cell and that we'd be far better utilized in that capacity. Effectively, he covered our "moonlighting."

In the end, fitting with the silent mantra of special operations "better to act first and beg forgiveness later," Vern and I never *really* asked permission from our special operations chain of command to take duties at the new strike cell. We simply did it; and let the chips fall where they may. Besides, once the commander of Iraq said he was going to use us to run his new strike cell, we didn't think many would argue. As it turned out, General Pittard was all too happy to have us—and the feeling was more than mutual.

CHAPTER 26

ISIS on a Silver Platter

DANA PITTARD
WITH REMARKS FROM WES BRYANT

In the days following the successful offensive at Haditha Dam, our coalition aircraft patrolled the skies above the area in order to thwart any ISIS counterattacks and hunt any remaining fighters we could find.

Through our Predator drones, we observed a lot of civilian vehicles moving across the Iraqi-Syrian border near the ISIS-controlled city of Al Qaim. However, we could not accurately determine if any of the ISIS fighters had *"hostile intent"* against coalition forces—a condition we had to meet before striking per our rules of engagement. Sometimes we just had to sit and watch until a determination could be made.

One night, three military transport trucks moving suspiciously through the border crossing at Al Qaim caught our eye. The trucks were about seventy kilometers west of the Haditha Dam, moving east along the major east-west highway that ran parallel to the Euphrates River between Al Qaim and the Haditha Dam.

Soon, they made their way to within fifty kilometers of Haditha. At twenty kilometers from the Haditha Dam, the trucks moved off the main highway and turned southwest onto a winding secondary road.

At the same time, we were receiving reports of multiple small ISIS counterattacks against various Iraqi Army defensive positions. There were numerous requests to move our Predator drone off the three trucks and allocate it to one of the reported skirmishes. Lieutenant Colonel John Barnett, our J2 intelligence officer, resisted those calls and kept tracking the trucks. He had my full support—John and his intelligence targeting team were on to something.

The trucks stopped about fifteen kilometers from Haditha. Approximately seventy people got out of the trucks, appeared to assemble, then started walking east. Their manner was very discreet. They walked in a single file and appeared to try to conceal themselves from observers on the ground by stealthily maneuvering through dry creek beds and folds in the desert valleys.

I looked at the Predator screen and asked John, "What do you think?"

He calmly replied. "Sir, it looks like an ISIS force preparing to attack the Iraqi defensive positions that are about ten or eleven kilometers away."

Colonel Ed Abisellan walked up to us at that moment. "Do you recommend we hit them?" I asked Ed.

"Yes," he answered without hesitating.

John intervened. "Sir, let's continue to observe them just a bit and see what happens."

Like Ed Abisellan, my gut feeling was to strike right then, but I agreed to wait. John Barnett was on to something—he was in the zone, I could feel it.

"Okay. Let's observe for now," I said. "Make sure we alert the Iraqi CJOC so they can inform their military leadership in Haditha what's going on."

I called General Kenani and told him about the suspected ISIS fighters approaching. He said his commander on the ground had his hands full with multiple ISIS counterattacks throughout the Haditha area. I warned him that the small counterattacks might be diversions, and that the seventy ISIS fighters we were watching could be a part of a larger planned attack. Still, Kenani told me they could not spare any fighters to interdict the ISIS force approaching from the west. He asked if we could just bomb them and be done with it. I wanted to be sure they were ISIS, though, and see if they would link up with an even larger ISIS force.

We waited and watched as the seventy fighters walked cautiously and deliberately through the night. About seven or eight kilometers from the Iraqi positions, they stopped. It looked like a rest stop. However, we quickly realized that something more sinister was happening. The seventy ISIS fighters had arrived at a weapons cache site deep in a small valley at the base of a hill. A small group of men met them. They handed each fighter a bulky package. The suspected ISIS fighters carefully put their arms through straps on the bulky packages and wore them.

I gave John a puzzled look.

"Sir, I believe those are suicide vests," he said.

I was shocked. "My God…seventy suicide bombers? That'll wreak havoc on the Iraqi positions."

Ed Abisellan looked at me. "Sir, I recommend we hit them right now."

I agreed. "Yeah. All right, John—call it in," I said. "Tell our JTACs to take them out."

But we didn't have any strike aircraft immediately available. Our concurrent support of the small diversionary attacks happening all around Haditha had all our strike assets tied up. Two F-16 Vipers could be on station and over the target area within about ten minutes, though. That was good news, since the suicidal ISIS fighters were likely two hours away on foot from the Iraqi military forces.

Within five minutes, the seventy ISIS fighters were back on the move. They were walking single file with about five-to-ten meters between each man over about a 600–700-meter span—almost seven football fields in length. We knew then that we had missed a huge opportunity to strike when they'd all been standing still and consolidated in one place. Their spread-out orientation presented a weaponeering problem for our pilots and JTACs. One pair of fighter jets simply wouldn't have enough bombs to cover such a long distance.

Ed Abisellan and the targeting team huddled with the JTACs. They came up with a strike plan. We would hit both ends of the column and then the center simultaneously with six 500-pound bombs. Then we'd destroy the remnants of fighters with additional bombs and 20mm gunfire from the Vipers. It was a sound plan.

The JTACs coordinated with our Viper pilots. They confirmed the location and orientation of the ISIS column and briefed the plan of attack. Both pilots acknowledged.

All eyes were on the Predator screen. The feed showed the seventy ISIS fighters within five kilometers of the nearest Iraqi Army position walking single file through a gulley. The timing and location were perfect.

The F-16s dropped two bombs.

The front of the column erupted, the tremendous explosions setting off a lot of secondary explosions from the suicide vests. At least ten fighters were killed. Two more bombs hit the rear of the column with the same explosive effect. At least eight more fighters were killed with more secondary explosives.

Near simultaneously, two more bombs hit the center of the column, killing at least ten more fighters. The rest of the ISIS fighters scattered quickly, running and hiding wherever they could—some discarding their suicide vests as they ran. Unfortunately for the survivors, we could still clearly see their heat signatures from the Predator drone and our F-16s. I gave the order for our JTACs to continue to track them down and kill them all.

The Vipers began rounding the ISIS fighters up with their 20mm cannons just as we received a fresh pair of F-16s on station hungry to jump into the fray. We watched as approximately twenty-five ISIS fighters hid in a small crevice. The pilots and our JTACs were all over it.

Two more 500-pound bombs from our freshly-armed Vipers went into the shallow crevice. The explosion and resulting secondary explosions were unbelievable. No one could have survived the barrage. Still, we were slightly surprised as we watched five fighters crawling out, wounded and dazed.

The JTACs asked me if I wanted to re-engage the surviving ISIS fighters.

"Yes," I firmly replied.

Another 500-pound bomb was soon dropped that ended all human movement at the crevice. Every ISIS fighter was killed.

While that was happening, a second Predator drone had been tracking some of the ISIS fighters that survived the initial strikes. Our JTACs controlled 20mm attacks onto those *squirters* (maneuvering ISIS fighters).

At that moment, Lieutenant General Terry—who'd been intensely watching from his remote screen in Kuwait and tied into our strike cell via teleconference—came across the loudspeaker. "Let them go, they don't have any fight left in them."

Everyone in the operations center looked at me.

I nodded. "Hold fire and continue to track them until I return," I instructed the team. I walked to my office and called Lieutenant General Terry right away for a private discussion.

"Good engagement, Dana," he answered.

"Thanks, sir," I replied. "But there are about ten more left to kill."

"I know…but I don't want to waste time or ammunition on squirters. They're clearly defeated."

"Sir, we need to kill every one of them. These are suicide bombers. They'll eventually try to kill our allies."

"Dana, I'm not budging on this one. Let them go and look for larger targets around Haditha."

Even though I disagreed, I understood General Terry's perspective and followed his logic.

Roughly eight ISIS fighters escaped that night. The next morning on Monday, September 8, the Iraqi Army sent heavily armed patrols into the area where the ISIS fighters had been hit. The ground patrols found remnants of fifty-nine dead ISIS fighters. That fact by itself was amazing—not just for the kill count but because ISIS rarely left their dead on the battlefield.

Remarks from Wes Bryant

Vern and I had dispatched a couple of our JTACs to assist the Embassy Strike Cell during the final offensive operation to take back the Haditha Dam. One was a young SEAL lieutenant, freshly JTAC-qualified. He'd gotten his certification only weeks before deploying with the CRF—a deployment that had unexpectedly turned into support of the Iraq crisis.

By chance, the lieutenant happened to be the controlling JTAC in the Embassy Strike Cell when our drones and intelligence picked up the vehicles carrying dozens of suicide bombers. In his first control in a combat zone, the lieutenant racked up a kill count of fifty-nine ISIS fighters! As far as we knew, that was a record for any first real-world control—and it was among the highest kill counts any JTAC could hope to get during a single mission in general.

Just a few months prior, I'm sure the lieutenant wouldn't have thought he'd be killing scores of America's greatest enemy from a strike cell in Baghdad. But that was the nature and beauty of special operations—you never knew where you'd end up or what craziness you'd be involved in on a moment's notice.

Because it was such a lucrative strike, the rest of the JTACs in the BIAP Strike Cell affectionately gave the SEAL lieutenant the nickname "Hero of Haditha" from that point forward. It was a nickname that stuck with him until the end of the deployment—largely, I'm pretty sure, to his dismay.

An IO (Information Operations) Win

The killing of fifty-nine ISIS suicide bombers constituted ISIS' largest single death-toll up to that point. The next morning, as an Iraqi patrol checked the bodies of the dead fighters, they spied slight stirring from the area of the crevice where we'd bombed. There they found three wounded, shell-shocked ISIS fighters and promptly captured them.

The Iraqi Army soldiers treated the ISIS prisoners with humanity. It was rare to capture ISIS fighters alive because normally the fanatical fighters either fought to the death or their comrades removed them from the battlefield once wounded. Later that day, the Iraqi military brought another huge media contingent with television cameras from Baghdad into the Haditha Dam area. The Iraqi government and military officials took pride in showing the world how humanely they treated ISIS prisoners—in stark contrast to ISIS' barbaric treatment of Iraqi prisoners.

The three captured and wounded ISIS fighters were interviewed on Iraqi television. They were very scared and shaken. Of the three surviving fighters, two were Saudi Arabian and one was Libyan. Listening to the prisoners gave us new insights into ISIS.

One of the Saudis was only twenty years old. He said he'd joined ISIS to fight Syrian President Bashar al-Assad and his "blasphemous" regime. He and several of his friends had originally driven a car from Saudi Arabia through eastern Jordan and into southern Syria. He'd been fighting in the

Deir ez-Zur area of eastern Syria in the Euphrates River Valley. After the Iraqi Army operations began in Haditha, he and the other seventy ISIS fighters had been ordered to board three trucks that then made their way from Syria to Iraq through Al Qaim. They said they were never told that they were going to Iraq. The Saudi insisted to the Iraqi media that he'd only wanted to fight in Syria.

"I would have refused to fight in Iraq," the fighter said. "Our fight is not with Iraq, it is with Bashar al-Assad and Syria."

Having the frightened young ISIS foot soldiers on Iraqi television was a huge propaganda victory for Iraq. Suddenly, the unstoppable, blood-thirsty, masked ISIS fighters became mere mortals. Unmasked, the ISIS fighters were just scared young men. It had a positive effect on the Iraqi national mindset—they understood ISIS could be beaten and humbled.

CHAPTER 27

The BIAP Strike Cell

WES BRYANT

The BIAP Strike Cell was definitely not the pillar of architectural glory one might have expected when imagining the sole location from which all airstrikes against ISIS in central and western Iraq were soon to be controlled.

Just a couple hundred meters down the airfield from the Glass House where our SOTF-I was headquartered, the new strike cell was set among a bunch of run-down mobile trailer units once used as troop barracks during the U.S. occupation in the Iraq war. The trailer was in a graveled dirt lot that was prone to forming large mud puddles after the frequent bouts of rain during that time of year. It had two entrances, one in front and one in back, with old, hastily constructed wooden stairs leading about four steps up into the doorways and offering just enough stair and porch to stomp most of the wet mud off of our shoes and boots.

It was field-expedient, yet highly effective.

Inside the trailer was a large main room, about fifteen feet deep by thirty feet long, that contained the nucleus of the strike cell. Two separate offices in the back housed the desks of Colonel Kehoe and his operations officer, Major David McRae—who served as the deputy director, second in command to Colonel Kehoe. The two would oversee the cell's operations 24/7. As our primary target engagement authority (TEA), General Pittard would be the only officer to give the final go-ahead to strike.

Three long rows of plastic-topped folding tables lined the room front-to-back. At the front-right were the three JTAC seats—the fulcrum of the cell. We placed a senior JTAC on shift at all times as the lead for targeting and "sensor management"—making the decisions on what to do with our aircraft to keep targeting in line with the intent of General Pittard and the directors. Vern and I would split that role along with a couple of my senior Combat Control JTACs, Josh and Adam, and our SEAL lieutenant. During our respective shifts we'd be the lynchpin for all decisions regarding how the cell would utilize the fighter jets, bombers, and drones tasked to us in order to most effectively find and kill ISIS targets. We'd also be the sole individuals charged with vetting targets before briefing the directors and General Pittard, advising them on strike considerations, and requesting authorization to strike.

We put at least one JTAC, sometimes two, on shift as the "primary controllers"—depending on the operational need for a given day. The primary controller was completely freed up to handle the "stacks" of aircraft flying for us throughout central or western Iraq, to support Iraqi ground operations or hunt ISIS independently. We let them focus solely on controlling so that during airstrike execution they were 100 percent dedicated to control of the mission, instead of becoming distracted by the need to back-brief the senior staff or the general while in the midst of an intense control. It turned out to be a great system.

Outside the trailer, large mast antennas of a multitude of frequency bands were connected to two Humvee-mounted radio communications pallets remoted into the cell. At the JTAC table inside the cell were three radio interface boxes cabled from the radio pallets in the trucks. That gave us the ability to tie-in to the amplified radios in the vehicles and talk to our aircraft on the multiple UHF-AM and SATCOM nets we utilized. Two secure phones at the desk, as well, enabled us to control drone crews back in the States, eliminating radio transmission delays.

Our coordination and planning for future operations was almost entirely accomplished by email traffic and secure chat and phone calls. Three secure networked computers sat at our workstation, vital for mission coordination with the various entities supporting us from all over the Middle East as well as our Special Forces teams embedded at the Iraqi operations centers who coordinated directly with the Iraqi ground commanders.

One computer was dedicated solely as the battle-tracking computer. It had secure Google Earth imagery and a database of marked points that we kept constantly updated. Day and night, our JTACs and intelligence analysts filled the database with reported and observed friendly positions and suspected enemy targets based on our intelligence reports as well as direct observation of the battlefield through our aircraft's sensors. The computer was tied-in to a big screen TV in the front of the cell that we'd use to brief the directors and General Pittard when requesting strike approval, or when further "developing" a target.

Lining the front of the cell were five more big-screen TVs, all of which could be tied to the line-of-site video feeds from our fighter aircraft when they were in range, and to the digitally-streamed feeds from our drones. With those we had the ability to keep eyes on multiple friendly and enemy units at the same time while still scanning other locations for activity.

To our surprise, the exceptional aerial surveillance capability we had from the strike cell would come to, at times, give us as good if not better situational awareness of the battlefield than if we were on the ground ourselves. Once our strike cell got heavy into operations, it became common for us to have four or five feeds going at once—all giving us sensor pictures from the multiple aircraft under our control overhead various objective areas and battlegrounds throughout Iraq.

Things could get incredibly intense. At any given point, we could have a stack of strike and intelligence-gathering aircraft controlled through our radio headsets, multiple drones controlled through secure phones, and other assets controlled through secure chat. The level of focus required to safely and effectively coordinate all those air assets, keep track of the oft chaotic friendly and enemy fire and maneuver on the battlefield (not to mention civilian or neutral-force activity), and culminate it all into hitting the right targets and successfully enabling Iraqi ground offensives would probably be mind-boggling to the outside observer.

The Strike Cell Team

Directly left of the JTAC seats sat our intelligence, surveillance, and reconnaissance tactical controllers (ITCs). These were our "left hands" assisting us with sensor management. Referring, most often, to the capabilities of an aircraft's targeting pod, the *sensor* was the piece of equipment that gave pilots and JTACs the capability to differentiate between individuals and objects on the ground, calculate coordinates with accuracy of a few meters, and guide air-to-ground ordnance onto targets from altitudes upwards of 20,000 feet.

ITCs also assisted us by controlling drones when we weren't actively controlling strikes or supporting Iraqi ground offensives. Exhaustively filtering through mounds of daily reported intelligence, using their training and experience as analysts they'd allocate drone sensors to what they deemed potentially credible reports in order to find targets for the JTACs to prosecute.

During strike prosecution, our ITCs would help manage all the airspace for us, aid in target acquisition for other strike assets (fighter jets and bombers, specifically), and hand-off drones to us when we needed to use their *Hellfire* missiles.

Our best ISR controller was Captain Marcellus McKinley, an Air Force special operations intelligence officer. Marcellus was the sole ITC tasked to SOTF-I and a part of my team over at the task force. His keen analytical skill and ability combined with immense previous experience hunting the Taliban in Afghanistan would help serve us up some extremely lucrative targets with high enemy kill counts. He split eight-hour shifts with two conventional Air Force ISR controllers. Though not nearly as experienced from the start, they also proved extremely valuable as time went on.

Left of the ISR controllers sat a small Army communications and airspace management team from Colonel Kehoe's 17th Field Artillery Brigade staff. The chief of the team was an older, soft-spoken U.S. Army warrant officer. He did an outstanding job as the sole individual in charge of both keeping all our communications and computer equipment running *and* tracking all the air traffic in Iraq to ensure our air assets were de-conflicted. The former was a formidable responsibility, and the latter was no easy task, to put it lightly.

The warrant officer worked odd shifts, timing them to the operational tempo of our strike cell operations. He tasked a couple of his junior soldiers to be in the cell whenever we needed in order to keep the communications equipment and computers running smoothly. We also relied on him and his crew to communicate with Iraqi airspace officials and ground artillery units and ensure our U.S. and coalition aircraft stayed de-conflicted from both Iraqi aircraft and Iraqi artillery fire. His small team of communications soldiers was truly an invaluable workhorse in the strike cell.

In the very center of the cell were seats reserved for the director, deputy director, and General Pittard. They'd be in the cell primarily during the execution of airstrikes, but sometimes they'd sit and observe—offering us guidance as we developed targets. During active ground offensives by the Iraqi military, they'd always be in the cell directing our operations.

As well, we had a military lawyer continually on-call. Two female Army lawyers, both extremely competent and focused, split twelve-hour shifts. The lawyers were charged with ensuring all of our targets were legal to strike and within our given rules of engagement. Colonel Kehoe and General Pittard nearly always consulted with them prior to approving strikes.

At the far left in the middle row sat a Navy SEAL or Army Special Forces team member (depending on the shift) from our special operations task force. They served as liaison (LNO) from the Special Forces teams we had embedded at the numerous Iraqi operations centers. They'd communicate with their teammates who were side-by-side the Iraqi commanders directly in charge of forward Iraqi forces.

The LNOs were our link between the strike cell and the Iraqi ground forces we supported. They informed us when the Iraqis were in a fight, passed the direct ground reporting on enemy positions and activity, and kept us updated on friendly force locations. During strikes, the LNOs were vital in relaying our guidance to forward ground forces to ensure we hit our intended targets as quickly and safely as possible. There were times, for example, when we'd need to direct the Iraqi forces to consolidate to a specified building prior to an airstrike if we thought they were too close to the target for our comfort. Our LNOs were our voice and ears to the Iraqi forces on the ground.

Straight behind the JTACs and to the right of the general and directors' seats in the middle row sat two collateral damage estimation (CDE) analysts. Their job was to run formal analyses of any potential for collateral damage for nearly every target we prepared. They would come to do this within an extremely limited window—during "troops-in-contact" situations between Iraqi and ISIS forces or with fast-moving vehicle targets.

A typical analysis from our CDE team might be to recommend a change of ordnance to a smaller warhead or a change of attack parameters to alter a bomb or missile's impact heading to reduce the risk of collateral damage to a nearby structure. Our CDE analysts were vital in enabling the strike cell to hit targets without causing collateral damage to surrounding infrastructure or inadvertent civilian casualties. They helped ensure that we maintained strict adherence to the rules of engagement and that we upheld the mandate we'd been given from CENTCOM to do everything we could to limit chances of collateral damage or civilian casualties resulting from our airstrikes.

Perhaps not surprisingly, CDE analysis would soon become so paramount in the evolving campaign against ISIS that, months later after I returned stateside, I'd attend formal training at the U.S. Central Command and become certified as a CDE analyst. On future deployments hunting ISIS then unforeseen to me in 2014, I would have the ability to perform CDE analysis in conjunction with my JTAC duties. That enabled me to target more effectively, and to speak more intelligently when advising senior commanders on potential risks of collateral damage.

• • •

The campaign against ISIS was as rapidly evolving as it was complex. Because of that, it truly took all these elements of expertise—synergized masterfully through the exhaustive efforts of each and every player involved—to transform the BIAP Strike Cell into the multiservice conventional and special operations killing machine it soon became.

PART 6

Unleashing
the Dogs of War

CHAPTER 28

Keeping the Iraqis on the Offensive

DANA PITTARD
WITH REMARKS FROM WES BRYANT

The liberation of Haditha gave hope to the Iraqi people that ISIS could be defeated even within a Sunni-dominated area like Al Anbar Province. The newly elected Iraqi Prime Minister, Haidar al-Abadi, declared Haditha to be a great victory for Iraq.

I knew we needed to keep the Iraqis on the offensive, so we were already planning the next set of operations. Following the victory over Haditha, I met with General Kenani and his staff at the Ministry of Defense.

"We must work our way to re-taking Mosul as soon as possible, sadey," I told him.

Kenani answered, "Isn't that a Kurdish problem?"

"No, sadey," I replied. "Just like the Mosul Dam, it's an Iraqi problem. We now have momentum, and ISIS is running scared. They are fearful of where the Iraqi Army will strike next. We must relieve the pressure on the Bayji Oil Refinery first, then take back Tikrit, Quyarrah, and on to Mosul and Tal Afar. Then we can retake Fallujah after Mosul is back in Iraqi hands."

"General Pittard, we need more equipment, vehicles, and weapons before we are in a position to retake Mosul."

"We will do our best to get you the equipment you need, sadey," I said, "but the most important thing you have to maintain is the *will* to fight and defeat ISIS."

General Kenani nodded. "Of course, general. But we will also need more troops. As you know, over seventy percent of our units are around Baghdad and not even under my command. They are under the command of Lieutenant General Abdul Amir. He is the Baghdad Operations Commander, and he reports directly to the prime minister. If you can help us get Lieutenant General Amir to send us some troops, I think we can support an offensive to the Bayji Oil Refinery."

Inwardly I rolled my eyes. "Sadey, I will meet with Lieutenant General Abdul Amir and get more troops, but you must continue to plan and focus on Bayji."

I met with Lieutenant General Abdul Amir at his headquarters on the other side of the Green Zone. He was a powerful man and a well-respected Iraqi military leader among both Sunnis and Shias. Amir introduced me to several Sunni sheiks who'd been fighting alongside his forces and who wanted U.S. airstrikes in support of their local tribal fights against ISIS. Unfortunately, I had to politely refuse because we barely had enough airpower to cover our major operations against ISIS. I recommended that they ask the Iraqi Air Force for support. Lieutenant General Abdul Amir also had good relations with Shia militias.

Amir informed me that the new Iraqi prime minister would only approve his sending Iraqi units to General Kenani if he felt that Baghdad was absolutely secure. I smiled as he spoke; I knew the next thing Lieutenant General Amir would be asking for was airstrikes against ISIS within his area of operations.

Like clockwork, he told me that he could possibly give up an Iraqi Army or Federal Police brigade from Baghdad—*if* I could help him with airstrikes to push out ISIS forces threatening the outskirts of Baghdad Province to the southwest and southeast of Baghdad.[1] He didn't beat around the bush. Amir showed me his operational plans for securing

---

1   Lizzie Dearden, "Isis 'just one mile from Baghdad' as al-Qaeda fighters join forces against Syria air strikes," *The Independent*, September 29, 2014, accessed April 24, 2018, http://www.independent. co.uk/ news/world/middle-east/islamic-state-crisis-al-qaeda-fighters-joining-forces-with-isis-against-air-strikes -in-syria-9761392.html.

southwest and southeast Baghdad. They looked pretty sound; however, they would need to be modified by our American operations planners to maximize the effects of our airstrikes.

I had a broader plan—to get the Iraqis to conduct a major offensive against ISIS in Bayji—but supporting offensive ground operations in the greater Baghdad area was proving to be the ticket to that show. We began drawing plans to support the Iraqi Army clearing ISIS fighters from their strongholds in southwest Baghdad, southeast Baghdad, and southeast of Fallujah.

At the same time, other special operations teams were supporting the Peshmerga in northern Iraq. They'd recently taken a key ISIS headquarters compound near the town of Zumar. And the Kurdish Peshmerga, Iranians, and Shia militias had been fighting some very tough battles against ISIS in the towns of Sadiyah and Jalula in northwest Diyala Province. All of this was in addition to the fighting against ISIS in several regions in Syria—the most significant of which was in the town of Kobani near the Syrian-Turkish border.

The senior leadership of ISIS was being forced to react not only to multiple attacks against their fighters in Iraq and Syria, but also to our relentless targeting against them with airstrikes. ISIS had been thrown off balance.

We planned the south Baghdad operation for mid-to-late September. It would be the first real test for the BIAP Strike Cell.

Remarks from Wes Bryant

A few days prior to the kickoff of the first operations of the BIAP Strike Cell, our newly-formed team huddled in the small trailer, talking through various game plans for the upcoming operations. General Pittard coolly walked in. Chatter quickly tapered off into silence as we all turned our attention to the ground commander of Iraq. It was my first time meeting General Pittard, or even seeing him in person.

The general was unpretentious but composed. He was tall, and under the short ceiling seemed even taller. He shook hands with each of us, smiling warmly as he did, and he projected an air of humility and dignity and respect toward all of us that I found comforting. I was relieved, because I typically found myself detesting and wary of officers—especially senior ones.

We listened intently as General Pittard relayed his vision for the BIAP Strike Cell and his operational plans for the first mission. As he spoke, eloquently and intelligently, any doubts I'd previously had in my mind about how well our special operations team might integrate with the general and his staff were completely dispelled.

I knew right then that we were going to get some good work done.

CHAPTER 29

The First Strikes in Baghdad

WES BRYANT

Mid-September 2014

The first operation for the BIAP Strike Cell: support an Iraqi Security Force ground offensive to take back the ISIS-controlled southwest and southeast Baghdad regions and thwart ISIS' encroachment on Baghdad.

Early on in the operation, as Iraqi forces slowly but steadily maneuvered their vehicle convoys into the region, we'd been witness to a massive civilian exodus. We watched on our drone feeds as hundreds of civilians left their homes and crossed the Euphrates River toward the west in order to avoid being caught in the inevitable crossfire that they knew would be coming as soon as Iraqi Security Forces advanced to fight ISIS.

That was actually a very fortunate thing for us in the BIAP Strike Cell—it meant we'd have far less worry over inadvertently causing civilian casualties. Even so, our attempts at targeting ISIS with airstrikes in the first couple of days were slow and cumbersome. ISIS fighters in the area were well dug-in and fortified. By then, ISIS forces were no longer as overt as they had been when we'd first kicked off the airstrike campaign a few weeks previous. They'd become far more cunning in avoiding our strikes within a very short period of time. Worse, the Iraqi ground units were tentative to advance and showed little motivation to fight.[1]

The Iraqi military leadership pushed for our strike cell to bombard the area with airstrikes ahead of their ground movement. They told us that they would not go on the offensive until we "dropped bombs for them"—yet they couldn't seem to give us any valid ISIS targets.

It was a struggle to get the Iraqi military leadership to accept how the modern U.S. military waged war. More likely, they just didn't care. But we were not going to budge. We needed "vetted" targets—with positive identification of an enemy force or entity, verification of all nearby friendly force locations, and confirmation that the target area was free of civilians.

We could not simply "drop bombs" randomly in and around villages and cities simply because they asked us to. That is the difference between the modern American military and those we call our enemies. We do not disregard the lives and well-being of anyone in our way for the sake of killing the enemy—we are calculated, precise, and go to great lengths to protect the local populace and infrastructure. It took time to get these points through to the Iraqi commanders running the offensive in southwest and southeast Baghdad, but we finally did.

We were frustrated with the Iraqi forces' apparent lack of motivation to advance, but part of their gradualness was because ISIS had emplaced a heavy concentration of IEDs on the routes their convoys were forced to take. Mostly made up of American Humvees and pick-up trucks, the Iraqi convoys were pretty vulnerable to the ISIS-emplaced IEDs. They were even more encumbered by the time it took to clear their routes. And they were still hitting IEDs even with all the exhaustive clearing, just because of the sheer quantity that ISIS had placed. That caused casualties and debilitated vehicles, further slowing the Iraqi Army advance.

To top it off, ISIS was well concealed—they didn't seem to want to come out and fight directly. They stayed in "hide-sites." They strong-pointed in buildings. At most, they'd throw a few sniper shots at the Iraqi Army troops just long enough to harass them but not long enough for

---

1   Kirk Semple and Eric Schmitt, "ISIS Keeps Up Pressure Near Baghdad as Iraqi Troops Hesitate," *The New York Times*, October 17, 2014, accessed April 24, 2018, https://www.nytimes.com/2014/10/18/world/middleeast/isis-keeps-up-pressure-near-baghdad-as-iraqi-troops-stumble.html?mtrref=www.google.com&gwh=9A28C33EF44659949C26D9B5DFA2DA2B&gwt=pay&assetType=nyt_now.

anyone to pinpoint where the shots came from. We deduced that ISIS must have been tipped off on our operation—likely by an insider in the Iraqi Army, which was not outside the realm of possibility.

Finally, on the evening of September 16 about three or four days into the operation, the first real fighting between ISIS and the Iraqi forces began. At last we got our chance to hit ISIS from the BIAP Strike Cell.

An ISIS heavy machine gun nest and rocket-propelled grenades rained down on a small convoy of Iraqi forces as they tried to maneuver toward a suburban area in southwest Baghdad. My right-hand man—a senior Combat Controller named Adam—was the primary controller. Using a flight of F/A-18 Super Hornets, he swiftly went to work.

Adam directed the Hornets to put a 300-pound *Maverick* missile into the doorway of the building where the ISIS fighters were popping out from shooting their RPGs. The first missile annihilated the fighters in the doorway. Then Adam coordinated a second strike onto the nearby ISIS machine gun nest and, within minutes, had obliterated it. He hammered ISIS fighting positions with more strikes from the F/A-18s as our Iraqi convoy pressed forward and aggressed.

Adam's strikes in southwest Baghdad were the first to fall under the newly-authorized U.S. mission to *offensively* hunt and destroy ISIS throughout Iraq—a mission that President Obama had announced just a few days earlier.[2] "Offensive" was exactly what we became. That first engagement set the precedent for the new BIAP Strike Cell—aggression was the name of the game.

Opportunities to target ISIS seemed to open ten-fold over the next few days as Iraqi forces continued to draw ISIS forces out from their hiding and take ground back. Iraqi forces quickly became emboldened by the support of our airstrikes, and ISIS was scrambling to resist against our combined onslaught.

Throughout the remainder of the operation we targeted ISIS command and control buildings (structures from which ISIS planned and directed combat operations), heavy weapons positions, armored vehicles,

---

2   Zeke J. Miller, "U.S. Launches First Strike in Campaign Against ISIS," *TIME*, September 16, 2014, accessed September 13, 2018, http://time.com/3380722/united-states-airstrike-campaign-isis/.

gun-trucks, anti-aircraft artillery, and dismounted fighters actively engaging and maneuvering on Iraqi Security Forces.

We destroyed ISIS supply boats and transport vehicles along the Euphrates River after we'd identified a robust waterborne operation to support ISIS front line fighters with ammunition, equipment, and food. We thwarted several attempted ambushes on Iraqi forces when we identified ISIS positions lying ahead in wait; annihilating the ISIS fighters before they ever knew what hit them. And when Iraqi forces called on us pinned down and under heavy fire, we destroyed ISIS forces within *danger close* of the Iraqi positions—close enough that they were within fragmentation range of our ordnance—without a single friendly injury from our strikes.

Within less than two weeks we had decimated the command and control infrastructure, fighting capability, and local logistical network of ISIS in the southwest and southeast Baghdad regions and enabled Iraqi forces to take back the majority of the ground.

The south Baghdad operation was an immensely successful first mission for the BIAP Strike Cell. The volume of our airstrikes in the ensuing weeks would only fiercely increase as we shifted our focus to taking out the ISIS footholds in and around the cities of Bayji, Karma, Hit, Ramadi, Fallujah, and elsewhere.

CHAPTER 30

The Foggiest of Wars

WES BRYANT

Running the BIAP Strike Cell by night, my existence quickly became a blur. My sense of day and night was distorted—the strike cell became a twilight zone in many ways. Time was a relative term, only kept up-to-date in my mind by the necessity to remember which operation we were covering at any given point. My entire being became wholly consumed with one objective: hunting and killing ISIS.

I'd wake up in the late afternoon in my single-room CHU, set among the old mobile units situated off the airfield about 500 meters from the strike cell. It was modest living. My most prized possessions were an electric water heater, a small French Press, and a fresh supply of my favorite local coffee that my wife had sent from the States. We always bought the coffee from the local grocery store in the little North Carolina town where she and I called home.

The local coffee was not only my staple—my morning vitamin—but it was a daily reminder of the life back home I sacrificed for. I got in a routine of waking up to a couple of cups of steaming pressed coffee while standing on my small, weathered wood porch in the early evening and watching the setting Baghdad sun. I'd try shaking the grogginess out of my head, usually to no avail until my second or third cup. Scenes of the previous night's strikes always streamed through my mind. I'd play the events over and over—thinking about what went well and what we could have done better. I'd fall asleep with a mind saturated with scenes from the night's strikes, and I'd wake up to more of the same.

As a JTAC, there was always a psychological and emotional toll—no matter how the killing was done. Even though this time I was killing remotely from a strike cell physically removed from the battlefield, the mission still had an impact. I was in a state of constant aggression—consumed with the hunt.

My wife knew when I'd had a busy night hunting ISIS. If she couldn't already tell from my demeanor over the phone, years back I'd established a code word that only she and I knew. When I slipped it into casual conversation, she knew I'd been doing my job—controlling airstrikes against our nation's enemies.

She was my rock. Through all my deployments over the years I would talk to her about everything I could—operational security permitting. By then, everyone knew America was slaying ISIS with airstrikes. That was no secret. My wife was just privy to the fact that I was one of the men doing it.

I'd found that the more she knew about what I was involved in while I was gone, the better she could handle my inevitable maladjusted quirkiness and generally aggressive mindset every time I came home. Keeping her in the dark about where I was and what I was doing never helped. I preferred her to at least have some understanding of my world across the ocean.

And in my world, we were soon killing nearly 300 ISIS fighters a week—just a little more than they could effectively recruit.

But it wasn't easy. The war against ISIS took place in a thick fog caused by language and cultural barriers, strict rules of engagement, the challenges of discerning friend from foe, and many other difficult factors. Our job in the strike cell was to cut through the fog—or at least rise above it.

Our requirements for targeting ISIS were strict, and our processes to meet those requirements were sometimes encumbered by the methods we had to utilize. Far from being on the battlefield and in the fight like we were used to as JTACs—with our own eyes on enemy targets as we destroyed them—strike cell operations were a whole different animal. But the fundamentals of close air support never changed, and the doctrinal requirements for authorizing air-to-surface fires onto a given target had to be met just the same.

Our two most vital precursors to any airstrike were valid targeting information and friendly force locations. And they came from a variety of sources. If we weren't actively supporting a ground battle between Iraqi forces and ISIS, where we could observe enemy positions and easily correlate information the Iraqis were passing to us, our targeting was difficult. We'd receive intelligence reporting from various military and government entities in Iraq on a near-constant basis. Part of our struggle was sifting through that steady flow of reported intelligence to find the viable reports that would lead us to enemy targets, while also ensuring we knew where our friendly forces were and where civilians were not. We had to screen the reporting in real-time, to rule out what was good and what was bogus.

Too often, intelligence just didn't pan out. Other times, reports from separate entities conflicted. It was not uncommon for one entity to tell us that a certain location was an ISIS position while another said it was a friendly force or civilians. At times, our reporting was so inconclusive and conflicting that we just disregarded all of it and went on the hunt ourselves without assistance from any so-called "intelligence." We'd simply direct our aircraft via our own intuition built from years of experience hunting insurgencies on the ground—and we'd do it with great success.

When we supported our Iraqi forces on ground offensives, targeting was easier in some ways but more difficult in others. Our special operations team liaisons were vital in maintaining direct communications with the Iraqi commanders in charge of the forward ground units, but there was still a very lengthy communications chain ridden with language and cultural barriers.

The communications flow had to go from a forward Iraqi field commander on the ground to his commander at one of the Iraqi operations centers—sometimes via multiple intermediary commanders—then to an interpreter with our embedded Special Forces team. From there, the communication would finally be relayed to our liaison at the strike cell and to us. Likewise, any amplifying clarification or guidance from our strike cell back to the Iraqi ground force commander had to take the reverse route.

Sometimes the chain of communication to and from Iraqi ground commanders went well, and others it surely did not. Those variables were based largely on the nature, competency, and aggressiveness of a given Iraqi commander, communications reliability between field commanders and their superiors at the operations centers, and the translation capabilities of interpreters. The communication delays were a huge challenge.

Adding to those challenges, a myriad of combat entities populated the battlefields of Iraq—and not all of them were Iraqi Security Forces. Some were neither our allies nor our enemies. Those included Shia and Sunni militias not associated directly with Iraqi Security Forces as well as Iraqi police units. With those entities, we often had spotty communication at best.

One night during the initial few days of the south Baghdad operation, we'd identified a suspected ISIS stronghold forward of our advancing Iraqi forces. It was a fairly large compound comprised of two adjacent, one-story buildings. We used a Predator drone to scan the area and counted roughly thirty armed fighters. The compound had machine gun positions reinforced with sandbags up on the corners of the rooftops. There was a mortar team in the main entranceway to the larger building, and a couple dozen fighters actively patrolled the grounds of the compound. Both the rooftop gun positions and the mortar tube were oriented toward our advancing Iraqi forces who, though a long way off, were to the north. Our ISF had slowly but steadily been making their way into the area and were still about two or three kilometers away—but that was well within range of the enemy mortar tube.

We needed to get verification that we were looking at an ISIS position. We asked the commander of the ISF unit to the north, but he couldn't confirm if the compound was ISIS. He knew it was not any of his own forces, at least, but nothing beyond that. We contacted the Baghdad Operations Center and the Iraqi Ministry of Defense. Those entities were responsible for verifying the identification and locations of Iraqi ground units in lieu of real-time information from our forward Iraqi commanders. They were our last stop for identifying friend or foe.

While we waited for word back, the commander of the forward Iraqi unit radioed again to assure us that none of his forces were near the compound. He was convinced it was an ISIS compound and wanted us to go ahead and strike it.

We were observing a large number of armed fighters, embedded machine gun positions, and a mortar tube, all oriented toward our Iraqi forces. We'd had a forward Iraqi commander verify that his forces were not at the compound. At that point, we held right in our laps what was legally termed *"reasonable certainty"* under our rules of engagement that the position was an ISIS stronghold.

Still, we couldn't always think in black-and-white terms. Things just didn't feel right quite yet. Prudence dictated that we shouldn't act, because the situation remained a little too ambiguous. Sure, we were looking at a large compound with a lot of armed personnel and heavy weapons, and it would be a really lucrative ISIS target. But we had to be far surer of the target before we struck.

It would have been really simple for us if the Iraqi forces just closed-in on the compound. That way, we could see if the fighters at the compound opened fire on our Iraqi unit. If they did, we'd have our answer and would have the authority to strike immediately in defense of the Iraqi forces. The Iraqi unit had no plan to do that, though; it was too risky for them. Most of the regular Iraqi forces were not equipped with night vision equipment like our soldiers in the U.S. military, so nighttime firefights were a little more perilous. Plus, they were still a few kilometers away and the movement at night would be long and difficult.

We needed either trusted intelligence or ground verification that the force at the compound was enemy in order to request and prosecute a strike. We kept watching…and waiting. Finally, word came back from the Iraqi MoD.

A senior Iraqi general from the MoD called our strike cell and said that they'd determined the location contained neither friendly forces nor neutral militia units. They concluded it was an ISIS position, and requested we strike.

It was exactly what we'd been waiting for. The target was as lucrative as they got. It was well-fortified, and the enemy force there would no-doubt inflict large casualties on our advancing Iraqi forces if we didn't take them out first. General Pittard had been waiting patiently along with the rest of us for word back from the MoD. He quickly approved the strike.

It was a clear-cut target.

Emotions in the strike cell ran high. We were all anticipating destroying the large ISIS compound. As JTACs, though, it was our job to temper emotions—that eagerness to "get the kill"—with professional objectivity. When emotions ran rampant, judgment could be clouded and mistakes made. Mistakes with airstrikes could be devastating to our mission and to the very people we were striving to protect.

Adam and I were tandem controlling with multiple strike assets that night. In the time that we'd been waiting on the MoD to come back with verification on the target, he and I had already coordinated the attack in advance so that we could execute as soon as we got the word. Adam had control of a drone crew over secure phone and I had our fixed-wing strike aircraft on the radio. We were inwardly salivating to kill the huge ISIS target, yet outwardly calm and level.

Overhead the ISIS compound, concealed by the night sky, an AC-130 "Whiskey" gunship orbited, armed with a 30mm cannon and a slew of 45-pound *Griffin* missiles. Above it, a Predator drone circled with a compliment of 100-pound *Hellfire* missiles. Both were ready to unleash fury on the fighters in the compound on our call.

Our plan was to hit the fighters in the open first with a slew of Griffin missiles from the AC-130 gunship, followed by 30mm, then destroy the mortar tube and machine gun positions with a second attack in sequence. Meanwhile, the Predator would be standing by to hit any squirters with its Hellfire missiles. It was the quickest way to pull off the attack—and it was going to be a beautiful strike.

I was just about to give final strike clearance to the gunship when Colonel Kehoe interjected with a change in plans. He wanted us to alter our strike plan to attack the mortar tube and gun positions first. I was a little irked at the demand—Adam and I knew from experience that the enemy typically couldn't move an established mortar tube and well-emplaced machine gun positions within the time it would take between strikes, especially when they'd be scrambling from the first one. Hitting the fighters in the open first was our best bet to round up as many kills as we could before they had a chance to maneuver and take cover. Then we could take our relative time destroying the heavy weapons positions that would, most likely, be abandoned at that point.

Colonel Kehoe was adamant. That was his prerogative as the strike cell director. I knew it wouldn't cause too much of a delay to re-brief the crews anyway, so I was fine with it in the end. I could see benefits from either game plan. The compound and the fighters in it weren't going anywhere any time soon. We had time.

It took a couple more minutes for us to brief the new strike plan to our gunship and Predator crews. The new game plan would be that our Predator would launch a single Hellfire missile at the mortar tube while the gunship simultaneously threw Griffin missiles onto the machine gun positions on the rooftops. Then the gunship would pull into a tighter orbit and rain down 30mm on any fighters in the open.

It turned out those couple of minutes we took re-briefing our aircrews were an incredible stroke of luck. We'd just finished relaying the new game plan, and had directed our strike assets to set up in position to execute the strikes, when we received an urgent phone call from the MoD.

"Don't strike! The compound is a Shia militia headquarters!"

Adam and I wasted no time. "All players—Abort, Abort, Abort!" we relayed to the Predator and gunship almost in unison. Both crews acknowledged.

I sat quietly for a few moments, a bit stunned that I had just come about *yay* close to having a strike on "friendly" forces under my belt. Aside from the moral issue of killing the wrong people with an airstrike, it was a huge mar on the reputation and professional pride of any JTAC. In all the strikes I'd controlled both in Iraq and Afghanistan throughout the years, I was proud to say that I didn't have a single bad strike—and I wasn't interested in changing that trend. Adam and I exchanged solemn, knowing looks and shook our heads at the close call, sighing relief.

From his very first moments upon hitting the ground, General Pittard had worked tirelessly to unite the tribal elements of Iraq in a common fight against ISIS. Thus far, he'd been pretty successful. During the operation to liberate the city of Amerli only a few weeks earlier, Shia militias had fought alongside Iraqis and Kurds in a near-miraculous multifaction coalition against ISIS. And after Amerli, senior leadership of the major Shia militia forces openly proclaimed that the militias did not intend on fighting the U.S. or its coalition, and that our common enemy was ISIS.

A strike on a fortified compound of Shia militia that night would have been detrimental in the effort toward uniting Iraqi tribal elements in the fight against ISIS. It could possibly have turned the Shia militias against us. That was the heavy fog we dealt with in the new kind of war we waged. And in the weeks and months to follow, we'd use that near-fratricide on the Shia militia force as a solemn lesson-learned in the campaign against ISIS.

CHAPTER 31

The Braveheart of Bayji

DANA PITTARD

Early October 2014

ISIS executed another western hostage, Alan Henning, on October 3 following their defeat in Kobani at the hands of the Syrian Kurd (YPG) forces assisted by coalition airstrikes from the special operations strike cell in northern Iraq.[1]

ISIS forces were now being fought on fifteen major battlefronts throughout Iraq and Syria, and they were beginning to feel the pressure from their numerous defeats.

By pushing the Iraqi military and Kurdish Peshmerga to conduct offensive operations throughout all of Iraq while the YPG simultaneously attacked ISIS strongpoints in Syria, we knew that ISIS would have an extremely difficult time reacting. In Iraq, it was time to set the conditions to relieve the ISIS siege of the strategically important Bayji Oil Refinery, 130 miles north of Baghdad.

The Bayji Oil Refinery was the largest oil refinery in Iraq. It was being held by a small contingent of Iraqi Security Forces led by the elite Iraqi Counter Terrorism Service. The small Iraqi Army contingent had been

---

1   "ISIS Releases Video Showing Beheading of Alan Henning," NBC News, October 3, 2014, accessed October 31, 2018, https://www.nbcnews.com/storyline/isis-uncovered/isis-releases-video-showing-beheading-alan-henning-n208816.

surrounded and besieged by a larger ISIS force since June.[2] They were holding on through sheer grit and will, but their force was getting weaker and we feared they might soon be forced to surrender.

We needed to break the ISIS siege and re-establish full control of the Bayji Oil Refinery. Although the Iraqi military leadership was gaining confidence from the recent offensive successes against ISIS, they were afraid to commit to relieving the siege of Bayji because it was so far away from their base of support in Baghdad.

Convincing the ISF leadership to commit to attacking ISIS around Bayji became a major undertaking. We had to press the Iraqi leadership hard, but they had finally committed by late September. Lieutenant General Abdul Amir kept his promise from our previous talks and allocated a brigade-sized Iraqi force—two federal police battalions and one infantry battalion—for the operation. We began planning the Bayji operation jointly with the Iraqi military leadership.

Then, out of nowhere, I got word from General Kenani that the Iraqi leadership had decided not to conduct the operation after all. I couldn't believe it. I let General Kenani know how deeply disappointed I was with him and with the Iraqi decision to call off the Bayji offensive operation. I strongly urged him to simply set a new date for the attack.

I threatened to withdraw all air support from the Iraqi Army and move my headquarters from Baghdad to Erbil where I could support the Kurds, who appeared to still have the will to fight. I understood, though, that General Kenani was under a lot of pressure from Prime Minister Haider al-Abadi and other senior Iraqi generals. He had said as much. Most of them wanted him to concentrate on protecting Baghdad only and to stop conducting offensive operations against ISIS.

To help General Kenani, I decided to accompany the new U.S. ambassador to Iraq, Stuart Jones (who I'd briefly worked with back in Jordan), to meet with Prime Minister al-Abadi. It was a good meeting. Abadi spoke perfect English, and with a distinct British accent since he'd spent decades in Great Britain. The prime minister told us that his priority was securing Baghdad. If I could convince him and his generals that the capital would

---

2   Mark Tran, "Isis insurgents attack Iraq's biggest oil refinery," *The Guardian*, June 18, 2014, accessed January 28, 2019, https://www.theguardian.com/world/2014/jun/18/isis-fighters-iraq -oil-refinery-baiji.

remain secure, he would support an offensive operation in Bayji. I told him that Lieutenant General Abdul Amir felt confident he and his forces could secure Baghdad, and that he'd even agreed to give up some forces to support the Bayji operation.

Al-Abadi finally gave his permission for Bayji—but on the condition that I myself could convince his generals. I took the prime minister's condition as a challenge.

General Kenani invited me to meet with him and thirty of his most senior generals from Iraq's Army, Air Force, Federal Police Forces, and other entities in order to discuss the Bayji operation. I brought my staff to help brief the plan for the operation. I knew it was my time to personally attempt to instill the will to continue to fight and defeat ISIS into Iraq's most senior military leadership.

We met at General Kenani's CTS headquarters at the former Italian Embassy in Baghdad. With Italian architecture, marble floors, and winding staircases, it was the most stylish interior decorum I had seen in Iraq.

My staff and I drove up to the compound in three black, armored SUVs. As we entered the main building on the compound, one of General Kenani's deputies met us and told me that the meeting was restricted to generals only. He signaled that the rest of my staff needed to stay put.

I put up my hand. "No way. We're all coming in."

General Kenani came out and greeted me. "General Pittard, it is very important that only you and Ali come into the session." He saw my hesitation and added, "At least initially…please." He had a grave look on his face.

Seeing the look, I conceded. "Okay, sadey, I will have my staff wait in the next room over." My staff was crestfallen.

Ali and I made our way to the meeting room. As I walked in, it felt strange—like I was walking into a lion's den. The room was set up like a typical Arab meeting room, with rugs and carpets on the floor and chairs and couches along the walls in a U-shaped configuration facing the center. There was a lot chattering, which ceased as General Kenani and I entered. Thirty Iraqi senior generals sat in the chairs lining the walls.

I said confidently, "Salaam Ahlakhum."

"Alakhum Salaam," most everyone in the room replied.

General Kenani sat down at a small table at the opening of the U-shape. I sat next to him. My trusted interpreter, Ali, sat to my right.

Kenani opened the meeting. "General Pittard has proposed that we attack to relieve the ISIS siege of the Bayji Oil Refinery...."

And so it went. I listened calmly for over an hour as Ali provided near-simultaneous translation. General after general stood up and talked about why they felt the Bayji operation was a bad idea. Even the Salah ad-Din operations commander, newly promoted Lieutenant General Wahab—who had previously been picked by Kenani himself to *lead* the Bayji operation—stood and recommended against it!

I thought to myself, *my goodness, do these people not want to defeat ISIS and get their country back?*

In the end, all the senior Iraqi generals in attendance recommended the operation be cancelled or postponed. They each had various reasons to justify it—that Baghdad must be protected, that they needed more troops, more equipment, more training, and on and on.

I was deeply disappointed, but I refused to show it. I felt strongly that the Iraqi military had enough troops and enough useable equipment and weaponry, and that the Iraqi soldiers were trained *at least* as well as the average ISIS fighter. What the Iraqi military needed was the will to keep fighting!

At the end of their long discussion, General Kenani turned to me. He asked if I wanted to address the thirty generals and give my opinion before he cancelled the operation.

I solemnly nodded and replied sharply, "Yes, sadey."

I stood up slowly to my full height. I could feel the tension in the room. A couple of Iraqi generals said in Arabic, "What the hell can HE tell us?"

I scanned the room. I placed my hand over my heart and bowed my head slightly in the common gesture of friendship and respect. Some put their heads down, others glared at me.

"Many of you in this room have known me and so many other American soldiers and Marines like me over the past eleven years," I began, as Ali interpreted next to me. "We were together in Iraq as brothers-in-arms before we left in 2011. Now, three years later, my soldiers and I have returned. We have left our homes and our families in America to come here to this war and support *you*, support *your* families, and to support *the great nation of Iraq* against ISIS. This is why I am here—why we are *all* here far from our loved ones with you today. No other reason."

I raised my hands up, palms inward. "The world says, 'The Iraqi Army will not fight!' I ask you…is that true? Is that true?"

Many of the leaders groaned. Some shouted, "No!"

I continued before they got too loud. "But you—all of you here—can show the world that Iraq can determine its own fate and destiny! You can show the world that ISIS can be defeated! Right now, you have unstoppable momentum. With the collective leadership in this room and your brave soldiers and our airstrikes, ISIS has been on the run for the last two months."

I paused for effect, then raised my voice. "It is time! It is time for you to take back all the territory ISIS has stolen from Iraq. You must do this! The brave troops who have been holding on to the Bayji Oil Refinery are surrounded by ISIS. They cannot hold on much longer. Together, let us attack ISIS and take back Bayji before it is too late!"

My voice elevated even more. "If you are all to sit here and tell me Iraq no longer has the *will* to fight, then maybe it is time for my soldiers and I to go home. Or, perhaps we will assist the Kurds—because I know for a fact that *they* want to fight and destroy ISIS."

Some appeared angry, others looked around the room at one another. Still others seemed thoughtful and listened to my words intently.

"I do not want to do that," I continued. "I'm not ready to go home. I have come to love the Iraqi people. They deserve to be free of the grip of ISIS, to be free of terror. It is time, generals…it is time to attack!"

I looked around the room again. "I don't know about you, but I have no fear. I will lead the attack on Bayji myself, if I must. By the grace of Allah, ISIS will be beaten, and everyone in this room has a duty and a role to play in the defeat of our enemy!"

Several of the generals grunted and nodded in approval.

I closed my discourse with one final sentiment. "The relief of the siege of Bayji could be Iraq's finest hour of 2014, but *you* must have the *will* to fight and win and take your country back from ISIS. I personally say shame on you if you cannot step up and fight for Iraq and our brave Iraqi soldiers holding on for dear life in Bayji…. *Shame* on anyone who shirks this fight for freedom. Because together, I know we can crush ISIS once and for all!"

I sat down, knowing that I had just given the best impromptu speech of my life. The room was eerily quiet, but my pulse was loud in my ears. I had fired myself up and I was ready to go. General Kenani initially looked down and appeared to be praying. He thanked me in low tones for my impassioned words.

Kenani looked around the room at all thirty generals. Most of them were shaking their heads or murmuring amongst themselves. I noticed a couple of them looking to the ceiling, fingering their Arabic prayer beads (sometimes referred to as "worry beads").

After a long pause, General Kenani sighed and stood.

"Okay, listen!" He addressed the room, putting up his hands to get their attention. "I think we all know General Pittard is right. The Americans and the coalition are here to help us, but *we* must take our own country back from *Daesh*! It is time for us to lift the siege of Bayji. No one can do this but us. Our country is depending on us."

A long silence followed. Suddenly, a couple of the generals voiced agreement. A few more joined in. Then, almost all of them began shouting warrior slogans of support for General Kenani—and for me! The group of Iraqi generals, who just moments before had been glowering at me, suddenly made an unbelievable turnaround. I sat back in my chair and smiled at Ali, who smiled in return. It was all quite strange, but the senior Iraqi military leadership was once again committed to the liberation of Bayji.

CHAPTER 32

A Relentless Enemy

WES BRYANT

We were at once honored and exhilarated to be part of the small group of U.S. forces pushing back the ISIS advance and thwarting their campaign of torture, terror, and genocide. Knowing the bloodshed and butchery that ISIS had been unleashing on so many innocent people throughout Iraq and Syria, and the subsequent threat they posed to the free world, incensed us with a deep vehemence toward them.

Frankly, we couldn't kill enough of them. We had a craving for ISIS blood that was satisfied only through our ceaseless airstrikes against them and our ever-increasing ISIS body counts as a result.

It was a crisp, clear night and we'd gotten notification from our Special Forces team embedded at Iraq's Anbar operations center that Iraqi troops were in a heavy fight with ISIS at a water treatment plant in Ramadi.

We sent a Predator over the area. Unfortunately, the drone wasn't armed *and* the fighter jets we'd just had on station were switching out with another flight of jets, and we were waiting on the new set of fighters to show up. It was a less-than-ideal scenario, but in the meantime we got eyes on the area to assess the situation.

We quickly pinpointed the water treatment plant situated off the south bank of a stretch of the Euphrates River. Its large circular basins provided easy identification. It was a large complex with multiple separate compounds inside. We soon found armed individuals maneuvering in and among buildings, firing on one another.

Handfuls of fighters—three or four separate squads—maneuvered in teams, periodically taking cover behind buildings as they engaged one another. But we didn't yet have enough information from the Iraqi commanders at the operations center. We had no idea who was who, and so we couldn't do much more than observe.

Those were some of the most frustrating moments in the strike cell—when we were forced to watch battles with our hands tied. But, in reality, we couldn't help the Iraqis fight off the ISIS forces because we couldn't tell for sure which ones were Iraqi forces and which were ISIS.

Our holy grail of information came after ten or fifteen minutes. Iraqi Security Forces clarified that one of their convoys was pinned down on a road right off the river. The convoy had tried to enter the main compound to counterattack ISIS positions when they encountered ISIS fighters in a strong defensive position on an embankment. The ISIS force was within 100 meters of the Iraqi convoy's location, battering them with recoilless rifle and rocket-propelled grenades. They'd disabled the Iraqi convoy.

The Iraqis sent us a rough grid to the location and we pushed our Predator drone sensor overhead. Right away we saw it—picture-perfect as far as target descriptions go. We identified the halted Iraqi convoy off a small road on the south bank of a stretch of the Euphrates. To the west, slightly over 100 meters and across an open area, a large berm provided ample cover to an eighteen-man force of ISIS fighters.

We watched as the ISIS fighters took turns sporadically running to the top of the berm and laying down AK-47 and machine gun fire at the halted ISF convoy, then withdrawing back to the west side cover of the berm. The Iraqi troops took cover behind and inside their vehicles, but they couldn't counter the heavy ISIS fire.

When we'd first received the report, I had dispatched a runner from the cell to fetch General Pittard for briefing and strike approval. He walked in just as we'd identified the ISIS force at the berm.

"What's going on, Wes?" Pittard asked as he came up calmly to Adam and me, his eyes on the drone feed in the front of the room.

We explained the situation. He was all about it. *Let's do this.*

A single ISIS fighter scrambled to the top of the berm, carrying a large tube on his shoulder. It was a recoilless rifle—which looks like a rocket launcher but fires modified artillery shells, not rockets.

BOOM!

We couldn't hear the explosion, but we saw it and all but felt the round explode out of the rifle to strike the Iraqi convoy. Most of us were all too familiar with the brain-splitting blast of a recoilless rifle shot. Our Predator feed had an infrared sensor, so we could see the heat reverberation from its huge rear backblast.

"Kill those shitheads, Wes!" Colonel Kehoe exclaimed.

I only wished it was possible in that moment. We were still waiting on our strike aircraft to arrive on station. Instead, I detailed to Colonel Kehoe and General Pittard the weaponeering plan that Adam and I planned on executing once our fighter jets showed up. All we could do until then was watch the situation develop and hope ISIS didn't either wipe out the entire Iraqi convoy or maneuver somewhere where we couldn't track them with our drone.

Luckily, ISIS never made a move away from their well-fortified position. They had the advantage, or so they thought. Of course, they had no idea that U.S. and coalition airpower was on its way to destroy them.

Ten or fifteen minutes had gone by since we'd pinpointed the ISIS location—but it seemed like hours. We finally had a flight of two F-16 Vipers check in on station. My biggest concern, though, was that they weren't American pilots—they were coalition.

Language barriers with our allied pilots sometimes proved to be a real problem. On top of that, the targeting abilities of some coalition pilots were not always up to U.S. standards. This would be a *danger close* mission, and we could not afford any error in targeting.

Fortunately, as I briefed the pilots on the situation and got their targeting verifications and weaponeering inputs, I was relieved to find that they had solid English skills and were competent and efficient pilots. I coordinated for the Vipers to drop two GBU-49s: laser-guided 500-pound bombs with optional GPS guidance equipped with warheads specifically designed to kill enemy forces in the open.

The ISIS fighters were divided into two groups north and south, on the west side of the berm. My plan was to put one bomb at each of their locations. Our Predator drone would laser-guide the target closest to our friendly Iraqi position. That would offer us the least risk of accidentally impacting friendly troops since it was the most accurate guidance option. The second bomb would guide by GPS only, targeted by the pilot's aircraft sensor. We couldn't lase in the second bomb because we'd risk the laser being obscured by the smoke and haze of the first impact and the second bomb never finding its mark. That wasn't a risk we could take.

I emphasized to the coalition pilots that it would be better to miss the target completely than to inadvertently injure or kill any of our Iraqi partners in the strike. But I also knew that if we didn't strike the ISIS fighters soon, they would overtake the Iraqi convoy. *Danger close* or not, there was some risk we had to take.

Still, I relied on quite a few "mitigation" techniques to reduce any chance of injuring our nearby Iraqi force: A combination of laser and GPS guidance for precision strike capability. Restriction on the attack heading of the F-16s to ensure the trajectory of the bombs was not in line with the Iraqi convoy. Keeping the bomb impact points on the west side of the berm in order to shield the Iraqis from fragmentation. And ensuring the pilots switched their selectable fuse option to "contact" versus "airburst" to keep the risk of fragmentation to our Iraqi forces at a minimum.

As I was planning the attack with our coalition pilots, Adam and our special operations team liaison had been coordinating with our Special Forces team in the Anbar operations center. We needed to ensure the Iraqi force knew that we were about to drop bombs on the ISIS position in front of them. We warned the ISF on the ground to stay with their convoy and take cover, and to not attempt to advance on the ISIS location until our strikes were complete.

I set our Vipers in position to strike, controlling them over satellite radio as Adam controlled the Predator drone crew over secure phone. The ISIS fighters continued their furious cycle, pounding the ISF convoy with gunfire and RPGs then maneuvering back down the berm to take cover before the Iraqis were able to effectively counterfire from their gun trucks. The ISIS force was still separated into two entities, more or less, with about thirty meters between.

General Pittard sat behind us, relaxed and still nursing a small lollipop, watching the Predator feed on the screen at the front of the cell.

That was his way. After giving his approval and guidance, he would sit back and quietly observe while casually snacking on a bag of pistachios or nursing a lollipop and drinking from a vat of iced tea. In fact, we had a running joke that if the pistachios or lollipops came out, the kill was on.

Steadily, I directed the fighter pilots to strike.

"Dash one—*cleared hot*. Dash one—*cleared hot*."

The lead Viper pilot called inbound with the first bomb. A few seconds later in heavily-accented English he came back, "One bomb away, south target, forty-five seconds to impact."

Adam had the drone crew on speakerphone. The Predator sensor operator came through and verified that he was lasing for the bomb. "Laser on...good lase," said the focused voice through the secure phone.

Adam and I took a few seconds to examine our Predator video feed and verify that the sensor operator was, indeed, marking the correct location and that the operator had the right laser code entered that matched the bomb's code. If he didn't, the bomb would never catch the laser energy from the Predator and wouldn't hit on target.

Over my radio the Viper wingman called in for clearance to drop the second bomb. I verified that he was inbound within my directed attack parameters, and cleared the strike.

"One bomb away, north target, forty seconds," came the equally thick-accented notice from the F-16 wingman.

Then came the waiting game.

Both bombs were in the air on their way down to impact an ISIS force barely 100 meters from our ISF convoy. The final seconds between weapons release and impact were always tense for me in these situations. It was the time when I hoped I hadn't screwed up, that my target didn't suddenly move, or that the friendly ground force didn't start advancing toward the impact point. Though only a matter of a few dozen seconds at most, it felt like an eternity. I nearly always second-guessed myself. My mind would race through the entire control process as I analyzed my performance within a consolidated timeline of microseconds.

It wasn't really because I doubted myself. Over the years I'd found that it was the mark of a good controller to have such anxieties—the bad ones tended to think they could do no wrong. Overall, I felt solid about the attack. My feelings were soon validated.

BOOM...BOOM!

We watched near-simultaneous impacts as the two bombs smashed their intended targets. Clouds of smoke obscured the west side of the berm where the ISIS fighters had been.

It was a tremendous strike. Everyone in the strike cell was ecstatic.

"Fuck yeah!" Adam and I yelled almost in unison.

We immediately directed our F-16s and Predator to search around the settling debris. Inevitably, we knew there would be squirters. It never failed to surprise me how often we had survivors even from 500-pound bomb strikes. Typically, we'd have to wait a couple of minutes to spot them—not only for the smoke, haze, and debris to settle, but for the shell-shocked fighters to come to their senses and get oriented enough to clamber to their feet and run.

The smoke slowly cleared in light winds. Soon we distinguished bodies strewn all over the west side of the berm—some with limbs separated and others in contorted positions. Those were always solemn moments, but ones that we were conditioned to appreciate as warfighters battling a bloodthirsty enemy. As strange as it may seem to some, for guys like us it was a scene of somber beauty to see our enemy cut down and lying in pieces on the ground in front of us.

I praised the pilots and the Predator sensor operator for their first-rate precision. No sooner had I done so than the drone feed displayed two ISIS fighters running west away from the strike location. We weren't done yet.

Since the coalition F-16s had unleashed all their weapons in the strike, we had to call in the follow-on team—a pair of U.S. Navy F/A-18 fighter jets that had been on standby just outside the airspace waiting to get into the fight. We also had another coalition drone that had checked in on station, an MQ-9 Reaper. It was unarmed as well—that particular coalition country had yet to approve arming their drones for the fight in Iraq. (That was unfortunate, because Reapers could carry a lot of firepower.)

We used the coalition drone as a second pair of eyes. Adam directed the pilot to search west following the Euphrates for more enemy activity. Before I could direct a strike onto the fleeing ISIS fighters with the new set of Hornets, I had to follow procedures—which included passing a targeting brief, setting safe attack parameters, and directing all the other air assets in the airspace to de-conflict from the approach of the attacking jets. Delays like that were sometimes unavoidable. It would have been nice of the enemy to wait until we were ready, but that was never going to happen. You had to play the hand dealt.

The lag between strikes was only a few minutes, and that turned out to be a good thing. We watched as the two fighters pushed further west and maneuvered through the thick vegetation on the bank of the Euphrates. They linked up with more enemy fighters and gave us an even better target.

At that moment, General Pittard directed us to continue hunting ISIS in the area until all the fighters were killed. We now had free rein to hunt and kill ISIS. Adam and I directed our fighter and drone pilots to find every ISIS fighter they possibly could. We wanted to eliminate as many of them as possible that night.

The F/A-18 Super Hornets carried a compliment of 500-pound bombs, 300-pound missiles, and on board 20mm cannons. I directed them to posture their aircraft to strike the maneuvering ISIS fighters with bombs. While our aircraft positioned, we watched in delighted surprise as even more fighters appeared and linked up with the same group. We now had twelve to fifteen ISIS fighters in our sights.

Strangely, the ISIS fighters began moving back toward the positions we'd just hit near the Iraqi convoy. We couldn't believe it! We'd known ISIS to be bold, but we were awestruck that they seemed to be reinforcing their original positions even despite our airstrikes. Maybe they thought we were out of bombs and ammunition? If that was the case, they were about to be in for a shock.

I directed the Hornet pilots to drop two GBU-54s: 500-pound bombs with both laser and GPS guidance capable of hitting targets that moved far faster than a squad of ISIS fighters in thick vegetation. The bombs were a direct hit. They killed all but one of the ISIS fighters.

The lone squirter ran west.

As we tracked the lone wolf, our coalition Reaper crew reported even more ISIS fighters making their way toward our two previous impact locations from further to the west.

Full night had fallen.

We watched as more squads of ISIS fighters maneuvered the tight trails of thick underbrush along the river. On the infrared video feeds, we saw them as stark black figures moving through lighter shades that depicted the water and vegetation around them. They weren't running anymore. They were moving more tactically and regrouping into smaller units, presumably so we couldn't hit them all at once. The ISIS fighters were clearly rattled and scared; but were determined to continue the fight and hold their ground.

We held off, biding our time until we could attack with maximum efficiency. After ten minutes or so they played into our hands, forming a group of about a dozen fighters. I immediately began coordinating for another strike as four of the fighters branched off again. The coalition Reaper tracked the four, and we kept eyes on the other eight with our Predator.

Within minutes in another adept strike, our Super Hornets killed the entire group of eight using two more 500-pound bombs. Meanwhile, the coalition drone pilot observed the four fighters fleeing into a building even further west along the river. While we'd been directing our strikes to the east, he had observed slews of ISIS forces coming and going from the building.

The Reaper drone had identified an enemy stronghold—likely a bed down for the local ISIS forces. It would have served as a living quarters, ammunitions and weapons storage, rear area command and control, and defensive fighting position. I turned and asked General Pittard what he wanted to do about the building, since targeting buildings carried more concern for collateral damage and civilian casualties. He was finishing the last remnants of his lollipop—iced tea in hand.

"I want that building destroyed, Wes," he told us. "And try to get as many ISIS fighters in it as possible when you drop."

He took a swig of his cold tea and stared intently at the screens displaying our two drone feeds. The coalition Reaper operator estimated at least eight enemy fighters were in the building. We watched two of them intermittently pop out of what appeared to be a covered porch at the main entrance. They'd periodically move to a position near the edge of the front wall and peer out east where we'd been striking, then quickly move back under the concealment of their covered porch. It seemed that they were trying to recon the area without moving too far from their cover and concealment.

I worked with the lead Hornet pilot to decide what firepower we wanted to unleash. The target was a single story, house-sized structure. Our plan was to hit dead-center with their remaining two 500-pound bombs. We'd drop the first with a delayed fuse, and the other would hit shortly after, detonating on impact. The combination would completely obliterate the building and all fighters inside.

I postured the aircraft for the strike. I held off briefly as the two roving ISIS scouts made their rounds. I wanted to give the command to strike once they went back inside the building—I was never interested in survivors.

Direct hit.

Once the smoke and dust cleared, no trace of the building remained except for the heat signature on the ground where the bombs had impacted and a few scattered pieces of incinerated debris. There were no survivors.

We'd been on the offensive for nearly two hours and killed more than forty ISIS fighters. We'd also destroyed what was most likely a key command and control stronghold in the area. But we weren't done yet. Our drones picked up more enemy fighters who'd been hiding among the thick underbrush along the river.

Our Hornets were out of bombs. We were down to using either their AGM-65 air-to-ground *Maverick* missiles or the on board 20mm cannons. The cannons weren't exactly peashooters, but my weapon of choice was the laser-guided Mavericks. 300 pounds of death-dealing destruction, I'd used Mavericks with great success plenty of times against enemy fighters both on the move and in the open. The missiles were always deadly accurate and devastating. Maverick missiles were, by far, my favorite weapon to use for their versatility, accuracy, and killing power.

We tracked a group of six ISIS fighters maneuvering erratically on the main trail along the river. They were in pure survival mode by then—careful to space themselves out to avoid giving us a consolidated target. We waited them out, knowing they'd eventually have to come together to pass information and plan what to do next. As anticipated, that's exactly what they did.

I cleared the Hornet flight to launch a Maverick.

In the forty or so seconds of the missile's flight, the ISIS group broke up and continued moving down the trail. I wasn't too worried. The exceptional laser guidance capability of the Maverick missile would allow the Hornet pilot to easily track the maneuvering personnel while the missile was in flight and adjust the impact point as the fighters continued down the trail.

The problem was, the group was separating further and further. The further apart they got, the less chance we would have of the missile's blast and fragmentation killing all of them.

IMPACT.

Four were killed instantly. One of the fighters who had pulled away from the pack in the last seconds survived the blast and ran for cover. Another got up from the ground a few seconds after impact, clearly injured but able to move, and ran to link up with his friend. We had one Maverick missile remaining. I wanted to use it to kill the two final ISIS fighters.

But Colonel Kehoe had an issue with that plan. He asked why we couldn't just use the 20mm guns and save the more expensive missile for another possible follow-on target that might present itself later. It was a valid question. But I knew the 20mm cannon of the F/A-18 was originally optimized for air-to-air use. Because of that, its effectiveness as an air-to-ground weapon at night against two fighters on the move and separated by at least ten meters would surely be poor. I'd had a lot of experience with 20mm cannons in similar situations. They often missed their target. I advised Colonel Kehoe to that end, but he was concerned about munitions resources.

"I just don't think it's worth wasting a Maverick on two guys," he said. "Try to kill them with the guns, Wes. If we miss, we've killed enough of them here anyway."

I continued to press for a minute or so longer, but the director insisted so I reluctantly complied. Unfortunately, what ensued after that was perhaps the most frustrating end to what had up to that point been nothing short of an awesome mission.

During the few minutes that the colonel and I had debated over what ordnance to use, the last two ISIS fighters kept moving. By the time we settled on our weaponeering decision, they'd traveled a couple kilometers from the original target area into a network of orchards with large trees. Their movement was now intermittently obscured by the trees.

I briefed the Hornet pilots the new plan: clean up the enemy squirters with 20mm guns. They didn't like the idea. They contended. They insisted on using their last remaining Maverick missile just as I had advised the colonel. After some arguing on their part—and understandably so—I plainly told the pilots that we had a directive from higher to use their guns and that was that. They reluctantly conceded.

The Hornet pilots couldn't make out the moving ISIS fighters in the orchard, but our Reaper was still tracking them. I now had to rely on "Plan B." I'd have the Reaper put a laser mark on the two fighters, tracking them with the mark as they moved down the trail. I'd direct the fighter pilots to strafe with their 20mm cannons right on the laser mark from the Reaper. It wasn't an optimal plan as we always wanted a pilot's eyes on a gun target for accuracy's sake. But it was the most viable plan I could go with at the time.

Within a few minutes, the Hornets came in from far above and behind the two ISIS fighters while they now almost casually walked a narrow trail through the orchard. Adam and I laughed that the ISIS fighters probably believed they were finally safe.

On my clearance, the jets fired two separate 20mm volleys right on the Reaper's laser mark. The rounds sprayed the dirt and trees around and in front of the fighters...but missed them both. They split up and ran frantically.

We lost sight of them as they hid among the trees. I advised the Hornet pilots to wait and re-position themselves for another volley of guns. I knew the ISIS fighters would move again. After a few minutes the two fighters began making short, quick bounding movements through the trees to link back up. Once they got back together, they half-walked/half-ran along the riverside trail—likely hoping in vain that they were safe and had survived the last of our onslaughts.

I requested another round of guns from our Hornets, but this time received no response.

I gave the order again.

No response.

I came over the radio several more times. Still nothing.

We watched, frustrated, as the two enemy fighters ran toward a thicker section of the orchard. We knew once they got there that they'd be even harder to track. And under such thick foliage, even if our drone kept its sensor on their general location, we wouldn't be able to effectively lase to direct another volley of guns—and the Hornet pilots surely wouldn't be able to pick up the fighters with their sensors.

Still, no response from the Hornets.

I had to wonder if my Hornet pilots were so pissed off about being forced to use their guns that they'd decided to call it a day and were intentionally ignoring my commands. They didn't know how forcefully I'd argued with the strike cell director. On the other hand, they didn't know the pressure Colonel Kehoe was under from higher to reserve our ordnance for the most optimal use.

My body could have made an effective weapon of mass destruction at that point. There was enough volatility boiling in me to wipe out a small army. We'd spent the last two-plus hours rounding up dozens of ISIS fighters—all of it frustrating, all of it intense, all of it exhausting. The last enemy standing needed to be killed, but I couldn't get our pilots to do the job.

"Does *anyone* on this net want to *kill* these two ISIS fighters?!" I yelled over the radio. "Request *immediate* reattack with guns. *HOW...COPY*?!"

Finally, the lead pilot came back over the radio with acknowledgement. Within less than a minute, he and his wingman swooped in to fire off another round of 20mm strafe onto the mark from our Reaper. Foliage from the orchard trees flew everywhere, but the luckiest pair of ISIS fighters on the planet was still on the run. They headed in different directions.

Then our F/A-18s called in low on fuel. They'd been flying for hours before even being tasked to support our mission, and they had to return to base.

I looked for something to punch in my immediate area that wasn't a valuable piece of communication equipment, but I couldn't find anything. I snatched my communications headset off and threw it on the table in front of me. I couldn't stand to leave enemy survivors. We didn't always know who we were letting live. For all we knew that could have been one of the most senior leaders in ISIS that we'd just let walk away unscathed into the orchard.

I gave begrudging credit to the two ISIS fighters who'd survived our onslaught, but I sure as hell didn't wish them well for the future. *You may have survived an encounter with the world's most effective killing force, but there will be another day of reckoning for you soon.*

Everyone in the strike cell gave me room to cool off. Well, except for Adam who was laughing. I muttered angrily to myself, shaking my head.

"You okay, Wes?" came a calm voice from behind.

I turned around to see General Pittard in his chair, casually placing his lollipop back in his mouth and offering a slight smile. I knew he'd stepped out earlier to take a phone call from his interpreter, Ali, and I thought he was still gone. I hadn't even noticed his return to the strike cell. I was a bit embarrassed and tried to laugh it off.

"Yeah, I'm good sir…" I started. "I just get a little heated sometimes." I continued offering excuses for my outburst. "I don't know what was going on with those pilots on the last few strikes—"

"It's alright, Wes," he said smiling. "Good mission."

• • •

As I later learned, the pilots began having communications difficulties at the tail end of the mission. They weren't getting most of my transmissions. The reality was that we couldn't always count on 100 percent clear communications—and sometimes there was just nothing anyone could do about it. Truly, the Hornet pilots had performed magnificently during the mission.

Within twelve hours of the strikes, communications intercepts and intelligence reporting confirmed that we had taken out a key ISIS leader along with nearly fifty of his fighters. In addition, we'd liberated the water treatment plant and safeguarded an Iraqi unit facing annihilation by the larger ISIS force.

The next morning, Vern and I stood at the edge of the crowded operations center at the special operations task force as Commander Black received his morning updates from the SOTF-I staff.

"Last night, the Iraqi Air Force killed fifty ISIS fighters along with a key ISIS commander at a water treatment plant in the vicinity of Ramadi," the intelligence analyst began.

Vern and I exchanged glances then listened in disbelief as the task force intelligence officer finished giving a completely inaccurate briefing to Commander Black and the dozens of SOTF-I staff huddled at the Glass House—that our strikes had been accomplished by the Iraqis using Iraqi strike aircraft.

We looked at each other and smirked. Our own task force didn't even know that their very JTACs—standing right there in front of them—were the ones who'd controlled the strikes they were briefing about. And all from a strike cell about 300 meters up the road.

Vern and I said nothing. We didn't feel a need to correct anyone that morning. We knew it was just a reflection of the general disconnect between our task force and everyone else. And, we knew who was making the difference in the fight against ISIS. We shook our heads, half smiling, as we walked out the door to get on with the hunt.

CHAPTER 33

Caged Dogs

WES BRYANT

ISIS was a brutal enemy, and inhumane to the core. They needed to be obliterated beyond all trace. But the terrorist army seemed fearless. Even as we hit them with airstrikes again and again, they quite literally fought to the last man. It was uncanny.

ISIS was certainly nothing if not zealous and aggressive. From the outside looking in, their spirit seemed nearly indomitable. Of course, we'd later learn a contributing factor was that they gave their fighters opiates and cocaine before battles and threatened punishment or torture for failure or cowardice. Religious extremism coupled with mind-altering drugs and fear of torture was certainly a way to create a seemingly indomitable force.

Still, we were often surprised at the level of capability ISIS showed even in comparison to some of the best-trained Iraqi ground forces. In fact, when we came across armed and maneuvering fighters we hadn't yet identified as friendly or enemy, the going rule became "if they move tactically sound, they're probably ISIS." Nonetheless, if ISIS prided themselves in being bold and aggressive, they were surely humbled once they realized what it meant to be on the receiving end of the wrath of the U.S. military.

Those of us in the BIAP Strike Cell had all sacrificed and bled with our partner forces during the previous Iraq War and the ongoing war in

Afghanistan. Most of us had lost friends and brothers- or sisters-in-arms over the years, and we'd watched our partner forces suffer the same. We'd helped both the Iraqis and the Afghans fight for their homes and their countries, and we witnessed their struggle to balance the well-beings of themselves and their families with the duties and sacrifices that came with being soldiers in perpetually war-torn nations. We knew what our Iraqi forces were enduring because we'd been there. In the strike cell, when we supported the Iraqis with airstrikes, we put ourselves on the ground with them.

The most difficult challenge was how differently we were doing business than what we were used to. It wasn't common for JTACs to work tandem and run strikes as a team. We were accustomed to being "the man" in charge—the sole JTAC attached to a special operations team, tromping through austere battlefields as the exclusive air and indirect firepower expert for the team. We were used to working independently and making tough calls on our own under intense circumstances. Because of those factors, our job tended to attract strong and independent individuals.

Admittedly, most of us had pretty controlling personalities. It was difficult at times to figure out how to take a crew of special operations JTACs and get them to work cohesively as one killing team. Compound that with the intensity of strike cell operations that were truly a perfect microcosm of everything that is war—and you had a recipe for volatility.

I paired my shift with Adam, the most senior Combat Control JTAC of my Special Tactics team. Adam was a bit rough around the edges. He was a charmer and a bit of a lady's man on one hand, and a hothead on the other. Extravagant and robust, his was a strong-willed personality that was often quick-witted and funny, but also pretty abrupt.

Even though our personalities seemed to be near polar opposite, Adam and I had an immediate bond and my respect for his abilities outweighed anything else. He was a smart, aggressive, and extremely talented JTAC. His past experience hunting insurgents on the battlefields of Afghanistan and Iraq—mirrored with my own—made us quite a good team.

But we butted heads fairly often, and our nights were not complete without a few fights. I was the senior enlisted JTAC for the strike cell. I had to make sure our JTACs were following the intent of General Pittard and Colonel Kehoe at all times. Sometimes, my idea of that conflicted pretty significantly with Adam's.

It was a particularly quiet night and we were waiting for the Bayji operation to kick off within a few days. Adam and I were using our air assets to hunt for ISIS targets of opportunity. It was so dead that Colonel Kehoe, his deputy Major McCrae, and the general were all out for the evening on other business.

In lieu of active ground offensives, intelligence on enemy locations, or any other information leading us to targets, we were still every bit as aggressive hunting ISIS. In fact, we were often as much if not more successful when let loose to hunt ISIS using our own intuition, past experience with insurgency tactics, and what we'd learned about how they operated thus far. We'd developed a growing database, nearly imprinted in our minds, of the patterned tactics and behavior of the ISIS forces we were hunting.

Adam was the primary controller. He'd been directing a couple of fighter jets and a Predator drone to search various locations that he suspected had ISIS fighters, based on historic patterns and some past operations we'd conducted. All of his searches were coming up dry.

After a while, I finally told him to shift to another specific area. I had a general plan for the night after my discussion with Colonel Kehoe earlier in the evening, and Adam hadn't really been following it anyway. He definitely didn't like my correction.

"Why do you wanna look there, man? We won't find shit there," he told me frankly.

I had particular locations I wanted checked out, and Adam had others he believed would give us a higher chance of finding ISIS. We argued off and on over the course of about twenty minutes or so, the tone of our argument growing ever more bickering as we went.

Little did I know, the tension was building in Adam. I didn't quite realize it at the time because I was also engrossed in the secure email and messaging traffic that I tended to on my down time, coordinating for future operations. Adam was growing increasingly agitated with each of my corrections.

Eventually he couldn't take it anymore.

"Just do your fires bullshit and let me control!" he snapped. "I'm the JTAC tonight, man!"

I stayed relatively calm. At least, calm in my *mind*—although I'm sure looking back I was outwardly pissed off. On the inside, I was immediately enraged. Still, I didn't act on my anger. I tried to explain my reasoning to him a little better, hoping to tame down the situation. Adam wasn't hearing it. He thought my plan was, in a word, "bullshit."

He may have been right...but I wasn't going to let up.

We raised our voices incrementally higher. I was insistent on following my agenda and Adam wouldn't budge on his. What started as a minor tiff quickly escalated into an all-out yelling match as I could no longer maintain the calm myself.

I turned toward him and leaned in close to his face. "Dude, just put the *fuckin'* aircraft sensors where I told you to—or I'll just control!" I bellowed.

The strike cell was suddenly like that cliché of the record screech in a dance club—dead silent. Up until that point, Adam had been coolly passing guidance to the fighter pilots and drone crews in-between arguing with me, remaining ever-the-professional JTAC even despite our heated pissing match.

But then, he abruptly stopped mid-transmission and ripped off his communications headset, slamming it onto the table. He shoved his chair back and shot up. Attached to his belt on the right hip of his jeans was a custom leather holster with an etched CCT crest holding his issued Glock 19 pistol. He ripped the holster off and smashed it onto the radio control box on the table between us. (I noted that he made sure not to de-holster his pistol and that the barrel pointed away from either of us.)

"Don't you EVER fucking tell me how to control!" he yelled as he jutted his head toward me. His eyes narrowed in a look that told me *I want to beat the shit out of you right now.*

Unfortunately, my anger got the better of me again.

"Fuckin' *leave*, then! Get the fuck outa here, I'm controlling now!" I shouted back.

Adam stood in anger for a few seconds, staring at me in silence as I donned the radio headset and ignored him. He stormed out of the back-side of the trailer. The back door thudded closed.

I felt my eyes had gone red with anger, I was so infuriated. My first instinct was to go outside, get back in his face and say things that surely would have led to us brawling it out. Luckily I held that urge back—really only because we still had aircraft to control, actively hunting for ISIS across central Iraq. Adam and I may have been on the verge of a full contact match in the middle of the BIAP Strike Cell, but we couldn't leave any of our pilots hanging.

I gathered myself and keyed the microphone. "All players be advised—*Vampire Zero-One* has control," I said relatively calmly over the net.

I gave the aircraft updated guidance...*my* guidance. And I sat at the desk, fuming. Then I despondently watched over the next several minutes as our aircraft feeds revealed absolutely no signs of enemy activity in my new search areas.

Everyone in the cell continued on in dead silence while I worked on quieting my temper that had almost raged completely out of control only minutes before. Luckily, controlling our aircraft in search of ISIS gave me something else to focus on. At the same time, I was laughing a bit inside at the tension in the cell. I kind of just wanted to blurt out, "Hey guys, it's just another day in our world...this is how we talk through things!" Ultimately, I didn't think that comment would be appropriate at the time, so I kept it to myself.

Adam and I were friends, and we were teammates as JTACs. But I was also the senior member of our team. After a few minutes I realized that, despite my anger, I needed to figure things out. I was upset with myself. I had nearly gotten in a fistfight with a subordinate and teammate while in the midst of what was probably the highest priority military tasking at the time—a mission straight from the President of the United States.

I knew we couldn't continue to act this way given the scope and gravity of our mission. It was one of those times when regardless of which of us was in the wrong, we just needed to pull our shit together and continue mission.

In my years as a noncommissioned officer up to that point, I had never really counted myself as the quintessential "inspirational" type of leader that others seemed to pride themselves in being. I had other strengths, and I'd at least picked up a few pearls of wisdom. If there was one thing I'd learned about working with and leading the kind of hardened, *Type-A*

individuals that abound in the JTAC and special operations community—it was that sometimes you just had to let men be men. And that's
not in the way some might think of the phraseology, but entirely in the
warrior sense.

I knew it wouldn't go anywhere to continue to get in Adam's face
or levy my superior rank or position. It would only make him angrier
and then resentful toward me for having to rely on rank to settle the
issue. In the culture of special operations there was this kind of unofficial commandment: respect was merit-based—it had to be earned. Your
teammates and subordinates respected you first for your skill, ability and
experience, and second for the respect you showed to theirs. Rank and
position were always secondary, at best, to those critical things.

I knew that truth from first-hand experience. I'd been on the opposite
side of the equation all too often in encounters with unsavory superiors
over the years, and I'd vowed to never do the same when I became a leader.

Ten or fifteen more minutes dragged by. I controlled our pair of
fighter jets and the Predator drone, monitoring the video feed in front
of me for any signs of ISIS. I was still having about as much luck finding
ISIS as Adam had.

In my periphery, I saw Adam stroll quietly back in. He sat down
next to me as calm as can be. Without exchanging anything but a couple
mutually understanding nods, I passed the headset back over to him. He
grabbed his holstered Glock—still sitting on the radio box where he'd
slammed it—and casually attached it back onto his belt.

He situated his headset as I passed him a brief update on the status of
our aircraft and the taskings I'd given them since he'd been out. A cardinal
rule in the JTAC world was to never hand off control without first giving
the new controller a current update on the battlefield along with a status
of the position of all aircraft and their sensor allocations. That rule super-
seded any fight we may have had.

"Got it," he said evenly.

He went back to controlling without skipping a beat. I slid back over
to my side of the desk, quietly resuming my secure email and message
coordination—or my "nerd work" as Adam would so often lovingly prod.
A couple of minutes went by. During a break in his radio communication
with the pilots, Adam finally looked over at me.

"Sorry bro," he said, breaking a sly smile. "I love ya."

I nodded and smiled back. "Love you too man," I replied. "Sorry if I was more of a dick than I thought I was being."

"It's cool, man."

He looked over at me briefly, then with a closed-lip smirk he coolly put his fist out toward me and turned his head to the front of the room to keep his eyes on the aircraft feeds. We fist-bumped, and drove on with the mission.

CHAPTER 34

The Bayji Oil Refinery

DANA PITTARD

Mid-October 2014

Lieutenant General Wahab, the designated Iraqi commander for the Bayji operation, never fully trusted Americans. He didn't think we would support him with intelligence or airstrikes in a timely manner, and he pointed to our slower response to the Iraqi requests for strikes during the Haditha operation as evidence for his conviction. If we were ever slow on prosecuting a target, though, it was because the Iraqi reporting and lack of accuracy hadn't been able to meet our strike criteria in a timely manner.

In the couple of days before the start of the Iraqi Security Forces ground operation to liberate the Bayji Oil Refinery, our strike cell began hitting a multitude of ISIS targets based off our own intelligence and targeting efforts in order to soften the battlefield for the Iraqi advance. Wahab had a target list, too—developed solely from Iraqi intelligence—which he requested we include in our pre-assault strikes.

Unfortunately, most of his targets did not pass our strict targeting criteria so we could not prosecute them. Deep down, I suspected Lieutenant General Wahab's target list was full of valid targets, but we needed more information to strike most of them. We did not want to risk hitting innocent civilians.

When I informed General Wahab that we needed more collaborative intelligence to engage his targets, he got angry. But, to his credit, he listened. To ensure he had more detailed intelligence for the remainder of the operation, he reinforced his very capable spy network in Bayji with even more agents. He also reinforced his intelligence operatives throughout the entire province of Salah ad-Din.

On October 16, the ground operation to relieve the ISIS stranglehold on the Bayji Oil Refinery kicked off. Iraqi forces departed their assembly areas near an Iraqi air base northwest of Tikrit, fifty kilometers south of Bayji. They moved along the south-north highway that linked the cities of Tikrit and Bayji.

Lieutenant General Wahab was brave to a fault. He led from the front and often placed himself in harm's way. For the assault, he positioned his mobile command post—an old American M113 tracked armored personnel carrier—as forward as possible. He was with the lead infantry battalion consisting of a tank platoon of four M1 Abrams tanks, an engineer road-clearing platoon, and two mechanized infantry companies in various armored vehicles and trucks.

Few Iraqi generals were as courageous as Lieutenant General Wahab. However, there were plenty of Iraqi generals who were smarter. Still, I admired his courage and stubbornness. At least he was attacking! To be honest, I wished I could have been on the ground sharing both the adversity and the danger with him.

In its entirety, Lieutenant General Wahab's huge fighting column had more than 3,000 Iraqi soldiers and Shia militiamen, about the size of an American army brigade. The column moved at an extremely slow pace as the engineers had to clear countless IEDs from the highway that had been emplaced by ISIS fighters.

From the BIAP Strike Cell, we watched the slow progress of the Iraqi approach to Bayji while simultaneously directing numerous strikes there and elsewhere in Iraq. We'd dedicated a Predator drone to the Iraqi column to be quickly available for any supporting airstrikes. We also had a drone covering the Bayji Oil Refinery fifty kilometers north of the column, in case ISIS decided to conduct an all-out attack to take the refinery before the column arrived. Because of that foresight, our Iraqi CTS defenders, with the assistance of our airstrikes, were able to beat back numerous attacks launched by ISIS before the main Iraqi Army force arrived.

We also turned the battle for Bayji into a hugely successful ambush on key ISIS leadership. As we had expected, senior ISIS leaders rushed to the Bayji battlefront to encourage their fighters. Within the first 24–48 hours of the operation, we were able to kill the ISIS *emir* of Salah ad-Din province as well as the senior ISIS leader in Bayji.

Though the operation was going well, we still needed to get the Iraqi column to speed up its pace. The slower the armored column went, the easier it would be for ISIS fighters to set up ambushes and IEDs and prepare their defenses. In fact, Wahab's large column advancing on a single axis was an inviting target.

In planning for the operation, we'd developed a plan for a multi-axis attack on Bayji, but the Iraqis had flat out refused to adopt it. They saw safety in having one large single approach, while I saw potential disaster. I eventually relented, and was just happy that the Iraqi Army was attacking. However, I still thought that the single avenue of approach was a huge tactical mistake, except for the fact that we could easily concentrate our airstrikes both to the front line and flanks of the single axis.

Any stationary defending ISIS fighters were quickly dealt with by our strike cell, but highly mobile suicide bombers in vehicles were another thing altogether. Known as *VBIEDs* (vehicle-borne IEDs), they were almost impossible to detect from the air until right before they struck, because they looked like normal civilian vehicles.

My interpreter Ali and I stepped out of the strike cell. We needed to urge Lieutenant General Wahab to move faster. Ali used his cell phone to call, and after going through the normal pleasantries in Arabic I asked the general for a situation update on the ground.

"Thanks be to Allah, we are progressing," he said. "There have been a lot of IEDs cleared today, and my intelligence agents tell me we should expect several *Daesh* suicide car bombers."

Almost on cue, I heard an eruption of yelling and screaming in the background. Lieutenant General Wahab yelled to his men in Arabic, "Fire on that car right now!"

We heard the staccato sound *rat-tat-tat* of machine gun fire, and the phone call dropped. Ali and I looked at each other and then rushed back into the strike cell. On our Predator video feed we saw a car moving from the east at a high rate of speed toward the Iraqi column. Luckily, the car was pummeled by Iraqi Army machine guns. It blew-up in a ball of fire.

Then a second car came from the west, and a third from the north. The one from the north was quickly blown apart by an Iraqi tank round. The car from the west detonated itself as it crashed into an Iraqi M1 Abrams tank. It was a horrific scene, but luckily the tank and its crew survived—with mere scorch marks on the side armored skirt of the tank. Even the tracks remained intact. God, how I loved the resiliency and power of the U.S. Abrams tank!

Lieutenant General Wahab called me back as I stepped back out of the strike cell. "I am so sorry that I had to get off of the phone," he said, "but we had three suicide car bombs attacking us from three different directions. ISIS is getting desperate and sending very valuable and critical assets like car bombs at me and my soldiers. So far, thanks be to Allah, we have been able to hit them with machine gun fire and tank fire before they caused any serious damage. By Allah's grace, may we continue to be so lucky."

I agreed. I told Wahab that we'd seen it on our Predator drone feed and that the attackers must have used either hastily-prepared car bombs or bombs that had been constructed weeks ago—since we'd destroyed ISIS' largest car bomb factory southwest of Bayji in a deliberate airstrike a week earlier.

Lieutenant General Wahab hesitated a few moments before replying. "General Pittard, your airstrikes last week were good, but you failed to strike a second car bomb factory that's right in the middle of Bayji. I have had some of my people watching an auto repair shop that is doubling as a car bomb factory. Will you please hit that target with an airstrike?"

"Sadey, you know the answer to that one. We can't hit that target with an airstrike because of the potential collateral damage to the surrounding buildings in the middle of the city."

The auto repair shop was long suspected as a possible car bomb-making factory. The Iraqis had told us as much, but we had such a high standard of proof for targets that we still hadn't verified it as a bomb-making facility. Plus, the fact that it was in the middle of a large population center prevented us from striking it. Even so, Wahab's spies in Bayji continued to watch the auto repair shop around the clock.

I changed the subject to the matter at hand. "Sadey, please be careful out there. Iraq cannot afford to lose you or any of your brave soldiers. It will be safer for you if you and your column move faster."

"I am moving as fast as I can, thanks be to Allah!" Wahab replied.

The Franken-Truck

On a side alleyway in the middle of Bayji, one of Wahab's spies watched as two ISIS fighters carefully opened the large garage doors of an auto repair facility—their suspected car bomb-making factory. Slowly, a large truck emerged through the opening. A third ISIS fighter came out of the facility, stepped up to the truck's cab and looked through the heavily armored door. He appeared to say a prayer to the driver.

The massive sixteen-wheeler truck and its cab were modified with armored plating throughout the front and side areas of the cab. The back of the cab was filled with what appeared to be a lot of thin metal plates and a massive amount of explosives. The front windows were paneled with armored plating as well, with only enough of a slit for the driver to barely see the road.

The driver gave a thumbs-up and the truck turned into the alleyway and onto a major street. The Iraqi spy knew he had to inform Lieutenant General Wahab immediately.

Back in the BIAP Strike Cell, I was talking with our chief JTAC on duty, Vern, when I got word that Lieutenant General Wahab urgently wanted to speak with me. I stepped out of the strike cell and saw Ali with the cell phone.

"General Wahab says he has intel that a large suicide truck filled with explosives is moving to attack his troops advancing on Bayji," Ali said.

I had Ali call Lieutenant General Wahab.

"Sadey, how are you? Are you making progress?" I asked.

He replied nervously, "All is well General Pittard, but I have intelligence that a huge suicide truck bomb is leaving Bayji and headed our way. It is the largest one we have ever seen."

Wahab's intelligence network had proven to be pretty good, but this seemed like a stretch. Still, I could hear the anxiety in his voice. A potential suicide truck bomb was a concern to all of us.

"Do you currently have eyes on the truck?"

A little agitated, he responded, "No, but the truck is headed to the Bayji-Tikrit highway. It is headed right toward my advancing forces!"

"Can you please describe the truck, so we can locate it?"

He gave a good description of it as a large, armor-plated trash truck. I had my aide, Captain Barrett Newsom, ask Colonel Kehoe to direct the strike cell to locate this suspected suicide truck that was apparently headed south toward the Iraqi column. Then I told Lieutenant General Wahab we would do our best to find it.

"What will you do when you find it?" Wahab asked.

"We will try to intercept it," I said simply.

I turned the phone over to Ali and darted back into the strike cell. As I walked in to the buzzing cell, Colonel Kehoe turned from talking to the JTACs and told me that he believed they'd already located the suicide truck. He gestured to one of our drone feeds in the front of the cell. "There it is, sir, and we already have two coalition F-16s in the queue."

The truck was a frightening sight and it sent a rare chill down my spine. We stared at a large, sixteen-wheeler truck barreling south at a fast rate of speed. The cab of the truck was covered with strapped-on armored plating—even the windows were armor-plated except for the slit only large enough for the driver to see through.

I'd heard numerous stories from the Iraqis and the Kurds about these huge suicide trucks, and I'd seen plenty of terrible aftermath scenes from their destruction, yet I had never seen one before it exploded. I had an eerie feeling as we all watched what we could only describe as a *Franken-Truck* barrel its way toward our Iraqi forces.

On my order, Colonel Kehoe directed our JTACs to destroy it.

We immediately ran into ROE problems from the CENTCOM staffers who were observing our drone feeds from Tampa. They asked question-after-question about the target, doubting our assertion that it was a suicide truck.

"How do you know the truck has *hostile intent*?"

"Why do you think it is an ISIS truck?"

"Are there civilians on board?"

"Do you really want to waste valuable ordnance on a truck?"

We were running out of time. The truck was now twenty kilometers from Lieutenant General Wahab's armored column and closing the distance rapidly. We estimated less than fifteen minutes until it hit the Iraqi forces.

The JTACs and Colonel Kehoe patiently answered all of CENTCOM's questions, but after a few minutes I'd had enough. I firmly informed the CENTCOM staff that I trusted the intel source. I was not going to allow this suicide Franken-Truck to halt our offensive operation to Bayji.

I turned to Colonel Kehoe. "Execute the mission, Tim."

The next problem came from the coalition pilots. Now *they* weren't sure that *their* nation's ROE would allow them to hit the truck. After more minutes of wasted time, the pilots finally received clearance from their individual country's chain of command. Unfortunately, each of their F-16s only had one Maverick missile remaining from having prosecuted previous strikes during their sortie. Even so, we thought that should be plenty of ordnance to halt the truck. After all, it was just a single truck!

Both F-16s fired at the Franken-Truck. We watched in anticipation as the missiles struck. The Predator feeds were immediately obscured with lots of smoke and debris. Then slowly, as the smoke cleared, we saw movement like a phantom on the screen.

It was the Franken-Truck, still moving—both missiles had missed!

Loud groans, cussing, and fists pounding on tables filled the strike cell. I looked at Vern who took a deep breath and offered, "The F-16s can still use their guns."

I nodded in approval.

Three more minutes went by as Vern and the JTACs coordinated a 20mm gun run on the truck. The Franken-Truck was only about four minutes from the Iraqi column.

As the coalition F-16s swept in for their gun run, the Franken-Truck appeared to speed up. The 20mm guns from the F-16s blasted toward the target. The truck swerved and increased speed as soon as the driver realized rounds were incoming. The rounds hit all around the moving truck, yet somehow missed it again.

"That is one fucking *lucky* truck!" someone yelled.

After one volley of 20mm, the pilots reported that all their ammunition was expended.

I was beside myself, angry and disappointed. Ali came into the strike cell holding the cell phone toward me. He said that Lieutenant General Wahab wanted to talk with me again.

I put up my hand. "Tell Wahab we see the Franken-Truck and we are developing a plan to stop it."

As Ali translated that back, Wahab yelled through the phone, "Developing a *fucking* plan?! Gracious Allah, the truck is almost within sight!"

Ali told Wahab we would call him back.

We had less than three minutes until the Franken-Truck impacted our Iraqi convoy. Vern turned to me and Colonel Kehoe. "We've got a flight of American F-16s that'll be on station in five minutes."

My face contorted into a pissed-off look. My reply came through clenched teeth, "We don't have enough time."

Adam—one of Wes's senior JTACs—interjected nonchalantly. "Sir, we can always have the Pred fire a Hellfire."

I almost rolled my eyes at that. Up to that point, our track record with some of the Predator operators hitting fast-moving targets with their Hellfire missiles wasn't all that impressive.

There was no choice, though. We had a little over two minutes until the Franken-Truck's impact.

I waved them on. "Do it. Immediately!"

As Adam coordinated the strike, we all watched the video feed anxiously. The Predator pilot and sensor operator got their drone postured to strike and locked the Hellfire onto the Franken-Truck.

It was taking too damn long!

The Franken-Truck driver was now in sight of the Iraqi armored column. The strike cell was silent with anxiety. You could feel the tension in the room. The Iraqi column began moving their vehicles into hasty defensive positions, orienting all their guns toward the advancing suicide truck.

One minute remained. The Franken-Truck sped up and crossed the desert highway median to point itself directly toward the now stationary Iraqi column. The Iraqis fired all they could—rifles, rocket-propelled grenades, machine guns, even tank rounds.

At thirty seconds to impact, a Hellfire missile launched from our Predator. The Franken-Truck was seconds from smashing into the Iraqi armored personnel carrier at the head of the convoy.

WHAM!

The Hellfire hit the suicide truck with a vengeance.

A massive explosion shook the earth around the lead vehicles of the Iraqi column. The strike cell erupted into uncontrolled cheering, clapping, and fist pumping.

"Hell yeah!" I heard Adam yell.

I stepped out of the strike cell with Ali and we called Lieutenant General Wahab. He was alive and well. I spoke to him myself this time.

"Thanks be to Allah, that was way too close for our comfort," he told me.

"I agree," I said. "If it wasn't for our Hellfire missile, you would have had a lot of casualties."

He sharply replied, "What do you mean by that? Our lead tank fired the round that stopped the truck!"

"No," I came back. "It was hit by an American Hellfire missile fired from one of our Predator drones."

"Well, I am on the ground, and I know what I saw!"

I smiled. I took a breath. *Okay,* I told myself. *It's* Okay. Then I congratulated General Wahab on stopping the Franken-Truck.

He and I went on to coordinate the operations plan for the next twenty-four hours. We still had a lot of tough fighting ahead, and there was no need to get into a pissing match.

Later, after the fighting had died down a bit for the night, Vern played back the Predator video feed from the Franken-Truck strike in slow motion. To our surprise, we could see an Iraqi tank round hitting the truck simultaneously with our Hellfire missile. We watched the replay over and over. It was an amazing sight!

It turned out that Wahab and I were both right.

The Siege is Lifted

The offensive operation in Bayji had a serious effect on ISIS. While they were fighting in Bayji, they stepped up attacks in the Baghdad area to divert the Iraqi government's attention and try to force them to withdraw from the Bayji offensive and reinforce Baghdad. Because of that, General Kenani came under intense political pressure from Iraqi politicians to bring Lieutenant General Wahab and his forces back to Baghdad.

We had both anticipated as much. I called Lieutenant General Abdul Amir to get an update on the ISIS attacks around Baghdad. Amir was concerned about the increased ISIS attacks, but said that the Baghdad defenses would hold and that he did not need reinforcement from Lieutenant General Wahab. I asked Lieutenant General Amir to tell Prime Minister Abadi what he had just told me.

Shortly after that conversation, the pressure on Kenani stopped and the Bayji offensive drove on without any further political hitches. We just had to keep Wahab and his troops moving. Our strike cell team continued to hunt ahead of Wahab's advancing column, thwarting ambush-after-ambush with dozens of airstrikes onto ISIS fighting positions and maneuver forces. The fight to re-take the strategic oil refinery ebbed and flowed over the next several weeks, but ultimately the Iraqis prevailed. With our assistance, the ISIS siege around the Bayji Oil Refinery was lifted by early November.[1]

A Hostage Killed—Peter Kassig

The loss of Bayji was a huge setback for ISIS. On November 16, 2014, ISIS brutally murdered American Peter Kassig—the friend and colleague of the journalist who'd passed Kassig's location to me in hopes of coordinating a rescue back in late June. Kassig's brutal beheading by the executioner "Jihadi John" caused worldwide condemnation.[2]

A global hunt ensued for "Jihadi John," who was actually a British Arab named Mohammed Emwazi. On November 12, 2015, U.S. Special Forces tracked him down in Raqqa, Syria, and killed the butcher with a drone strike.[3]

---

1   "Iraq troops 'push Islamic State from oil town of Baiji,'" BBC News, November 14, 2014, accessed April 24, 2018, http://www.bbc.com/news/world-middle-east-30052714.
2   Brian Eason, "U.S. confirms Indy native Peter Kassig killed by Islamic State," *Indianapolis Star*, November 16, 2014, accessed April 24, 2018, https://www.indystar.com/story/news/2014/11/16/islamic-state-claims-killed-indy-native-peter-kassig/19135479/.
3   Gordon Rayner, "This is how the US and UK tracked down Jihadi John," *The Daily Telegraph*, November 13, 2015, accessed April 24, 2018, http://www.businessinsider.com/this-is-how-the-us-and-uk-tracked-down-jihadi-john-2015-11.

CHAPTER 35

Sharp Shooters

WES BRYANT
WITH REMARKS FROM DANA PITTARD

Many challenges faced us in the campaign against ISIS, but as a military there were some we brought on ourselves. It's no secret that as a culture we are perpetually bureaucratic and in conflict with one another. And it seems that the hindering bureaucracy and infighting that exists within our social and political system somehow managed to creep its way into our warfighting complex.

Who knows when that happened—perhaps it has been there all along. Nevertheless, it often keeps us from winning. Unless, of course, we pay it no attention.

The Bayji operation was no exception. While we battered ISIS targets day and night from the BIAP Strike Cell, enabling Iraqi forces to advance and take ground, we were inundated by sharp shooters from other agencies who constantly questioned our decisions.

On one night, after we'd tracked a group of ISIS fighters maneuvering west of the Bayji Oil Refinery, we fired two 45-pound Griffin missiles from an AC-130W gunship to take them out. We put the missiles through the top of a small house-sized structure we'd tracked the fighters to. The missiles, by design, were optimized to kill troops in the open or take out lightly armored vehicles at the most. They were not meant to penetrate thick-roofed structures and kill everything inside.

We knew that. We had far better weapons on board the gunship to do the job. I would much rather have utilized one of the 250-pound "low-collateral damage" bombs that the gunship carried—but our collateral damage analysis still showed that the risk of damaging nearby structures would be too high. Even breaking through the top of the small building with the gunship's 30mm cannon would have been a better option, effects-wise, but the potential fragmentation of the rounds and the fact that the cannon was not a precision weapon still presented too high of a risk to the nearby buildings and any potential civilians in the area. We were hamstrung to either use the Griffin missiles or to not strike at all.

Prior to the strike, we'd asked the gunship crew what weapons effects they thought we'd get by throwing two Griffins through the top of the building. They were a little irritated at our intent to use the Griffins, and understandably so. They argued the weaponeering choice, but once I explained that it was the only legal option, they understood and complied. They were pretty sure the missiles would punch through the roof, but they couldn't say how much damage would occur inside.

We fired the missiles. They penetrated the center of the roof and likely tore up whoever and whatever was in the immediate vicinity of the impacts, but they surely didn't affect the entire space inside the building. In the end, we couldn't be certain if all the enemy inside were killed as intended but we'd done what we could given our restrictions.

Within thirty minutes after the strike, I received a call to my desk in the cell. It was the squadron weapons officer for the AC-130W gunship crew that had just launched the missiles. The tone and nature of the call was pretty accusatory. The lieutenant colonel on the other end inferred that either we did not know what we were doing as JTACS, or that our ground commander, General Pittard, was remiss in directing the use of such a non-optimal weapon for the target.

The conversation didn't end well.

On yet another night, we killed four ISIS fighters maneuvering in an open field with more Griffin missiles from another AC-130W gunship. I received a call this time from the *director of operations* for the gunship squadron, another lieutenant colonel. He was angry that I'd requested the launch of *two* of their low-inventory, highly sought-after Griffin missiles to take out a group of "only four" ISIS fighters. He asked why I'd made the request to use two missiles instead of one.

I knew from experience that just one of the small 13-pound warheads on the Griffin would have left too big a risk of survivors, especially if the fighters heard the missile inbound before impact and scattered—which often happened. Two missiles, on the other hand, raised the kill probability considerably. In fact, the collective experience throughout the JTAC community with groupings of enemy personnel surviving strikes from a single munition was so commonplace that we'd adopted an unofficial weaponeering mantra: "*two is one, and one is none.*"

I replied curtly to the officer, deliberately leaving out the obligatory "sir" before addressing him. "I used two Griffins because it accomplished exactly what General Pittard wanted—which was to kill the ISIS fighters with no chance of survivors."

My reply did not rest well with the lieutenant colonel and started an argument between us that continued on for the next few minutes, until I'd finally had enough. I cashed in my hand. "Sir, if you really want to address this at the source, the commander of Iraq who authorized the strike is sitting right behind me. I can pass him the phone if you'd like."

General Pittard had been sitting there the whole time, quietly listening as I begrudgingly squabbled with the gunship squadron's director of operations. Curiously, the lieutenant colonel abruptly ended our discussion and hung up. The general and I had a good laugh at that.

Frankly, we were all just sick of the sharp shooting. Strike cell operations were a hundred miles a minute—extremely fast-paced and sometimes rolling from target-to-target and operation-to-operation. We simply didn't have time for armchair quarterbacking.

Those weren't the first officers outside our strike cell to make such accusations and judgments, and they wouldn't be the last. But the critics either lacked understanding of our operating environment or simply didn't care. We made decisions based on priorities established from the president down, and ill-informed criticisms of our operations often hindered our mission almost as much as the political constraints did.

All in all, our AC-130 gunship crews gave us outstanding support, and as the campaign against ISIS evolved over the coming months the gunships would come to kill hundreds—nay thousands—of ISIS forces. And to be fair, there were plenty of other agencies and entities that gave us an equal amount of grief about our strike decisions and weaponeering choices. (Enough to fill an entire second book, frankly.)

As angering as it was at times, we were sure that they were all well intentioned. We understood that the various leadership of the myriad agencies and units supporting the campaign against ISIS had to weigh their own priorities and concerns, and they saw it as their place to fight for them. Still, in the end the petty conflicts only detracted from our mission.

Remarks from Dana Pittard

Throughout our massive airstrike campaign against ISIS—a campaign that would soon extend across the three major theatres of Iraq, Syria and Afghanistan—the last thing we needed was to have officers in the rear sharp shooting the decisions of those of us carrying out the mission. During the initial months of the campaign in 2014, I refused to let that stop us from killing ISIS.

I was even "cautioned" on several occasions after authorizing and directing airstrikes that the strikes "could have come close to causing collateral damage." And I received more than a few phone calls warning me about munitions conservation. My commander, LTG Terry, was getting heat from the commanders of both the U.S. Central Command and the U.S. Air Forces Central in regards to both issues.

Still, I was never overly concerned. Our mission was to kill ISIS fighters and support the Iraqi Security Forces taking ground from ISIS. Accordingly, I instructed our strike cell team to aggressively attack and kill ISIS wherever found, in whatever way they deemed necessary, while reasonably adhering to our rules of engagement and collateral damage considerations. I trusted the expertise and judgment of the JTACs in the strike cell. In all our strikes, we killed our intended targets without collateral damage, and we were never excessive in our use of ordnance.

Eventually, additional munitions were acquired from the U.S. Air Force's worldwide pre-positioned munitions stocks, and more funding was allocated by Congress to increase production. However, as the campaign against ISIS expanded over the next few years, we'd come to see shortages again as we began utilizing so much ordnance throughout Iraq, Syria, and Afghanistan that the manufacturers could not keep up with the demand.

CHAPTER 36

Vampire Village

WES BRYANT

Halloween Night, 2014

We were covering operations simultaneously in multiple locations throughout Iraq. The pace was lightning at times. We'd often have two strikes going at once in completely different parts of the country, with JTACs sitting tandem and controlling intelligence and strike aircraft annihilating ISIS wherever and whenever we could find them.

Every evening before leaving for my shift, I'd fill a large travel mug full of French-Pressed brew to sip on throughout the first hours. I needed that to keep my edge, for better or worse. I'd catch the dinner meal at the chow hall, sometimes linking up with my JTACs off shift or in-between missions with their Special Forces teams. We'd bullshit about the last few days' events, at least as much as we could in the non-secure environment of the chow hall dining room that bustled with a mix of conventional soldiers, State Department personnel, and military contractors.

Vern and I would try to link up for dinner when we could since it fell toward the end of his shift. That was nice when it happened. He'd be able to fill me in on what had gone on during the day in order to expedite our handover an hour or so later. It was also our only real time to small talk. We'd chat about our lives back home, our families, and the job.

If I didn't see Vern at the chow hall, I knew he was on a busy shift and hadn't been able to break away for dinner. That gave me a feel for how much more coffee I should guzzle down before I pushed out to the cell. On those nights, I knew we were likely going to step into chaos.

Our shift changes could be incredibly busy. Sometimes the incoming crew would come in during a strike in progress. In those cases, our established rule was that they stand by and observe, quietly absorbing all the details of the situation so they could jump in and replace the on-shift JTACs seamlessly and take over at the best opportunity without affecting the operation or any of the strikes.

Other times, the previous shift was actively targeting or tracking enemy forces but not yet at the point of requesting strike approval. There might be a few more pieces of information yet needed to close the loop— such as the location of the closest friendly forces or final verification that we weren't looking at a neutral militia group or some other unit that no one was previously tracking. There were times when it took hours, even days, to fully develop a target.

Those instances always created a bit of amicable jealousy on part of the outgoing crew. We'd shake hands and pat shoulders, and the guys on their way out would affectionately nudge "you're welcome for the target on a silver platter, fuckers." JTACs always wanted to get the kill for themselves, it was our nature and what we trained for. But that was just how it went sometimes.

There was one incredibly frustrating target we'd been building intelligence on for weeks. None of us had been able to pinpoint any enemy forces at a place where the Iraqis insisted was saturated with ISIS. Then the opportunity finally came.

In a suburb of Ramadi, ISIS had previously taken control of two large Iraqi Army compounds. Weeks before, they'd driven out or killed most all the Iraqi forces in the area. North of the largest compound, only about 200 meters and across a main road, was a third compound. There, a handful of stubborn Iraqi forces were strongpointed and continued to defend.

At best, a platoon-sized element of Iraqi forces remained at that northern compound—around thirty-to-forty soldiers. To complement their force they had one M-1 Abrams tank and a couple of armored Humvee gun trucks. The number of ISIS fighters at the other two compounds wasn't known for sure, but we knew from intelligence reports that it was more than the Iraqi contingent and that they were well-fortified.

We deduced that the ISIS force was also utilizing the suburban residential area further to the south to hide most of their fighters and mask their activities. Time and again over the course of the preceding weeks, we'd receive word that the Iraqi holdout forces were being attacked. Yet, every time we pushed aircraft overhead we were unable to identify any ISIS forces or positions.

Numerous times over those frustrating weeks, the Iraqis had asked us to just strike the remaining compounds. But they were huge, multi-storied structures that used to house multitudes of Iraqi troops. We couldn't just destroy the compounds without real-time verification of ISIS occupying them. Not only was that against our ROE, it would be an irresponsible use of ordnance and a detriment to the Iraqi forces' ability to eventually re-take the compounds and utilize the facilities.

Finally, that Halloween night as our children back home trick-or-treated through the relative safety of our American neighborhoods, the commander of the small Iraqi holdout force in the Ramadi suburb decided he'd long had enough of being caged-in by ISIS. He relayed to our strike cell that he was going to aggress the ISIS positions in a bold counterassault. He declared he would take his remaining tank, gun trucks, and his soldiers and retake the compounds to the south—and that he'd be manning the tank himself. He adamantly requested airstrikes from our strike cell to support the maneuver.

Hell yes! We relayed our enthusiasm back to him. We were ecstatic to finally see some aggression by those Iraqi forces!

The Iraqi field commander took time to ensure that he was in direct contact with his rear operations center before he pushed out, so he could keep good communications with our strike cell throughout the assault. His senior commander at the Iraqi operations center was side-by-side with our embedded Special Forces team, and the team was in-turn on a secure conference call with our liaison in the strike cell. The communications flow for the operation from the forward commander to us and back would be near real-time.

Within an hour, we watched as the Iraqi commander's modest force of one tank, a couple of armored Humvees, and a squad of dismounted

Iraqi soldiers pushed out from their strongpointed building to engage the fortified ISIS fighters to their south—a force that we well knew outnumbered them.

"This guy's a *fuckin'* badass!" one of the guys in the cell yelled out.

The small Iraqi assault force made its way across the road toward the largest ISIS-held compound, landmarked in the center by a 100-meter long, three-story building. Immediately upon crossing the main road, the Iraqi force got into a couple of skirmishes—taking fire from ISIS fighters holed up in the large center building and a couple smaller buildings to the east and west.

We couldn't tell where the ISIS positions were at the time, though. ISIS was holding ground easily and we had a difficult time identifying their firing positions in order to strike. Even though we were watching the firefight through our drone and aircraft feeds and we could see rounds impacting our Iraqi forces along with their counterfire, we still couldn't pinpoint the origination of the enemy fire. After weeks of enduring our airstrike campaign in Iraq by that point, ISIS had become incredibly adept at masking the muzzle flashes of their weapons inside buildings so that we couldn't make out their positions with our aircraft.

Our liaison that night, a keen and forward-thinking Navy SEAL, interjected with a simple but ingenious idea. He told us he was going to direct the Iraqi commander to start pointing the tank's barrel at the enemy locations as soon as they took fire, so that we could shift our aircraft sensors to the identified ISIS positions immediately instead of waiting for an information relay through the Iraqi operations center.

The tactic worked perfectly. The Iraqi commander maneuvered the M1 tank and its barrel like a boss, pointing the cannon at every ISIS fighting position he needed us to strike. As soon as we'd see the Iraqi tank maneuver and point its barrel another direction, we'd direct our drone sensor and inevitably pick up ISIS ground fire directed toward the Iraqi forces. With that overt of a verifier, we knew we were looking at an ISIS fighting position. We were able to quickly identify the ISIS fighters before they withdrew back into their concealment.

What transpired was a night of pure, unadulterated annihilation against a series of long-standing ISIS fortifications. We soon came into a beautifully harmonized effort between our strike cell and the forward

Iraqi force. We began destroying ISIS machine gun positions and building strongholds with strikes while the Iraqi gun trucks and dismounted soldiers maneuvered into flanking positions and suppressed ISIS fighters at every turn. We pummeled machine gun nests and fighting positions in the main building compound as well as multiple buildings to the south that we'd previously had no idea ISIS even occupied.

Soon, we began massing ground fires with our airstrikes—synchronizing gunfire from the Iraqi tank's 120mm cannon, the machine guns of their Humvees, and bombs and missiles from our American F-16s, coalition fighter aircraft, and Predator drone. Eight 500-pound bombs, three 100-pound missiles, and countless 120mm cannon and heavy machine gun rounds later and we'd taken out five ISIS command and control buildings, a slew of ISIS fighting positions, two 23mm direct-fire artillery nests, a sniper hide-site, and at least a few dozen more ISIS fighters.

The mission was, in a word, *epic*.

Because of our success that night, the small Iraqi force was able to take back the two Army compounds to the south and, within days, drive the remaining ISIS fighters from the urban area further south—where it was soon discovered ISIS had established an extensive command and control network.

I was one of only a couple of JTACs in Iraq at the time with the call sign *Vampire*. My Combat Control JTACs used the call sign *Titan*, and our SEAL and Special Forces JTACs had completely different call signs. Our call signs had been utilized throughout the previous Iraq War for all SOF TACPs and CCTs in country, but they'd been decommissioned upon U.S. withdrawal in 2011. They had a whole lot of history behind them, so we'd had them re-assigned as soon as we pushed in for the crisis back in June.

Since our strikes that night had decimated what could viably be termed a small *village* of ISIS fighters, I unofficially labeled the objective area "*Vampire Village*" in a fitting term of reverence for the legacy of the Vampire call sign and that epic Halloween night mission.

• • •

The successes of *Vampire Village*, and of all the operations we'd accomplished from the start of the campaign against ISIS, were a reflection of what the American-led coalition would evolve into over the ensuing months and years. They were testament to the fact that, with courage and aggression from our partnered and allied forces combined with assistance and air support from America and its coalition, we were an absolutely unstoppable force regardless of the enemy we faced.

CHAPTER 37

Shock and Awe: First Strikes in Syria

WES BRYANT
WITH REMARKS FROM DANA PITTARD

Backtrack to Mid-September 2014

I remember vividly the night we began the shock and awe campaign into Syria. We were deep into our airstrike campaign in Iraq. At the BIAP Strike Cell, most of our air assets had been taken from us for the night in order to cover down on the planned barrage of Syria strikes.[1]

Our strike cell was essentially shut down for the night for lack of aircraft—but we'd known for a while it was coming. The BIAP Strike Cell hadn't taken part in the targeting for the initial airstrike campaign in Syria—higher headquarters and another special operations task force had accomplished all the targeting. They were going to be controlling all the strikes, and they needed all the air assets in theatre to do it.

With not much else to do, we flipped on one of the TVs in the strike cell and watched the news back home as it reported, almost in real-time, on the first attacks in Syria. At the same time, we monitored our air traffic display that showed us all the aircraft activity over the skies of Iraq and

---

1   Barbara Starr, "U.S. ready to strike ISIS in Syria, military officials say," CNN, September 18, 2014, accessed April 24, 2018, http://www.cnn.com/2014/09/18/politics/us-ready-to-strike-isis-in-syria/index.html.

244 *Hunting the Caliphate*

Syria. Then we programed our drone feeds to watch the sensors of the drones that were soaking the first targets in Syria to be hit within just a few hours.

Later that evening, we watched on our air traffic display as dozens of coalition aircraft pushed toward the border of Iraq and Syria to prosecute the first strikes in Syria ever by the United States.[2] It was reminiscent of the bombing hordes of World War II. None of us had witnessed such a huge aerial offensive in all our years of war up to that point. It was an awesome and surreal sight to see—even on an air traffic feed.

As those first strikes happened, we watched live via our drone feeds.

One of the first targets was an extremely large building reminiscent of the stately brick or stone buildings you see on fancy college campuses. It was sitting by itself on a hilltop and was at least four stories high and around 200 meters long. It sat at the end of a winding road that led up to the crest of the small hill it sat on. It had a huge wraparound parking lot where a single car was parked. We'd been watching the building for hours before the strike, and we'd seen absolutely no activity at or around the building.

Soon, a flight of American F-22 Raptor fighter jets carried out the first strikes on the building, dropping a handful of 500-pound bombs. But the bombs did relatively little damage to the giant building. We noticed immediately that there was no *post-strike activity* as we would typically see with a strike on an occupied, multi-story structure. If there had been any ISIS members inside, we should have seen a lot of squirters from the building—ISIS fighters running for their lives after those first unsuccessful bombing runs.

Later that night, more strike assets were sent in to wipe out the building, but in the meantime we watched as the drone continued to observe the damaged building and the hilltop it sat on. Within twenty minutes or so after those first strikes, a vehicle drove up to the compound. A man exited and walked a few feet toward the collapsed entrance to the

---

2 Craig Whitlock, "U.S. Begins airstrikes against Islamic State in Syria," *The Washington Post*, September 23, 2014, accessed April 24, 2018, https://www.washingtonpost.com/world/national -security/us-begins-airstrikes-against-islamic-state-in-syria/2014/09/22/8b677e26-42b3-11e4- b437-1a7368204804_story.html?utm_term=.08f3f3e4d43b.

building. He stood staring toward it for some time. He must have been in shock at what he was looking at, wondering how it had happened.

After a few moments, the man slowly walked toward what had once been the large front entrance of the building, appearing as if he were trying to figure out if he could get inside. Shortly after, he just gave up any attempt at whatever he was doing—the front of the building was in near-ruins after all. He seemed to be a bit scared as he quickly made his way back to his car and drove off back down the hill.

Later that night after another barrage of strikes toppled the building completely, portions of that first strike were shown on U.S. news back home. The news reported the strikes as the successful destruction of an "ISIS command center in Syria." U.S. military spokespeople touted it as a great coalition success.

We found that funny in the strike cell, as we watched the news reporting on a strike that we'd observed in real-time. We knew, most likely, that ISIS had abandoned the building well before the strike—if it was ever even occupied at all. We all had a good laugh at the hype. We knew it was definitely a *dry* target—a target that maybe at one point was valid but wasn't by the time it was hit.

Maybe we'd hit that building for the psychological effect against ISIS, or to keep them from using the facility in the future? We really didn't know what the justification was, but both scenarios would have been perfectly valid.

Still, from our vantage point there was no discernable reason to feed that particular footage to the news. There were plenty of other strikes that same night that would have been better to feed to news outlets in my opinion—strikes where it was extremely evident that we'd killed actively maneuvering ISIS fighters.

The only reason we could think of was that any footage of people *actually* being killed might be deemed too much for American television. In that case, a benign strike on an unoccupied building would have been the choice footage to distribute to the media. We were puzzled by it, still.

But we were more puzzled at our sudden massive military involvement in Syria. With the Syrian regime in the midst of a civil war, and ISIS having infiltrated the eastern portion of the country, many of us wondered how and why our government was simply entering a sovereign nation and striking the hell out of it with zero permission from its government?[3]

What would the long-term outcome of the U.S. decision to initiate a bombing campaign against ISIS in Syria, without the Assad regime's consent, be? And what would our evolving mission become as a result?

Remarks from Dana Pittard

We must remember that virtually all wars are fought for some type of political end state. The image of four Arab nations' air forces—Saudi Arabia, Jordan, UAE, and Qatar—striking ISIS in Syria along with the United States was huge. It went way beyond the immediate tactical value of the targets. It demonstrated that the coalition, including Sunni Arab nations fighting the largely Sunni-led ISIS, were showing the world that the Middle East was united in stopping ISIS.

That said, I still felt strongly we should have conducted some level of coordination with the Syrian military. I understood why we could not do it openly. If we had any official coordination with the Syrian military, we would have lost the support of the Sunni Arab nations in the region who were all vehemently against Syrian President Bashar al-Assad and wanted to eliminate him and his regime. At that time, we needed the support of the Sunni Arab nations against ISIS. However, we actually did assist at least one of the Syrian regime forces fighting ISIS in eastern Syria.

There was a Syrian Army commander of a large military base of around 6,000 Syrian military personnel near the Syrian town of Deir el-Zour along the Euphrates River. His name was Major General Issam Zaher al-Deen. General Issam had two nicknames within the Syrian Army: "The Bone Cutter" and "The Lion of the Republican Guard."

Earlier that year, ISIS had surrounded Deir el-Zour and attempted to assault and overrun his base numerous times. General Issam's forces

---

3   Anne Gearan, "U.S. rules out coordinating with Assad on airstrikes against Islamists in Syria," *The Washington* Post, August 26, 2014, accessed April 24, 2018, https://www.washingtonpost.com/world/national-security/us-rules-out-coordinating-with-assad-on-airstrikes-against-islamists-in-syria/2014/08/26/cda02e0e-2d2e-11e4-9b98-848790384093_story.html?utm_term=.ecd36207e79f.

constantly counterattacked and successfully defended Deir el-Zour from multiple pounding ISIS attacks. His command was literally alone in a ferocious fight against ISIS.

We grudgingly admired General Issam's grit and determination from afar. We realized that, if Deir el-Zour fell, it would allow ISIS freedom of movement along the Euphrates River Valley—from the ISIS capital of Ar Raqqa all the way south and east into western Iraq. We could not let that happen.

During the planning for the first strikes in Syria, we quietly offered our help to General Issam through some of our coalition contacts, and we were able to strike some targets that he provided us intelligence on. The *Lion of the Republican Guard* was very grateful for our assistance. General Issam and his soldiers were eventually able to defeat the ISIS fighters in the Deir el-Zour area.

CHAPTER 38

A Visit from Senator John McCain

DANA PITTARD

Christmas 2014

In November, I moved back to Kuwait from Iraq and resumed my position as the deputy commander of operations for 3rd Army and ARCENT. Major General Paul Funk, with his large and very talented 1st Infantry Division staff, took over as the ground commander of Iraq.

Through mid-to-late December I oversaw the fight against ISIS in Iraq and Syria from Kuwait while Lieutenant General Terry was in the States. As the holidays approached, I heard a rumor that U.S. Senator John McCain planned to visit Baghdad the day after Christmas to receive a briefing on the status of the fight against ISIS.

There was a bit of a freak-out from the White House to the Pentagon and Central Command. Senator McCain was a harsh critic of President Obama and the general state of the fight against ISIS up to that point.[1] He was about to assume the chairmanship of the powerful Senate Armed Services Committee and he was already serving on the Senate Foreign Relations, Homeland Security, and Government Relations Committees.

---

1   Rory Carroll, "McCain urges ground troops to defeat Isis: 'They're winning, and we're not,'" *The Guardian*, October 12, 2014, accessed April 24, 2018, https://www.theguardian.com/world/2014/oct/12/mccain-isis-syria-iraq-strategy.

Major General Funk had assumed command in Baghdad, but there was concern of the need for a CENTCOM and ARCENT senior leader to be present for the visit. Shortly after getting word of the impending visit, I received a phone call from General Austin.

"Dana, I will not be able to meet with Senator McCain in Iraq due to other commitments," he spoke in his deep, baritone voice that sounded so much like the voice of Darth Vader. "Can you represent me and CENTCOM in Baghdad?"

"Sir, I think Paul Funk has a pretty good handle on things," I said. "I would hate to get in his way."

His tone deepened. "No one has your recent experience or understanding of the fight against ISIS. We need to put our best foot forward with Senator McCain."

The Force was not with me, by any means. I could literally feel General Austin's grip on my shoulder from thousands of miles away in his office in Tampa, Florida. When I replied, I felt like I was under the spell of a Jedi mind trick. "Yes, sir. I would be happy to go back to Baghdad and brief the Senator."

I was a little tired from my nearly two-year deployment that had culminated in a virtual non-stop undertaking to push and support the Iraqi military to conduct offensive operations against ISIS. I'd handed off the reins to an extremely capable and competent commander in Major General Funk, and I'd hoped to spend the holidays decompressing in Kuwait. That was not to be.

Instead, I saluted my commanding officer from afar and prepared to go back to Iraq. I returned to Baghdad on Christmas Eve and spent a relatively quiet Christmas with our troops. I went to meet Senator McCain on the tarmac at the Baghdad Airport the next day.[2]

I was surprised to see Major General Mike Nagata, commander of the Special Operations Command Central, on the tarmac waiting for the senator's plane as well. It was the first time I had seen Major General Nagata in Iraq since the Iraq crisis began back in June. Known as a skilled political operator and military leader, Nagata had been spending a lot

---

2   Amre Sarhan, "U.S. Senator McCain Visits Baghdad," *Iraq News*, December 28, 2014, accessed April 24, 2018, https://www.iraqinews.com/baghdad-politics/u-s-senator-mccain-visits-baghdad/.

of time in Washington D.C. trying to sell his New Syrian Forces (NSF) concept which many people, including me, thought was an awful idea.

I'd always had great respect for John McCain. He was an American hero in the flesh. I had first met him in 1998 when I was President Clinton's military aide. I briefly saw him again in Iraq in 2007. Being a West Point graduate, I'd given him slack about his alma mater, the Naval Academy. I admired McCain's grit, leadership, and bi-partisan approach over the years, his five years as a POW in North Vietnam, and the fact that he had been a Presidential candidate in 2008.

I stood in the background as Senator McCain came off the plane and met everyone. I was a little surprised at how much he'd aged since I had last seen him in 2007. Still, he appeared to be full of energy and in a good mood. He was smiling as he spoke to us.

We left the tarmac and packed into a little room at the nearby Special Forces compound. About twenty people filled the meeting room—mainly Special Forces officers and sergeants.

It was not a fancy setting. We sat on white plastic chairs and I joined Major General Nagata, one of his brigadier generals, and a colonel around a plastic table with Senator McCain. The senator made his position clear from the start: he wished President Obama and the administration had been more supportive of our efforts against ISIS. I thought it was a little strange to say that as a senator briefing senior military leaders—but I can't say I disagreed with him.

Major General Nagata and one of his officers addressed the senator. They outlined the special operations role in the fight against ISIS up to that point. They said they wanted more boots on the ground in order to do a more effective job of advising and assisting the Iraqi Security Forces and Sunni tribes.

At that McCain proclaimed, "See, just like I said. I wish you'd gotten more help from the president to defeat ISIS. We should have sent combat troops to fight on the ground."

Before the meeting, I'd resolved that I would not make any comments while the Special Forces officers briefed. As it turned out, I couldn't hold back. I had a very different outlook on the state of the fight against ISIS and our best way forward than they did.

I interjected, "Senator McCain, as long as the Iraqi and Kurdish forces are fighting ISIS and getting their own country back, I think we can support them without sending in a large number of U.S. ground troops."

The Senator appeared unhappy at my comment. Beyond that, he ignored me. He asked the group about upcoming Iraqi operations, saying there was no time to waste because ISIS had to be defeated quickly.

"Actually, time is on our side Senator," I replied. "Each day we have been getting stronger, and ISIS has been getting weaker."

I went on to tell him that two of ISIS' vulnerabilities were that they needed to take over territory in Iraq and Syria to keep up their momentum and prestige, and that they were lousy at governing captured territory. We had effectively stopped most of their capability to carry out the first and, over time, the second vulnerability would require them to use more fighters to secure rear areas and control the populations under their rule. That would take away much-needed fighters from their forward battle-grounds where they faced the anti-ISIS coalition.

Senator McCain took exception to my comments. "Time is on our side?!" he yelled. "How can you say that when there are people being terrorized throughout Syria by ISIS? What are you going to do about that, General Pittard? Who is going to stand up for those innocent people in Syria?!"

I was sure the Special Forces personnel were enjoying watching a U.S. senator try to berate me. I kept my cool. I looked at him but didn't answer his rhetorical questions. After all, it wasn't specifically our mission to protect the people of Syria from ISIS. Our mission was to *defeat* ISIS—which would eventually help both the people of Syria and Iraq.

I let the heat in the room settle down a bit before I replied. "The campaign against ISIS will take a lot of time. We don't want to rush to failure."

That only seemed to agitate Senator McCain. His face reddened, and he grumbled something that probably wasn't complimentary. The short briefing ended before he was able to let loose on me again, but I wasn't out of the fire yet. I still had to go on a helicopter ride with him to the embassy.

Senator McCain said goodbye to Major General Nagata and the Special Forces staff. He and I walked with our assistants over to the tarmac and boarded the helicopters to the U.S. Embassy in Baghdad. During the seven-minute flight from the Baghdad airport to the embassy, I tried to build some rapport with him. I pointed out the old U.S. Camp Victory and Al Faw Palace where we'd once housed more than 60,000 troops during the "surge" in 2007.

He looked and nodded his head, but he didn't offer any comments.

Once we arrived at the U.S. Embassy, Major General Paul Funk, U.S. Ambassador Stuart Jones, and I all met with Senator McCain at the ambassador's residence. We intended to give the senator a briefing on the overall fight against ISIS in Syria and Iraq.

I used what we called a "placemat slide" to brief the senator. I put a single, large slide the size of a placemat on his lap and then went over our strategy and the current state of operations. I emphasized how the Iraqis and Kurds had successfully begun the counteroffensive against ISIS with strong support from our strike cells and coalition airpower.

He appeared to be impressed, but he was still skeptical.

"You act as if we are beating back ISIS. We are losing this fight!" he declared.

I looked at Major General Funk, and we both looked back at Senator McCain and smiled.

"No, Senator, we have placed ISIS on the defensive in Iraq. The Iraqis and Kurds are conducting offensive operations and beginning to regain territory. It will take years to defeat ISIS, but I think we are seeing major progress."

McCain's face reddened again. "Why don't you ask for more American ground forces?" he said. "Don't you need more forces to fight ISIS here? We had over a hundred-and-fifty-thousand troops in Iraq at the height of the surge in 2007."

"Over time, we may need more troops to advise, assist, and train the Iraqi Security Forces," I replied, "but I don't think we would ever need more than about five thousand. This is a different fight than back in 2007. I was here in Iraq at that time. The Iraqis and Kurds must now take back their own country, with the *help* of the coalition. We now have strike cells—that are pretty impressive—to support the Iraqi Security Forces and the Kurdish Peshmerga."

My low troop figures did not seem to fit McCain's pre-conceived notions on how to fight a war. He insisted we needed a massive U.S. ground force in Iraq. He raised his voice at me and exclaimed, "If you really wanted to win, you would use every advantage that American military power offers—and that is with U.S. troops on the ground!"

I responded calmly. "We will defeat ISIS in time, and it will be with indigenous forces. Then the victory against ISIS will mean much more because the Iraqi Army, the Kurds, the Sunni tribes, the Shia militias, and others will have done it themselves—only with our assistance. We don't need a massive U.S. troop presence on the ground to defeat ISIS."

The Senator scoffed at that. He reconfirmed, "We are not winning!"

I bent forward from my seat next to him. I looked the man directly in the eyes. "That is simply not true, Senator," I said firmly. "The counteroffensive against ISIS began almost a year earlier than most military 'experts' thought possible. Our advisors and strike cells are making a huge difference. ISIS is now facing pressure from at least fifteen different battlefronts in Syria and Iraq. ISIS is losing and, yes, we are making significant progress."

I kept my eyes on his, and he scowled at me.

"*Humph*...I'll see what the Iraqis and Kurds themselves tell me later today and tomorrow."

Senator McCain spent the rest of the day meeting with senior Iraqi and Kurdish political and military leaders.

That evening, I was invited to join Senator McCain at the ambassador's residence for dinner. Because of the intensity of the morning's discourse with the senator, I thought of declining the invitation, but I ended up attending anyway. To my dismay, the ambassador seated me right next to McCain, putting me in the hot seat again.

I was greatly surprised when, before the first course was served, Senator McCain went out of his way to publicly apologize to me for his negative attitude and remarks earlier that day. He announced that he'd since spoken to Prime Minister Haider al-Abadi and many Iraqi senior leaders, and that they all thought ISIS was losing. He was far humbler than before as he proclaimed that we needed to tell the American people about the great progress we were making.

"Thank you, General Pittard—for setting me straight," he added.

"You are welcome, sir," I said, relieved.

I was extremely impressed that the senator publicly acknowledged his mistakes. John McCain was a powerful and respected leader who listened. That was a rare commodity. Even more important, he was a man of honor and dignity who cared about our troops and loved and served our country. I felt honored to interact with him.

The next day I received a phone call from Lieutenant General Terry back in the States. "What the hell did you do with Senator McCain yesterday?"

"Sir," I said, "it was not the most pleasant day of briefings, but what do you mean?"

"The Washington Post and a lot of news outlets are reporting that John McCain just gave a news conference in Iraq in which he changed his view on the fight against ISIS. He now supports President Obama's efforts! He said Iraq is heading in the right direction in the political and security spheres—especially in fighting *Daesh*. He praised our efforts against ISIS!"

In later months Senator McCain would renew his call for more boots on the ground and a U.S. troop surge, but at least we were able to show him that we were making significant progress against ISIS.[3]

Our support for Iraqi Army and Kurdish Peshmerga offensive operations continued and increased. By January 2015, under the leadership of Major General Paul Funk and the 1st Infantry Division along with the work of our special operations forces, an average of 1,000 ISIS fighters were being killed each month by our airstrikes. The month of February 2015 saw an estimated 2,000+ ISIS fighters killed.

When the Iraq crisis first kicked off in the summer of 2014, no one had expected our small team to get the fight against ISIS started so early. No one thought we would be able to force ISIS on the defensive so soon... but we did. There would still be some dark days ahead and tough fighting over the next three years, but ISIS as a state would eventually be defeated in Iraq by early 2018. All in all, I was very proud of what we collectively accomplished to stop the ISIS offensive juggernaut.

---

3   "McCain: 'Ugly Truth Is We Will Need U.S. Ground Troops Against ISIS,'" Fox News, February 12, 2015, accessed April 24, 2018, http://insider.foxnews.com/2015/02/12/mccain-ugly-truth-we-will-need-us-ground-troops-against-isis.

PART 7

Chaos into Syria

CHAPTER 39

A Proxy War

WES BRYANT

Fall 2015

By now, a new special operations task force had been stood up to run operations against ISIS in north and southeast Syria. The mission of the Combined Joint Special Operations Task Force-Syria (CJSOTF-S) was to select, train, and employ an all-Syrian surrogate force in combat operations against ISIS—called the New Syrian Forces (NSF). Special Forces teams dispatched throughout Turkey and other Arab nations were tasked with recruiting, vetting, training, and advising the NSF.[1]

Because of my experience a year prior helping to initiate the airstrike campaign against ISIS in Iraq, I was hand-chosen to be among the first assigned to the new task force as the lead Special Tactics JTAC to run the strike cell in support of the NSF mission.

There were several entities conducting strikes against ISIS throughout Iraq and Syria by then. The two strike cells in Iraq—in Baghdad and Erbil respectively—were now being run by conventional Army commands with TACP JTACs controlling the strikes. The Combined Joint Forces Air Component Command (CJFACC) had a team down in Qatar that

---

¹ Nick Paton Walsh, "Syrian rebels: This is what almost $1m of U.S. training looks like," CNN, August 18, 2015, accessed April 24, 2018, http://www.cnn.com/2015/08/18/middleeast/new-syria-force-fighter-abu-iskander/index.html.

257

prosecuted "deep" strikes against ISIS targets—targets outside the prox-
imity of our partner or allied units. Another special operations task force
executed strikes both in support of the Kurds in northeast Syria and
against high-value targets throughout Syria and Iraq.

Almost serendipitously, my best friend and neighbor in the States,
Marshall, was attached to our brother special operations task force. While
I hunted ISIS targets in north and southeast Syria, he was tracking down
the senior leadership of al-Qaeda's infamous *Khorasan Group*.

The primary objective we'd given our NSF was to hold and take
ground in a key region in northern Syria. About thirty kilometers northwest of the major city of Aleppo, in the far reaches of northern Syria near
the Turkish border, sat the major city of Mar'a. Mar'a was the largest city
in the region and housed the strongholds of our NSF. Because of that, our
task force had aptly named our primary area of operations the *Mar'a Line*.

At the Mar'a Line, our NSF held an east-facing front about fifty kilometers north-to-south, from the Turk border all the way down to the
northern outskirts of Aleppo. East of the Mar'a Line, ISIS held every
city edging the Turk border all the way to Jarabulus at the banks of the
Euphrates River. Further east of the Euphrates, Kurdish forces battled
ISIS with support from our brother special operations task force.

For ISIS, the Mar'a region was key for two reasons: First, it was the
location of the holy city of *Dabiq*. Dabiq sat only a few kilometers northeast of Mar'a and was believed by ISIS to be destined as the location for the
final battle of the "Great Holy War" against the West. Such was written in
the ancient Islamic texts that ISIS subscribed to. ISIS had even named its
major propaganda magazine, *Dabiq*, after the city. Second, ISIS' control
of key border crossings to and from Turkey was vital in order to continue
their unimpeded flow of foreign fighters, equipment, weapons, and logistical aid to support the front lines in both Syria and Iraq.

Because of those reasons, the Mar'a Line was of strategic significance
to our task force and needed to be secured. To accomplish that mission
we employed our NSF to take back the ground east of the Mar'a line and
keep the ground west from falling further under ISIS control. But running
a surrogate force on the ground in Syria came with a host of problems.
Syria was, to put it simply, a mess.

Dozens of militia groups were simultaneously fighting against the Syrian regime, ISIS, and each other. And the opposition forces we recruited consisted of a hodgepodge of tribal militias with so many conflicting loyalties that they often had as much hostility toward one another as they did against ISIS.

A host of anti-ISIS militias that we did not actively advise or coordinate with were also on the battlefield. As a group we called these militia units *moderate* Syrian opposition (MSO) forces. Once any of the MSO forces earned our trust—proving themselves loyal to our interests by fighting ISIS and not being associated with a terrorist organization or the Syrian regime—they would earn the label *vetted* Syrian opposition (VSO) forces. Under our ROE, that would enable us to support them with airstrikes a lot easier. Even so, we could not always count on their intelligence reporting or their allegiance to our cause.

Then there was the presence of our long-time enemy, the al-Nusra Front. They held the far northwest pocket of Syria, and they were actively fighting against ISIS and the Syrian regime. Strangely, as the "enemy of our enemy" we were directed to leave al-Nusra fighters alone.

Last, who could forget the active civil war going on in Syria? Syrian Regime forces were off limits for us—a "neutral player" if you will. We had strict orders not to intervene inadvertently in the civil war. At the same time, we knew that our opposition forces were pushing at least semi-regularly down to Aleppo to combat the regime.

In the course of their civil war against "rebel" forces, the Syrian regime had been pounding Aleppo with artillery and airstrikes for some time. Anti-regime rebels had been putting up heavy resistance. We would often watch our NSF gun trucks push south from the Mar'a Line toward the regime-contested city of Aleppo when they were in-between offensives against ISIS. We'd see their vehicles go right into areas known to be held by the Syrian regime.

Within a day or two, reports of major battles between the Syrian regime and rebel forces in the *same* area we'd seen our NSF gun trucks would confirm our suspicions. When we asked our NSF commanders about it, they insisted that they'd occasionally go down to Aleppo only to "refit" or "take care of family members in the area." We couldn't outright confirm that they were fighting the regime, but they were probably doing all of the above. Everyone knew our NSF recruits were also anti-regime, and so it only followed that they'd be using the weapons and training we provided not just to fight ISIS but to fight Assad's forces as well.

Our silence was consent.

Such was the American-backed proxy war against Bashar al-Assad's regime. To be clear, his regime was and is brutal and inhumane—and that's the plain truth. It really should have been ended long ago. Still, I felt that if we wanted the regime taken out then we should have been more upfront about it. But perhaps that was just my naiveté.

CHAPTER 40

Politics on the Front Lines

WES BRYANT
WITH REMARKS FROM DANA PITTARD

In Mar'a, our NSF held a very weak line.

The dimensions of the line were ever in flux, with ISIS continually taking villages and cities west of the line and our opposition forces eventually taking them back with support from our Special Forces advisors and our airstrikes.

We routinely decimated ISIS positions up and down the Mar'a Line to enable our surrogate Syrian fighters to take back towns and cities. But, time and again, ISIS would just move back in a day or two later when we weren't watching and kill any opposition forces still holding there or force their retreat.

The operating environment in Syria was *incredibly* different than what I had experienced in Iraq a year before. As opposed to the large, relatively well-equipped ground forces of the Iraqis, in Syria we were running hastily-trained units that fought in squad-sized elements at the most (six to twelve men). In addition, our NSF were a surrogate force composed partly of fighters who had no previous military background. Many did not have the years of experience fighting an insurgency behind them that our Iraqi forces did.

A lot of the Syrian recruits were previously educated professionals— doctors, lawyers, teachers, skilled workers, and even college students. These were people who'd had no thoughts or inclinations to join a military effort before the civil war. Topping it off, our NSF were pitted against a highly-trained, well-equipped, and extremely experienced fighting force that, by then, was not operating nearly as overtly as it had been a year previous when the campaign against ISIS began. After enduring months of the coalition airstrike campaign in Iraq and Syria, ISIS had learned something about how to mask movements from us. Targeting had become far more difficult.

To complicate matters more, different government entities ran surrogate forces in the region; entities that we had to coordinate with before striking and from whom we also gained intelligence. These different government entities also ran surrogate forces that we occasionally supported with airstrikes against ISIS. We had special operations liaisons embedded with those agencies, but it upped the ante considerably for the level of coordination needed before we cleared any strikes. On any given mission, we'd often have to coordinate with three or four separate ground entities running their respective militia forces in order to meet conditions for a safe and vetted strike. To complicate matters more, sometimes reports from the various entities would contradict. So, the sifting and vetting of information needed in order to get to the point of actually striking was *exponentially* more tedious than it even had been in Iraq.

Undermanned and Underequipped

Some of the worst struggles we had in our mission in Syria were essentially self-inflicted. Well, at least by higher leadership. At various junctures during the mission, there were constraints imposed by Washington directing us to cease resupplying and reinforcing our surrogate forces.[1] That had drastic effects on our mission and our forward Syrian forces fighting ISIS.

---

1   Greg Miller and Karen DeYoung, "Secret CIA effort in Syria faces large funding cut," *The Washington Post*, June 12, 2015, accessed September 14, 2108, https://www.washingtonpost. com/world/national-security/lawmakers-move-to-curb-1-billion-cia-program-to-train-syrian-rebels/2015/06/12/b0f45a9e-1114-11e5-adec-e82f8395c032_story.html?noredirect =on&utm_term=.905a0bf671b3.

On the frontlines in Syria, our NSF fighters found themselves continually in the cold because of the stalls in our task force's authorizations to reinforce and resupply them as promised. We often had situations in which a small number of our supported Syrian fighters became overwhelmed on an ISIS-infested battlefield with no hope for resupply from us (as promised) and no trained reinforcements on the way.[2]

The Syrians we'd recruited to fight ISIS had chosen the side of democracy and freedom. They were patriotic Syrians who'd joined our cause to fight a common enemy and take back their country. America gave them the hope and promise that we would help them. We owed them what we promised. But the ever-changing political climate in Washington and shifting directives from the Pentagon constantly prevented us from fulfilling those promises. It enraged us all that so often we simply could not deliver.

Our trouble was compounded in September.

We'd had a newly trained NSF force standing by in Turkey for weeks. We'd been waiting on approval from Washington to push them into Syria to reinforce the fight on the Mar'a Line. Along with more fighters they'd bring in more gun trucks, weapons, and ammunition sorely needed to resupply their NSF brothers on the line. On the Mar'a Line a small unit of NSF had been holding a highly contested town south of Mar'a for days. The NSF fighters were down to one rifle magazine of ammunition per man.

Authorization to push our NSF into Syria had to come directly from President Obama. His delays in approval were tied to a political climate in Washington that reeked of confusion and indecision toward both the NSF program and the general intent of our mission in Syria in the first place. Eventually, the president finally authorized the insertion.

On the night of the infill, our strike cell was tasked with covering the NSF movement across the Turkish-Syrian border, at an insertion point that happened to be in territory owned by another, unfriendly militia force. As it turned out, the commander of our new NSF team, and most of its members, were from a tribal faction that was the historic enemy of the force holding ground on the Syrian side of our intended border crossing.

---

2   Jeffrey White, "The New Syrian Force: Down but Not Necessarily Out," *The Washington Institute*, August 11, 2015, accessed September 14, 2018, https://www.washingtoninstitute.org/policy-analysis/view/the-new-syrian-force-down-but-not-necessarily-out.

As soon as the NSF tried to cross into Syria, they were denied entry at gunpoint by the armed force of rival militia fighters. The commander of the militia force on the Syrian side maintained that his fighters would open fire on our NSF team if they refused to go back into Turkey.

When we got word about the threat, our task force commander directed us to posture our drones to be ready to kill any militia fighters on the Syrian side of the border if they opened fire on our NSF. It was an incredibly ironic turn because, on any other night, we would have been supporting the same militia fighters with airstrikes against ISIS. On that night we had an armed MQ-9 Reaper overhead ready to bury its Hellfire missiles into all of them.

Luckily, the situation resolved after a couple of hours. The NSF commander and the leader of the militia force at the border checkpoint came to an agreement. The new team inserted along with their vital resupply of vehicles, ammunition, and equipment.

Then, as if the mission couldn't have gotten worse, the next day we heard reports that fighters from the famed al-Nusra Front had been handed some of the gun trucks, M-4 rifles, and a large portion of the ammunition we'd sent in with our new NSF unit. Somehow that news got out to mainstream media. Soon enough it was reported that our U.S.-backed Syrian fighters had betrayed us.

That couldn't have been further from the truth. Unbeknownst to us at the time, our small band of NSF fighters had been stopped at an al-Nusra Front checkpoint while on their way to Mar'a, hours after we'd gotten them safely through the border checkpoint and had stopped overwatching their movement—assuming they were safe in friendly territory (we only had so many assets and we couldn't be everywhere at once). Outnumbered and outmatched by the al-Nusra fighters, the NSF were forced to give up some of their weapons and ammunition in exchange for their lives and safe passage.[3] That misinformation would only convolute the political perceptions toward our mission even more.

---

3   Yeganeh Torbati, "U.S.-trained Syrian rebels gave equipment to Nusra: U.S. Military," *Reuters*, September 26, 2015, accessed April 24, 2018, https://www.reuters.com/article/us-mideast-crisis-usa-equipment/u-s-trained-syrian-rebels-gave-equipment-to-nusra-u-s-military-id USKCN0RP2HO201 509 26.

A Lost Objective

Our task force also had the mission of monitoring the desolate desert wastelands in southeast Syria where ISIS continued to maintain ground. There at the infamous *Tri-Border* region where Iraq, Syria, and Jordan meet, we watched for months as ISIS held several cities and border crossings between Iraq and Syria.

We began hunting for groups of armed ISIS fighters in the Tri-Border region after we'd gained intelligence that ISIS held the major border city of Al Tanf, Syria as a stronghold. We learned that ISIS was moving freely between Iraq and Syria through the Al Tanf border crossing and resupplying fighters at the front in Iraq. We soaked the area for days with our drones, and eventually tracked a small group of armed fighters after they'd held a meeting in Al Tanf and then loaded a pick-up truck to head east across the Iraq border.

Our strike cell coordinated a set of F-16s to drop a 500-pound GBU-54 on the truck of six ISIS fighters as it traveled east. The bomb was the best in U.S. inventory for hitting fast-moving vehicles, but unfortunately it didn't hit its intended aim point at the center of the cab and impacted slightly off the truck. The blast threw the truck into the air and killed the fighters in the cab, but the ones sitting in the bed of the truck were thrown out. Two survived. They were injured, and trying in earnest to get to their feet and scramble away from the vehicle.

Our strike cell director was a smart and aggressive Special Forces major who I enjoyed working with. He ordered the Army JTACs on shift to re-attack the surviving ISIS fighters with another strike. But the task force lawyer, who'd been quietly observing from behind, chimed in. He insisted it would be a war crime to prosecute another attack because the enemy was "clearly wounded" and "trying to flee."

Out of caution, the director called off the strike. Furious, our JTACs were powerless to affect the decision of the task force lawyer. They reluctantly watched as the ISIS fighters lived to fight another day. The two ISIS fighters regrouped and fled further east to take safe-haven at the next border town in Iraq.

Within a day after that strike, we received intelligence that one of the surviving fighters was a high-profile ISIS leader—one of the "named objectives" we'd been after for quite some time. Unfortunately, our lawyer's call that day had inadvertently allowed a senior ISIS leader to live. That would make the ISIS commander a hero in the eyes of his men.

After much heated discussion in the days following, including some phones calls to higher headquarters lawyers, our JTAC team proved that the task force lawyer had been wrong on his call. The rules of engagement actually authorized us to strike maneuvering enemy personnel, to *include* those "fleeing or exfiltrating from a previous attack."

The lawyer—though obviously well-intentioned—had made a call based on a subjective interpretation of the rules of engagement that truly stemmed from a general culture of apprehension, rooted in a political climate of wavering support for the mission in Syria combined with an enduring fear of public perception toward America's airstrike campaigns. It was a culture pervasive throughout America's war on terror, and it reared its head quite often.

A Massacre in Paris

ISIS had complete freedom of maneuver at the Tri-border region for months. We could have smashed identified ISIS strongholds with airstrikes a lot earlier on, but we weren't given the go ahead to target any of them. We lacked approval from Washington to actually push NSF teams into the region, and any offensive operations to take out entire ISIS compounds or fortifications had to be tied to our NSF ground offensives. The NSF *themselves* had to take back ground—only with our assistance.

We had another newly-trained NSF unit on hold. They'd been sitting and waiting for weeks to enter southeast Syria and push ISIS out of their strongholds in Al Tanf. Time and again we had them staged and ready to go across the Syrian border, only to get word that the mission was on hold because Washington had reneged on approval.

Our Special Forces teams handling the NSF were faced with the challenge of keeping an understandably angry Syrian militia force from abandoning the NSF program altogether—along with their alignment to our cause. Most of the fighters were on the verge of quitting. If we weren't going to help them fight ISIS, they were going back to Syria to protect their families. No one blamed them for that. We weren't coming through on our promises.

On Friday, November 13, we had the NSF unit staged for what we thought would be final approval to push them across and oust the ISIS strongpoints in Al Tanf for good. We waited anxiously all night for approval from President Obama. We had strike aircraft postured for the mission.

Approval never came.

That same night in France, an ISIS-coordinated suicide attack at six different locations around Paris took the lives of at least 130 inno-cent people.[4] It was a terrorist-prosecuted massacre unlike anything the modern world had ever seen. President Obama became so engrossed with the political and diplomatic emergency of that event that the approval we'd been waiting for on our end wasn't going to happen.

On one hand we understood completely. But on the other we thought: what better thing to do in response than push our guys across the Syrian border and annihilate ISIS in their strongholds that night? Man, how I wished I could have called President Obama to tell him as much. And I surely would have if ever given the chance.

On November 15 we finally gained the president's approval. Our Special Forces team infilled the NSF into southeast Syria and together we decimated the mass of ISIS strongholds with airstrikes from an AC-130W gunship and mortar fire from our NSF team on the ground.

Meanwhile, French fighter jets executed a separate bombing mission in the Ar Raqqah region of Syria in retaliation against ISIS for the Paris Massacre.[5]

The next day, I caught on the news that Senator John McCain had asked a pointed question in reference to the French retaliatory airstrikes along the lines of "if we'd had all of these ISIS targets just sitting there, why had we not already struck them?"

It was a valid question.

---

4   "Three Hours of Terror in Paris, Moment by Moment," *The New York Times*, November 13, 2015, accessed April 24, 2018, https://www.nytimes.com/interactive/2015/11/13/world/europe/paris-shooting-attacks.html.
5   Alissa J. Rubin and Anne Barnard, "France Strikes ISIS Targets in Syria in Retaliation for Attacks," *The New York Times*, November 15, 2015, accessed April 24, 2018, https://www.nytimes.com/2015/11/16/world/europe/paris-terror-attack.html.

Often, higher headquarters would mandate sitting on vetted targets for a while in order to tie the strikes into a ground offensive or particular agenda, like we had just done with the strikes in Al Tanf. Other times, they'd request to further develop targets by watching them for longer periods—tracking activity around them to gain more information that could lead to additional or more lucrative targets.

The targets the French attacked had already been approved as vetted targets, but they were being sat on for one of those reasons. Because the Paris Massacre was such a huge and significant event, those vetted targets were handed over to the French to strike immediately as retribution against ISIS.

We did that to help conciliate our allies. They wanted blood-for-blood just like the rest of us, it was only natural. But as a warfighter I had to side with Senator McCain's sentiments—I saw no use for political pretenses.

Remarks from Dana Pittard

Back in 2013 when I'd heard the initial proposal for the New Syrian Forces pitched by the highly respected Major General Mike Nagata, my gut reaction was that it was a bad idea and would be doomed to failure. I certainly appreciated the concept of using Syrian fighters as a surrogate force against ISIS. However, my experience as the senior U.S. military leader in Jordan gave me a different view of any potential NSF training program.

I'd had lengthy discussions with our personnel who were then responsible for conducting the training and support of the moderate Free Syrian Army (FSA) fighters.[6] The small, limited program was effective. However, they could barely find enough fighters who would voluntarily leave Syria to train in Turkey and elsewhere. Although there were tens of thousands of military-aged Syrian males in refugee camps in Jordan, very few of them were interested in going back to Syria to fight. Understandably, they were trying to escape the bloodshed in Syria and take care of their families.

---

6   Agence France Presse, "REPORT: The CIA Has Been Secretly Training Syrian Rebels For Months," *Business Insider*, June 21, 2013, accessed September 14, 2018, https://www.businessinsider.com/cia-secret-training-syrian-rebels-2013-6.

The NSF concept was rife with potential problems from the start. There were not enough recruits available, and the inevitably small units would have little effect against ISIS. In addition, most recruits were more interested in fighting the Syrian regime than ISIS. Then there was a major question that was never fully answered: How would we support them when they got into a fight with Syrian Army units?

Even with my reservations, I'd had faith that if anyone could pull the NSF program together it was the extremely talented and politically savvy Major General Nagata. Mike Nagata briefed congressmen, inter-agencies, and national leaders in the Middle East region on the NSF program. It had certainly briefed well but, unfortunately, in the end it just did not work out.[7]

---

7   Seifu Al Midhadi, "The 'New Syrian Forces': A Failed U.S. Initiative," *The Middle East Magazine Online*, August 05, 2015, accessed April 24, 2018, http://www.themiddleeastmagazine.com /?p=5485.

CHAPTER 41

Enter the Russians

WES BRYANT
WITH REMARKS FROM DANA PITTARD

In my fifteen years involved in America's war on terror, by then across three major countries in the Middle East, I had really never seen such a unique and complex battlefield as Syria. I didn't think things could get much more convoluted, but I was soon proven wrong.

In September the Russian military came in with all its might, and the situation in Syria devolved into pure madness. While it was already challenging enough running militia forces and controlling strikes against ISIS throughout Syria in the midst of its civil war, the encroachment of Syria-aligned Russia into the fold presented even more problems.

Russian president Vladimir Putin had publicly stated their involvement in Syria was solely to help the Assad regime battle ISIS, and that they had no objectives to intervene in the civil war. However, we knew that was a lie.[1]

Putin had made it well known that he believed toppling Assad's regime would create more instability than it was worth. Plus, in Syria, Russia had the use of key naval ports to the Mediterranean Sea as well as forward air

---

1   Landon Shroder, "Why the Hell Did Russia Intervene in Syria?" VICE News, September 28, 2015, accessed April 24, 2018, https://news.vice.com/article/why-the-hell-did-russia-intervene-in-syria.

bases. Geographically, Syria was key for the regional defense capabilities of the Russian homeland, so Putin had valid interest in assisting Assad against the rebels and keeping Syria stable.

Still, we figured there was no way Russia would become robustly involved on any military level in Syria while the U.S. was already saturating Syrian skies with combat airpower and running militia forces against ISIS.

We couldn't have been more wrong.

By mid-September the Russians were there in full force, having primarily arrived through the airfield at Latakia in western Syria and the naval port of Tartus off the Mediterranean Sea. By the end of September, Putin had authorized airstrikes and emplaced Russian ground forces to assist Assad's military.[2]

We thought for sure the U.S. mission in Syria would be shut down overnight. With such conflicting interests between two historically adversarial superpowers, we couldn't imagine our political leaders would want to risk armed conflict with Russia over Syria. But the reaction from higher was nothing short of "Oh, shit...what do we do now?"

From the start of Russia's involvement in Syria, our military and civilian leadership back home had almost no contact with Russian authorities. There were no discussions between the U.S. and Russia to establish any semblance of an agreement or to de-conflict military interests—not on any level that filtered down to us, anyway. We had absolutely no understanding of exactly what our continued role was going to be in Syria.

Would Russia become our ally in the fight against ISIS, but our foe in a not-so-secret proxy war?

Were we going to work with the Russians, ignore them, or oppose them?

In lieu of those answers, senior military command directed us to avoid conflicting with Russian ground objectives and any of their air assets to the same degree we were already avoiding Syrian regime forces. That proved impossible, though. We soon saw Russian fighter jets shadowing our drones and strike aircraft, and bombing near our own objective

2   Andrew Osborn and Phil Stewart, "Russia begins Syria air strikes in its biggest Mideast intervention in decades," *Reuters*, September 30, 2015, accessed April 24, 2018, http://www.reuters.com/article/us-mideast-crisis-russia/russia-begins-syria-air-strikes-in-its-biggest-mideast-intervention-in-decades-idUSKCN0RU0MG20151001.

areas. A lot of us had the overarching feeling that we were on the brink of another world war.

What the hell are we doing here?

In lieu of any political coordination between our governments, the Combined Joint Forces Air Component Command ordered that all U.S. aircraft operating over Syrian skies maintain a particular standoff distance from Russian air presence. And our pilots and aircrews were given strict directives to not inadvertently posture their aircraft in any manner that could be misconstrued by Russian pilots as aggressive.

Meanwhile, at our special operations task force we were directed if we observed any of Assad's anti-rebel forces making their way from Aleppo toward our objective areas in Mar'a that we were to stand down any strikes in the vicinity. That contrasted with our previous guidance—that if we witnessed regime forces aggressing our NSF we were cleared to engage to defend our Syrian partner forces.

From then on we were to assume that all Syrian regime forces would have Russians attached either as advisors or augmenting their fighting forces. None of our strikes were deemed worth inadvertently killing Russian troops. No one wanted to have to admit they started World War III.

The situation in Syria only escalated. Russian fighter and bomber jets began hammering Syrian ground targets in droves. It was astonishing to see the number of Russian combat jets and drones flooding the skies daily through our air traffic monitor. But, as surreal as it was to witness firsthand the Russian air campaign in Syria, I soon became angered and disgusted. It didn't take long for us to realize what the Russians were actually doing. In contrast to Putin's stated intent of "only targeting ISIS," Russia's first targets were actually against "rebel" forces actively opposing the Assad Regime—many of which were our own opposition forces.[3]

On top of that, Russia demonstrated incredible recklessness and brutality against the Syrian populace with their airstrikes. We knew Russia did not possess the advanced targeting systems or experience comparable to the U.S. to carry out the kind of precision strikes we routinely

3   Jack Stubbs, "Four-fifths of Russia's Syria strikes don't target Islamic State: Reuters analysis," *Reuters*, October 21, 2015, accessed April 24, 2018, http://www.reuters.com/article/us-mideast-crisis-syria-russia-strikes/four-fifths-of-russias-syria-strikes-dont-target-islamic-state-reuters-analysis-idUSKCN0SF24L20151021.

accomplish. Even so, their air campaign reeked of cruelty, targeting incompetence, and an utter disregard for humanity.

Russia seemed to have no consideration for civilian casualties in their bloodthirsty hunt for any forces opposed to Assad's regime. Accordingly, they often targeted densely saturated civilian areas—justifying their strikes by insisting the areas were solely occupied by ISIS forces. They seemed to make no effort to limit civilian casualties even when it was clearly possible. Their bombing was indiscriminate. It was no coincidence that news reports of inhumane bombing and shelling of civilians and anti-Assad militias in Syrian cities exponentially increased right after the Russians arrived.[4]

The Russian bombing campaign in Syria was far more robust than ours at the time, mostly because of the indiscriminate nature. Sadly, many back home in the U.S. came under a skewed perception of the Russian efforts in Syria because of that. (Likely also due in large part to the highly effective propaganda machine of Russian intelligence, which we'd later discover was in full-force.)

Instead of condemning the brutality of Russia and the conflicts that their actions presented to U.S. efforts in the region, a sentiment circulated that Putin was doing to ISIS what President Obama hadn't yet been able to do. All over certain news outlets and social media, President Obama was portrayed as frail and weak while Putin was "strong and manly" in the fight against ISIS in Syria. It was sickening for me to see such egregious views being propagated en masse back home.

Regardless of one's political leaning, I felt that the elevation of Putin for his military actions in Syria couldn't have been more amiss. To me, it seemed toward the dark abyss of treason to raise-up the leader of one of America's most dangerous and long-standing adversaries. Unfortunately, the man who would soon become our next president—Donald J. Trump—was one of the loudest voices in that regard.[5]

---

4 Jared Malsin, "Russian Airstrikes in Syria Seem to Be Hurting Civilians More Than ISIS," *Time*, November 30, 2015, accessed April 24, 2018, http://time.com/4129222/russia-airstrikes-syria -civilian-casualties-isis/.

5 Philip Bump, "Why Donald Trump is praising Validimir Putin," *The Washington Post*, October 1, 2015, accessed September 14, 2018, https://www.washingtonpost.com/news/the-fix/wp/2015/10/01/ why-donald-trump-is-praising-vladimir-putin/?noredirect=on&utm_term=.b24a1b45edcd.

Russia had never been our friend. And as I watched the response to the Russian campaign back home, I wanted so badly to reach back to the outlets propagating the nonsense and the people who subscribed to it, shake them by the collar, and yell some sense into them: *"Vladimir Putin is NOT your friend!"*

Remarks from Dana Pittard

It was obvious that the Russians entered Syria to help the Assad regime and not to fight ISIS. Russia's bombing campaign in Syria may have had a negative impact on ISIS, but the biggest problem was that President Vladimir Putin's attacks also targeted rebel troops opposed to embattled Syrian President Bashar al-Assad, including some U.S. surrogates. This was further complicated by the recklessness of their bombing campaign that led to such sharp increases in civilian casualties in Syria.

CHAPTER 42

Russia and Turkey: The Bear and the Wolf

WES BRYANT

The Bear

Our pilots in Syria were cautioned frequently about responding aggressively to the harassment and interference from Russian aircraft. Accordingly, as Russian drones, fighter, and strike aircraft regularly encroached into our areas of operations and engaged targets within our battle space, our own aircraft were forced to move out of the airspace.

On quite a few occasions in our strike cell we had to postpone strikes in order to wait for Russian air presence to leave. That sometimes resulted in a loss of target when, by the time we were able to push aircraft back overhead, ISIS had changed positions and we'd lost them. Those were hindrances to our mission, for sure—but soon came the more dangerous games.

Russian Su-30 fighter jets had been shadowing our Predator drones and other low-speed intelligence-collecting aircraft in overt shows of force for some time, often coming treacherously close. In one instance, one of our Predator operators snapped a sensor picture of a Su-30 flying so near his drone that the silhouette of the Russian jet took up the entire screen shot.

Our aircrews would attempt to hail the Russian fighter pilots over the radio in accordance with standard international air traffic etiquette. Fitting with their evident power play, the Russians rarely answered any transmission attempts. The Russians were deliberately harassing our aircraft and our pilots.

Things only got worse, and soon the Russians became even more bold and started going after not just our drones but our fighter jets.

The most audacious incident took place over the Mar'a Line in our task force airspace—against one of the F-16 Viper pilots who regularly supported our operations. Our Viper pilot was tailed and aggressively maneuvered on by a Russian Su-30 fighter jet. The Russian postured his aircraft in a manner that was fighter-talk for "*I can shoot you down right now if I wanted to.*" All the while, the Russian refused to answer our pilot's multiple radio hails.

Little did the Russian know, our Viper pilot was an F-16 weapons officer—the Air Force equivalent to the Navy's "Top Gun" fighter pilots. When he realized the Russian was serious, he quickly counter-maneuvered on the Su-30. He postured his own jet to make it clear to the Russian that he was the "Alpha Male" in the equation.

For a few tense moments, our Viper pilot considered the possibility that he may have to shoot down the Russian jet. It was the last thing he wanted to do, mostly because of the well-understood political sensitivity of such an event. Luckily, the Russian pilot broke away soon after he was out-maneuvered by our F-16 pilot.

The next day our Viper pilot vented to me over a phone call. He was a trusted colleague of mine who I talked to almost daily as the senior Air Force JTAC at the task force. As he relayed the story of the stand-off with the Russian pilot with immense frustration in his voice, I imagined some surly Russian laughing deviously in his cockpit as he maneuvered to break away from the engagement with our American F-16, satisfied in knowing that he'd just gotten some U.S. pilot's adrenaline rushing.

Our pilot felt constrained by the mandate to avoid conflict with the Russian. Deep down, though, he'd wanted to blast the Russian pilot out of the sky. And, really, he should have been able to. Our military leadership emphasized that all U.S forces had the "inherent right to self-defense," but that statement was discounted by a strong culture to the contrary, one that emanated throughout the chain of command: "if you *do* engage, you'd *better* be able to back up your actions, or else." That was the real, unofficial guidance.

I knew full well how that Viper pilot felt about the rules of engagement and the politics of the situation in Syria. I'd been there plenty of times in the past as a JTAC on the ground subject to some of the most handcuffing ROE in history. I could hear the same anger and frustration in his voice that I'd often felt as he vented to me about how surreal it was to have an enemy fighter jet conducting aggressive combat maneuvers against him while he was effectively unable to counterattack for fear of retribution from his own chain of command.

That day in the skies over Syria, a Russian fighter pilot engaged in the ultimate game of "chicken" with an American F-16, playing out decades of pent-up tension between the world's greatest superpowers while Washington and our senior military command wringed their hands wondering what to do.

After that I became more and more indifferent to the prospect of ending up in a fight with Russia. With their indiscriminate bombing of civilians, deliberate targeting of our surrogate forces, and now the harassment of our pilots—I was even more contemptuous of them than ever.

Fuck Russia. We'd smash them to pieces anyway.

Through the absence of any substantial political discussion or agreement by either nation, both the Russian and U.S. militaries had effectively been left to work things out on their own over the skies and on the battlefield of Syria. It was a sad fact that really reflected gross irresponsibility on the part of both Washington and Moscow. Perhaps it was a testament to the warrior ethos of both militaries that we never *actually* engaged one another, even with such fiercely conflicting and opposing objectives as we had in Syria.

On October 20, 2015, the United States and Russia finally signed a formal memorandum of understanding.[1] The agreement stated the intent by both parties of non-aggression toward one another and non-interference in each other's objectives in Syria. It also provided de-confliction

---

1 Lisa Ferdinado, "U.S., Russia Sign Memorandum on Air Safety in Syria," *U.S. Department of Defense News*, October 20, 2015, accessed April 24, 2018, https://www.defense.gov/News/Article/Article/624964/us-russia-sign-memorandum-on-air-safety-in-syria/.

guidance for the regulation of combat air traffic in order to avoid conflicts within Syrian airspace.

We were relieved that our respective governments had finally talked and apparently decided not to continue allowing their militaries to chest-poke one another on a faraway battlefield.

The Wolf

Compounding the already convoluted situation in Syria was our strange alliance with the Turks. It was really an alliance based largely on our need to use Turkey's airfields and airspace, in order to forward-stage our air assets to more efficiently conduct operations against ISIS in Syria and Iraq.

On one hand the Turkish government supported our campaign against ISIS, while on the other they had their own agenda. And they viewed our strongest ally—the Kurds—as their longtime enemy. The Turks also refused to formally join our coalition, a coalition that included many European and Arab allies. To top it off, they had their own heated history with Russia so our alignment with Turkey did not help much when the Russians entered the picture.

Still, from our special operations task force, we supported Turkmen ground forces with airstrikes against ISIS as they pushed down from Turkey to take control of several Syrian border cities edging southern Turkey. Understandably, the Turks viewed ISIS' control of those border cities as a threat to their security.

Turkish F-16s soon began supporting our strike cell, albeit on a limited basis, and we controlled them in strikes mostly against well-prepared targets because of the intense language barriers we encountered when controlling their pilots. It was all par-for-the-course in trying to strengthen a newly formed unofficial "coalition" with the Turks.

Then on November 24, 2015, the Turkish military did the unexpected. Turk F-16s shot down a Russian Su-24 strike aircraft near the Turk-Syrian border in northwest Syria over our task force's area of operations.[2] The Turkish government quickly announced that the Russian pilot

---

2   "Turkey's downing of Russian warplane–what we know," BBC News, December 01, 2015, accessed April 24, 2018, http://www.bbc.com/news/world-middle-east-34912581.

had violated Turkish airspace and had ignored multiple radio warnings to return to Syrian airspace. There were conflicting accounts of the event.

The fact was we all knew that Russian jets had been carrying out strikes in Syria near the border with Turkey on a regular basis. That was nothing new, yet every time the Russians flew anywhere near the Turk-Syrian border, the Turkish military and government would complain and claim violations of their border sovereignty by the Russians. The reality was Turkey's sovereignty probably wasn't being threatened in the least by the actions of the Russian jet, and the Turks likely recklessly shot down that Russian Su-24 strike aircraft.

In my opinion, Turkey had thumbed its nose at its longtime foe Russia while sitting on the shoulders of the United States. I hardly believed that the Turks would have taken such a bold step against Russia if they didn't already have their alignment with us in Syria and Iraq. In so doing, they hid behind the power and might of the U.S. military fully knowing that Russia would not retaliate against them for fear of U.S. action. It was an irresponsible move that put the U.S. in a compromising situation, even further degrading our mission in Syria.

But, then, what less could we expect from the chaos that had truly come to define America's war on terror in the Middle East....

Leadership and JTACs of the BIAP Strike Cell. From right to left: MG Dana Pittard, Josh (CCT), Josh (CCT), MSgt Wes Bryant, Mikey (SEAL JTAC), Vern (Fires Officer), Blake (SEAL JTAC), Aaron (CCT), Adam (CCT), "LT" (SEAL JTAC), Murph (Special Forces JTAC), COL Tim Kehoe (Director). Missing from picture are Major Dave McRae (Deputy Director) and CCTs JB, Kyle, Richard, and Logan. December 2014.

Colonel Tim Kehoe, Major Dave McRae, and the staff of the 17th Field Artillery Brigade at the Baghdad International Airport base complex. Colonel Tim Kehoe (center), Major Dave McRae (second from right). Fall 2014.

(Left) Colonel Tim Kehoe, BIAP Strike Cell director and commander of the 17th Field Artillery Brigade, stands next to his unit sign on Baghdad International Airport base complex. Fall 2014.

(Bottom) Senator John McCain walks off the tarmac of the Baghdad International Airport with senior leaders on a visit to assess the state of the fight against ISIS. From left to right: Jonathan Cohen (Deputy Chief of Mission, U.S. Embassy Iraq), Navy Captain—(JSOTF commander), Senator McCain, Major General Mike Nagata (SOCCENT commander), Major General Dana Pittard (JFLCC-I), Brigadier General Kurt Crytzer (SOCCENT deputy commander), unidentified, Lieutenant General Mick Bednarek (OSC-I commander). December 26, 2014.

General Lloyd Austin, commander of U.S. Central Command (2013–2016).

*Lieutenant General James
Terry, commander of U.S. Army
Central Command (2013–2015)
and Operation Inherent Resolve
(2014–2015).*

*Major General Michael Nagata,
commander of U.S. Special
Operations Command Central
(2013–2015).*

Major General Dana Pittard meets President Barack Obama aside Air Force One during the president's visit to soldiers of the 1st Armored Division at Fort Bliss, Texas. August 2010.

Major General Dana Pittard, deputy commanding general of operations for U.S. Central Command/Third Army, briefs General Martin E. Dempsey (left), chairman of the Joint Chiefs of Staff near Amman, Jordan (reference Chapter 3). August 15, 2013.

Then Staff Sergeant Wes Bryant holds overwatch on a commandeered Taliban fighting position atop mountain peak in Kandahar Province, Afghanistan (reference Chapter 2). Winter 2005.

Then Technical Sergeant Wes Bryant conducts overwatch in mountains of eastern Afghanistan after conducting an overnight raid on a Taliban safe-haven. Spring 2012.

Then Technical Sergeant Wes Bryant rests with members of his Special Forces team after an overnight raid on a Taliban-controlled village in eastern Afghanistan. Spring 2012.

Then Technical Sergeant Wes Bryant requests air support while controlling overwatch from atop an Afghan Police compound overlooking the Spin Ghar mountain range and Tora Bora region of eastern Afghanistan (reference Chapter 4). Spring 2013.

Then Technical Sergeant Wes Bryant controls overwatch alongside Afghan Special Forces team leader while on patrol. Spin Ghar mountain range in the backdrop (reference Chapter 4). Spring 2013.

Then Technical Sergeant Wes Bryant waves field-crafted American flag while atop former command center of a Taliban regional leader that was captured by U.S. Special Forces (reference Chapter 4). Spring 2013.

(Right) The white teddy bear with burkha that Wes Bryant bought for his daughters while tasked at the JSOTF-GCC in Bahrain, just before pushing into Baghdad to initiate the campaign against ISIS. Summer 2014 (reference Chapter 17).

(Bottom) Major General Dana Pittard (USA Ret.) presents Master Sergeant Wes Bryant with his certificate of military retirement from the Air Force. Spring 2018.

Major General Dana Pittard with the commander of the Iraqi Joint Forces and Iraqi Counter Terrorism Service, General Talib al-Kenani (center), and vice chief of the Iraqi Air Force, Lieutenant General Hassan Falah (right). Fall 2014. This is a snapped picture of a framed photograph that sits on Lieutenant General Falah's desk to this day, and was sent to Dana from LTG Falah specifically for use in this book.

"Dear Sir,

Thank you for everything you did for the future of Iraq. I remember, and I always mention every single event.

Without you and the Honor Soldiers, we could not crush ISIS—"

—Email sent from Lieutenant General Falah to
Dana Pittard on April 4, 2019

PART 8

State of the Hunt and the Way Forward

CHAPTER 43

The Fate of Iraq

WES BRYANT

The BIAP Strike Cell, as we had created it in 2014, was unprecedented in the *ad hoc* group of multiservice conventional and special operations forces coming together as one killing team. But there was one fundamental problem that Vern and I knew would later present itself—there was never really a clear understanding of the specific lines of effort tasked to each military entity in relation to the new strike cell operations.

From the special operations command, we were essentially "on loan" to the commander of Iraq to assist him in the air campaign that supported the *advise* and *assist* mission of our special operations forces. To Vern and me, that mode of thinking was not a long-term solution.

We had levied up our chain of command that SOCCENT needed to establish a formal, long-standing agreement for task force JTACs to continue to lead strike cell support of task force operations. We'd even personally addressed the deputy commander of SOCCENT, Brigadier General Kurt Crytzer, when he visited the strike cell from Tampa around October 2014. But none of our efforts went anywhere.

By 2015, U.S. support to Kurdish Peshmerga forces in northern Iraq became even more robust. We attached more Special Forces, Navy SEAL, and even Marine special operations teams to key locations in the north to support the Kurds taking and maintaining ground from ISIS. Our teams were at forward locations with partner Kurdish Peshmerga units but given strict orders to *advise* and *assist* the Pesh units only. They were told that under no circumstances would they accompany Kurdish forces on combat operations.

Senior military commanders even established various distances the teams were told to keep back from the FLOT (forward line of own troops). This catered to the Obama administration's continued guidance that the U.S. would not participate in ground combat operations. But it was sorely misguided. In counterinsurgency warfare there was never a true FLOT. The term was invented in the days of conventional warfare, when the armies of entire nations faced off on the battlefield in comparatively delineated fights. In those wars, lines could quite literally often be drawn in the sand to differentiate friendly and enemy held areas. In asymmetric warfare, lines are constantly in flux if they even exist at all.

The reality ended up that our forward special operations teams often found themselves in the mix, with eyes on ISIS targets or first-hand witness to firefights between their Peshmerga forces and ISIS positions and, at times, under fire themselves from ISIS forces. Because of the directives from our chain of command, the teams were forced to keep those facts quiet, or at least mute the full story in their reports to headquarters. If they did not, they would risk being pulled off the mission and the team leader fired for violating orders.

In 2015 the Special Operations Task Force-Iraq migrated solely to the mission of *advise* and *assist* to the Iraqi and Kurdish forces, along with a limited high-value targeting mission. Both the Erbil and BIAP Strike Cells transitioned to sole operation by conventional force commands. The fact that conventional forces were running the strike cells was not the issue. The main issue was in the fundamental application of fire support in warfare. The new strike cell ownership had no real relationship with the forward special operations teams they supported with airstrikes. That would turn out to be a detriment to the advise and assist mission and, at times, a danger to the special operations teams forward.

The new strike cell leadership became adamant about maintaining strike approval authority and control from their strike cells miles away from the fight, even with U.S. troops and JTACs on the ground. The strike cells consistently refused to hand over control of air assets to our forward special operations JTACs even when they had eyes on targets *or* were taking fire from ISIS. Instead, the strike cells would take the unnecessary time to gather all the information from the forward JTAC over the radio, run it through their formal "strike approval process," and eventually prosecute the strikes from their end.

More often than not, the extended time that process took put our U.S. ground forces under unnecessary risk. On a couple of occasions, strike cell commanders even risked the lives of forward teams under fire from ISIS, insisting on maintaining control of air assets then delaying strike prosecution for one reason or another or never striking at all.

It was all in direct opposition to the ROE change I'd seen pushed through in summer of 2014 when the campaign against ISIS first began. And it was actually in violation of the *U.S. Standing Rules of Engagement and Rules for Use of Force*, which state that on-scene commanders always have the "inherent right to self-defense." (I found, over the years, that the U.S. military has a knack for often taking two steps back before going forward.)

The bottom line was, the risks that we *had* to accept in strike cell operations supporting forward partner Iraqi forces—that daisy-chain of communication from the ground force up to us that so often caused confusion and delays in targeting—were being accepted with our *own* U.S. forces on the ground. I couldn't fathom it.

We'd been forced to accept such risks in support of our partner Iraqi and Kurdish forces because we couldn't just hand over control of coalition air assets to Iraqi and Kurdish units and allow them to hit targets of their choosing under U.S. authority and with coalition airpower. But transferring that same limitation and level of risk to our own U.S. forces on the ground was grossly irresponsible.

Still, things got better with time. Even with those early hitches in the evolution of strike cell operations in Iraq, and the extreme challenges that persisted within the operational environment on the ground, the fight against ISIS intensified. By early 2018, of the three countries in which the U.S. was waging major combat operations against ISIS, Iraq was definitely going the smoothest. That was directly attributable to the fact that the Iraqi government and military were the most developed, stable and capable of the three. Since 2014 we'd helped the Iraqi and Kurdish forces liberate the key cities and regions around Baqubah, Abu Ghraib, Fallujah, Ramadi, Tikrit, Mosul, and Tal Afar. And we'd kept ISIS from getting anywhere close to Baghdad or the Kurdish capital.[1]

But to this day, there are major operational roadblocks to the Iraq mission.

Iraq continues to be a morass of tribal factions with varying degrees of loyalty to the government and one another, where a small U.S. troop footprint has the challenge of uniting Kurds, Sunnis, and Shias in a sustained fight against ISIS. And the hope of a long-term Iraqi-Kurdish unification was at least temporarily shattered when Kurdish and Iraqi forces battled again in October 2017 over the long-contested oil-rich region of Kirkuk.[2] Add to that a heavy influence of Iranian special operations forces training and equipping the Shia militias toward their own interests, and there is still quite a quagmire in the region.

In July 2018, Lieutenant General Paul E. Funk—who replaced General Pittard as the commander of Iraq in 2014—wrote a commentary emphasizing the progress made since we initiated the campaign against ISIS. In it, General Funk states:

> *For the first time, many of us are optimistic of their [the Iraqis'] long term success and confident that the Iraqi brothers and sisters we fought next to for so long are heading along the right path.*[3]

We will have to see what the future of Iraq holds. Until then, we sincerely hope that General Funk's words ring true.

1 Sarah Almukhtar et al., "The Islamic State: From Insurgency to Rogue State and Back," *The New York Times*, October 22, 2017, accessed April 24, 2018, https://www.nytimes.com/interactive/2017/10/22/world/middleeast/isis-the-islamic-state-from-insurgency-to-rogue-state-and-back.html.

2 Maher Chmaytelli and Raya Jalabi, "Iraqi forces complete Kirkuk province takeover after clashes with kurds," *Reuters*, October 20, 2017, accessed April 24, 2018, https://www.reuters.com/article/us-mideast-crisis-iraq-kurds-clash/iraqi-forces-complete-kirkuk-province-takeover-after-clashes-with-kurds-idUSKBN1CP0PT.

3 Lt. Gen. Paul E. Funk, "Commentary: Iraq endures the crucible, and emerges transformed," *Army Times*, July 9, 2018, accessed August 13, 2018, https://www.armytimes.com/opinion/2018/07/09/commentary-iraq-endures-the-crucible-and-emerges-transformed/.

CHAPTER 44

Entangled in Syria

WES BRYANT

June 18, 2017

A Russian-made Su-22 fighter jet maneuvers under the heads-up display of an American F/A-18 Super Hornet in the skies over Syria. The Hornet pilot pulls the trigger and launches an AIM-120 AMRAAM missile toward the Syrian-piloted jet.[1]

Anti-missile chaff and flares thrust out from the Syrian jet. The American air-to-air missile blasts just past the Su-22 fuselage, missing by a few feet. The Syrian pilot's maneuvers worked. Or, maybe he had just driven his jet wherever he could—erratically pulling out all stops knowing that a U.S. fighter pilot was on his tail and targeting him.

The Hornet pilot re-maneuvers to lock up the Syrian a second time, all the while coolly narrating the status of his dogfight over the radio to his wingman. His voice is muffled under the constraints of his oxygen mask and further strained by the tension of the moment and the extreme focus required to control his jet's combat aerial maneuvers.

Within less than a minute, he has the Syrian fighter jet locked again. The targeting icon on his heads-up display blinks rapidly. Notifications

---

1 Michael R. Gordon and Thomas Erdbrink, "U.S. Fighter Jet Shoots Down Syrian Warplane," *The New York Times*, June 18, 2017, accessed April 24, 2018, https://www.nytimes.com/2017/06/18/world/middleeast/iran-syria-missile-launch-islamic-state.html.

sound that the second missile is within acceptable targeting parameters to launch.

The missile seems to wind its way to the target. Suddenly, a huge black blast appears in the screen where the Su-22 had just moments before been in the sky.

A direct hit.

• • •

In summer of 2017, I was the lead Special Tactics JTAC for the Special Operations Task Force-Afghanistan when the shoot-down over Syria took place. I watched our pilot's strike recording a few days afterward with my pilot friend and colleague—Major Greg Balzhiser (call sign "Smack"). Smack was an incredible F-16 fighter pilot and weapons officer who'd flown for my task force two years previous supporting the Syria mission, and he was now leading the squadron of F-16s supporting our mission in Afghanistan.

It was a pretty surreal video to watch. It was the first air-to-air kill accomplished by the U.S. military in eighteen years, since an American F-16 had shot down a Russian-made MiG-29 over the skies of Yugoslavia during Operation Allied Force.[2]

But a standoff in the skies over Syria had been a long time coming.

Back on April 6, President Trump had authorized the launch of fifty-nine naval Tomahawk cruise missiles against a Syrian air base, constituting the first official attack by the U.S. against the Syrian regime.[3] The cruise missiles targeted Syria's Shayrat military airfield, believed to be the base from which the Syrian military had launched a chemical weapons attack against civilians in the western city of Idlib two days prior. The chemical attack had reportedly killed eighty-six Syrians, to include dozens

2   Eric Schmitt, "CONFLICT IN THE BALKANS: THE AIR WAR; Nighttime Training and Awacs Capitalize on MIG's Weak Spots," *The New York Times*, March 27, 1999, accessed April 24, 2018, https://www.nytimes.com/1999/03/27/world/conflict-balkans-air-war-nighttime-training-awacs-capitalize-mig-s-weak-spots.html.

3   Everett Rosenfeld, "Trump launches attack on Syria with 59 Tomahawk missiles," CNBC, April 6, 2017, accessed April 24, 2018, https://www.cnbc.com/2017/04/06/us-military-has-launched-more-50-than-missiles-aimed-at-syria-nbc-news.html.

of children.[4] President Trump ordered the strike utilizing his executive power, as a show of force to the Assad regime that the U.S. wouldn't tolerate any further chemical weapons attacks.

Then from mid-May to early June, our special operations forces in Syria coordinated at least three separate airstrikes against pro-Assad Syrian coalition forces that had pushed beyond the U.S.-demanded "de-escalation zone" in southeast Syria.[5] Iranian-backed militias, loyal to the Syrian regime, had advanced toward the Tri-Border city of Al Tanf which was by then fully occupied by our partner Syrian Democratic Forces (SDF). Adding even more urgency, we had U.S. special operations teams on the ground with the SDF.

We'd made it abundantly clear to both Russia and Syria that they were not to approach our ground forces. But they and the Iranians who backed them viewed our SDF as rebel forces. They disregarded our warnings and continued to advance. The pro-Assad militia force came within seventeen miles of our SDF in Al Tanf and continued closing when our special operations commanders finally gave the order to strike.

A friend and colleague of mine, a senior Combat Controller named Dave, was the lead JTAC at the Syria task force while I was the lead in Afghanistan. Dave controlled the strikes against the pro-Assad militia forces and told me about it afterwards during a phone call. I can't say I wasn't *incredibly* jealous when I found out that he got to deliver the hate to Assad's henchmen! But I was glad for it, and glad for Dave's accomplishment.

Fast-forward again to mid-June 2017. In the minutes leading up to the U.S.-Syria dogfight, armored Syrian ground forces had again been advancing on our SDF. Senior U.S. military officials tried to use the "de-confliction hotline" that had since been established between U.S. and Russian military channels to avoid just such a scenario—but they got no

4   Kareem Khadder et al., "Suspected gas attack in Syria reportedly kills dozens," CNN, April 7, 2017, accessed April 24, 2018, https://www.cnn.com/2017/04/04/middleeast/idlib-syria-attack/index.html.
5   Thomas Gibbons-Neff, "U.S. conducts new strikes on pro-Syrian-government forces threatening U.S. Special Operations base," *The Washington Post*, June 6, 2017, accessed April 24, 2018, https://www.washingtonpost.com/news/checkpoint/wp/2017/06/06/u-s-conducts-new-strikes-on-pro-syrian-government-forces-threatening-u-s-special-operations-base/?utm_term=.3cf8b1710c2f.

response. Senior command then quickly authorized the task force to act in defense of the SDF.

The task force JTAC first directed a set of coalition fighter jets to strafe between the frontlines of the SDF and the Syrian forces as a warning to make U.S. intent known. That halted the advance of the Syrian ground forces. Shortly thereafter, however, the Su-22 was observed maneuvering in the airspace over our SDF and posturing as if targeting for an airstrike. Then it launched a bomb that impacted close by the SDF positions.

And the rest is history—at least, that Syrian fighter pilot is.

· · ·

Really, the situation in Syria had devolved into exactly the mess we had foreseen back in 2015 when talk first began about increasing U.S. ground involvement. The coalition strikes against pro-regime forces through May and June 2017, pinnacling with the U.S. shoot-down of a Syrian fighter jet in June, further intensified tensions between the U.S. and the Syrian regime, Russia, and Iran.[6] That added to the danger, because by then we had special operations teams on the ground in Syria running various opposition forces against ISIS, along with a host of other U.S. forces providing advisement and support.

In February 2018, the brooding situation on the Syrian battle-field came to a head. Near the city of Deir el-Zour in eastern Syria on the south side of the Euphrates, a pro-regime militia estimated at 500 troops advanced on a tiny U.S. special operations outpost with tanks and armored vehicles. The pro-Assad militia attacked the U.S. team with tank fire and artillery and mortar rounds. For the next four hours, the JTACs on the ground crushed the battalion-sized force with U.S. artillery and airstrikes—killing an estimated 200-300 pro-Syrian regime fighters and thankfully ensuring not a single U.S. casualty.[7] Intelligence later revealed

---

6   Luis Martinez and Katherine Faulders, "White House: US wants to 'de-escalate' Syria situation as Russia warns it will treat jets as targets," ABC News, June 19, 2017, accessed April 24, 2018, https://abcnews.go.com/International/us-shoots-syrian-fighter-jet-syria/story?id=48119895.

7   Eric Shmitt, Ivan Nechepurenko, and CJ Chivers, "The truth about the brutal four-hour battle between Russian mercenaries and US commandos in Syria," *The Independent*, May 26, 2018, accessed January 29, 2019, https://www.independent.co.uk/news/world/battle-syria-us-russian-mercenaries-commandos-islamic-state-a8370781.html.

that the militia force was made up of Syrian militia and Russian contract mercenaries; even though the Russian military denied involvement.

Yes, we've made progress against ISIS in Syria. The U.S. and its coalition have taken plenty of land from the caliphate. In northeast Syria we liberated Kobane and moved on to take back Jarabulus and Manbij—key ISIS strongholds that once housed deeply embedded ISIS command and control networks. The coalition was successful in releasing ISIS' stranglehold in northern Syria as well, even liberating the symbolic city of Dabiq in 2016.[8] And we mounted a counterassault on Ar Raqqa—ISIS' self-proclaimed capital that sits in the heart of Syria—and liberated it in October 2017.[9]

But to this day it is still political and military pandemonium on the ground and in the skies of Syria. Nearly every entity is at odds with one another as our warfighters wrangle dozens of separate military and militia forces—forces that regularly fight with one another and have wholly conflicting interests. The Iranian Quds Force and the Russian military are sole agents of the regime and relentlessly attack our surrogate forces. And our small footprint of U.S. troops is still under constant threat from Iranian, Russian, and Syrian ground and air presence, and has to balance mission objectives with the ever-complex task of avoiding direct or indirect involvement in the Syrian Civil War.

We're also forced to work with the Turks, who have their own objectives. In fact, the Turks have attacked their longtime enemy the Kurds so often that we named the "SDF" largely to dissuade them from assaulting Kurd forces. (Dubbed an "Arab coalition" of anti-ISIS forces, in actuality the SDF are comprised mostly of Kurdish YPG forces.) This was not lost on the Turks for long, though. As of late 2018, the Turks have been openly attacking our SDF, further complicating the mission in Syria.[10]

8   "ISIS suffers huge symbolic loss in Dabiq, Syria, to Turkey-backed rebels," CBS News, October 16, 2016, accessed January 31, 2019, https://www.cbsnews.com/news/isis-suffers-huge-symbolic-loss-dabiq-syria-turkey-backed-rebels/

9   Hilary Clarke et al., "ISIS defeated in Raqqa as 'major military operations' declared over," CNN, October 18, 2017, accessed April 24, 2018, https://www.cnn.com/2017/10/17/middleeast/raqqa-isis-syria/index.html.

10 Ryan Browne, "Key US allies 'temporarily' halt campaign against ISIS in Syria following clashes with Turkey," CNN, October 31, 2018, accessed November 1, 2018, https://www.cnn.com/2018/10/31/politics/sdf-halt-syria-isis-turkey/index.html.

President Trump's posture toward Syria has proven to be no better than his predecessor, President Obama. In April 2018, Trump stated his determination to withdraw U.S. troop presence from Syria—contradicting long-standing messaging from the State Department, the Pentagon and his own past assertions. [11] Yet only days later he ordered a second round of retaliatory strikes against Syrian President al-Assad in response to another reported chemical attack by the regime, then backtracked on his initial statement and signaled a more sustained troop presence after all. Yet, he has still failed to deliver any semblance of a long-term plan, strategy, or over-arching intent for the mission in Syria. [12]

Then in December 2018, after a phone call with Turkey's President Erdogan, President Trump abruptly announced that all U.S. troops would soon depart Syria—*and* claimed that ISIS had been defeated. It was a proclamation so unforewarned and audacious that it finally prompted esteemed Secretary of Defense James Mattis to submit his letter of resignation, in a historic and striking outplaying of political melodrama. [13]

In reality, ISIS as a caliphate has been beaten, but as a terrorist organization is by no means fully defeated.

---

11 Karen DeYoung and Shane Harris, "Trump instructs military to begin planning for withdrawal from Syria," *The Washington Post*, April 4, 2018, accessed June 22, 2018, https://www. washingtonpost.com/world/national-security/trump-instructs-military-to-begin-planning-for-withdrawal-from-syria/2018/04/04/1039f420-3811-11e8-8fd2-49fe3c675a89_story. html?utm_term=.d06e883a4a78.

12 "Trump announces 'precision' strike on Syria's chemical weapons capabilities Friday," CBS News, April 14 2018, accessed June 22 2018, https://www.cbsnews.com/news/strike-on-syria-trump-us-led-britian-france-bombing-missiles-trump-us-live-stream-2018-04-14/.

13 Grace Segers, "James Mattis resigns as defense secretary," CBS News, December 20, 2018, accessed January 29, 2019, https://www.cbsnews.com/news/james-mattis-resigns-as-defense-secretary-today-12-20-2018/.

CHAPTER 45

ISIS-K and the Resurgence of the Taliban

WES BRYANT

Summer 2017

The final combat deployment of my career as the lead Special Tactics JTAC for the Special Operations Task Force-Afghanistan. In 2014, I'd helped stand up the Baghdad Strike Cell in the onset of the war against ISIS. In 2015, I'd hunted ISIS throughout north and southeast Syria as the campaign against the caliphate expanded. I hadn't been to Afghanistan since the summer of 2013.

Although the landscape of the battlefield had changed immensely, the fluctuating nature of our strategy remained fully intact. We lacked a clear-cut strategy then as much as we ever had. After sixteen years of warfighting and nation-building efforts by the United States, Afghanistan was still an unstable nation-state.

We had a new enemy, then called *ISIS-K*. The "K" stood for *Khorasan*—a historic name for the area that once encompassed what is now Afghanistan, Pakistan, and Central Asia.[1] Our tunneled focus on

---

1 The Editors of Encyclopaedia Britannica, "Khorāsān," *Encyclopædia Britannica*, accessed April 24, 2018, https://www.britannica.com/place/Khorasan-historical-region-Asia.

ISIS in Iraq and Syria since 2014 had enabled ISIS to take a strong hold in Afghanistan.

ISIS-K ran a heavy recruitment campaign to draw in disgruntled Taliban fighters and other Afghans disillusioned by the Taliban, as well as foreign fighters. The most dedicated of the Taliban, however, couldn't be swayed. Instead, those Taliban forces became strengthened and emboldened by the threat of ISIS-K. What followed was a massive reinvigoration of Taliban across much of Afghanistan.

When I'd last been to Afghanistan in 2013, Taliban presence in the north was nearly entirely suppressed. By the summer of 2017, the north was a hotbed of revived Taliban activity and subsequently one of our biggest operational focuses aside from the threat of ISIS-K in the east.

The Taliban saw ISIS-K as a competitor for regional and state power. This not only intensified our fight against the Taliban, but an insurgency tribal war broke out between the Taliban and ISIS-K. Although the Taliban fought ISIS-K, they were far from our friends. Any temporary alignments between us were only in the moment, and fleeting.

In Afghanistan we were still plagued by the continual *green-on-blue* epidemic that had seen our soldiers killed time and again since the start of the war. During my deployment to the special operations task force in Syria back in 2015, our team in Afghanistan had lost two Combat Controllers to a green-on-blue attack. Though they fought back valiantly, Captain Matthew Roland and Staff Sergeant Forrest Sibley were shot and killed by an infiltrator at their camp in the first days of the deployment.[2]

Then in June of 2017, within the span of a week, our task force endured two major green-on-blue attacks when infiltrators within our partner Afghan commando units killed several of our soldiers and wounded several others. One of my best JTACs, a SOF TACP named Ivan, was among the wounded when he was shot at near point-blank range by an RPG from one of the very Afghan commandos he and his team had been training.[3]

2 Kelly Humphrey, "Two Special Tactics airmen killed in Afghanistan," *NWF Daily News*, August 27, 2105, accessed November 4, 2018, https://www.nwfdailynews.com/article/20150827/NEWS/150829343.

3 Jay Croft, "7 US Troops wounded in insider attack in Afghanistan," CNN, June 17, 2017, accessed April 24, 2018, https://www.cnn.com/2017/06/17/politics/us-casualties-afghanistan-attack/index.html.

Ivan and his team survived that attack only because the first rocket-propelled grenade didn't detonate, allowing the team to maneuver and giving time for one of the Green Berets to swiftly advance on the shooter and close-in just as he fired another round. The second RPG soared so close to the advancing Green Beret that its tail fin glanced off and slashed his forearm as he raised his weapon to return fire and kill the infiltrator.

A Microcosm of Failure

"We're *troops-in-contact*! I repeat, *troops-in-contact* from the south!"

Jeremiah, one of my SOF TACPs, was yelling over the radio net we had bridged into our task force operations center. He was knee-deep in the fight in ongoing *Operation HAMZA*.

Op HAMZA was a mission to root out ISIS-K through three valleys set amongst the foothills of the harsh mountain range bordering Pakistan in eastern Afghanistan's Nangarhar Province. The operation had famously made the news a couple months earlier when, on April 13, our task force had coordinated the drop of the MOAB, or *Massive Ordnance Air Blast*—otherwise known as the "mother of all bombs."[4]

Jeremiah spent the next couple of hours controlling airstrikes onto ISIS fighters surrounding his position using F-16 fighter jets, AC-130U gunships, Apache helicopters, and drones that we dispatched to him from the task force. Meanwhile, we coordinated GMLRS artillery (Guided Multiple Launch Rocket System) barrages onto ISIS targets within *danger close* of his position when he passed us targeting information in-between his communication with strike aircraft.

It was a tad bit of craziness—but really just another day in Op HAMZA. The operation saw our teams on the ground in near-constant fighting spread across three major valleys with ridgelines between. We racked up a pretty good ISIS-K kill count, and that kept leadership content that the operation was a major success. But I saw Op HAMZA as a microcosm of the fight in Afghanistan as a whole—a reflection of our failure there.

---

4   Barbara Starr and Ryan Browne, "US Drops largest non-nuclear bomb in Afghanistan," CNN, April 14, 2017, accessed April 24, 2018, https://www.cnn.com/2017/04/13/politics/afghanistan-isis-moab-bomb/index.html.

Originally slated to last ten days, the operation had been ongoing for about three months. I'd watched our teams sit on the frontlines for weeks, barely making any progress forward despite our constant air and artillery strikes against ISIS positions day and night. Every few days our teams would try to push further into ISIS territory with their Afghan partner forces—Afghan commando and police units. The Afghan forces would slowly clear ground, inevitably taking fire from multiple ISIS positions and then relying almost solely on our JTACs and long-range artillery to bail them out. Most of the time they'd fall back to their original positions.

HAMZA became a "whack-a-mole" operation—a rinse-and-repeat cycle to virtually nowhere. Our guys were literally sitting in austere valleys, holding ground for extended periods and relying on airstrikes and artillery to defend them from the ISIS forces that snaked through the hills and valleys like ghosts.

ISIS had become adept at using the huge network of long-abandoned talc mining tunnels to conceal their movements. Eventually they even patterned the timing for our airstrikes and artillery and figured out exactly how much of a window they had in order to be able to rain down fire on our positions before withdrawing or maneuvering to another firing position to avoid being targeted by our strikes.

Our teams became sitting ducks for organized attacks by ISIS fighters. HAMZA saw U.S. special operations forces using tactics wholly contrary to the very tenets of special operations, and that soon proved detrimental. By August we had several U.S. wounded and killed as a result of extremely well planned and well executed attacks by ISIS-K. I'd believed that was only a matter of time, and I had voiced that opinion often to the task force leadership—to no avail.

One of the green-on-blue events that June happened in the midst of Op HAMZA, when an Afghan soldier opened up on a squad of infantrymen in the early morning as they slept at their small forward patrol base that held the "line" in one of the valleys. The gutless attack killed three U.S. soldiers and wounded one.[5]

---

5   Ahmad Sultan, "Three U.S. soldiers killed, one wounded by Afghan soldier," *Reuters*, June 10, 2017, accessed September 14, 2018, https://www.reuters.com/article/us-afghanistan-attack -idUSKBN1910OL.

The Afghan forces on the ground had no real stake in Op HAMZA. They knew as soon as they and the American firepower that was with them withdrew from the valleys, ISIS-K would re-establish in full force.

"HAMZA is an American fight, not an Afghan one," an Afghan commando vented to one of my JTACs as they sat at their small patrol base in the valley one afternoon.

To me, the operation was a perfect reflection of the U.S. mainstay throughout our years of war in Afghanistan: We pressured the Afghan forces into holding and maintaining ground that they had no real stake in, across enemy-saturated parts of the country that were both rugged and non-permissive. We were often entirely too predictable in our tactics and operational focus. And, we endured constant and ever-increasing green-on-blue attacks as if they were an acceptable risk.

• • •

In June 2017, U.S. military leadership publicly acknowledged failure in Afghanistan. During an address on Capitol Hill, then Secretary of Defense James Mattis somberly admitted that the U.S. was "not winning in Afghanistan."[6]

Things haven't gotten much better since. Especially now that our most recent strategy, incredulously, is to broker a "peace" deal with the Taliban—the terrorist group that was our very reason for going to Afghanistan in the first place.[7]

Either way, if our last eighteen years prove one thing, it's that we need an entirely new approach to Afghanistan, or ISIS and others like it will continue to thrive there.

---

6   Connor O'Brien et al., "Mattis: 'We Are Not Winning in Afghanistan,'" POLITICO, June 13, 2017, accessed April 24, 2018, https://www.politico.com/story/2017/06/13/jim-mattis-not-winning -afghanistan-239488.

7   Mujib Mashal, "U.S. and Taliban Agree in Principle to Peace Framework, Envoy Says," *The New York Times*, January 28, 2019, accessed January 29, 2019, https://www.nytimes.com/2019/01/28/ world/asia/taliban-peace-deal-afghanistan.html.

CHAPTER 46

Our Country

WES BRYANT

Since the beginning of the campaign against ISIS in 2014, we've killed tens of thousands of ISIS fighters. We've destroyed their infrastructure and strongholds across three different countries and elsewhere. We've degraded their funding sources, sullied their information campaign, and demolished their equipment and weaponry.

By February 2019, ISIS had lost 99 percent of its held territory in Iraq and Syria, and we saw an estimated 7.7 million Iraqis and Syrians liberated from ISIS rule.[1] That is a remarkable accomplishment.

Still, ISIS continues to gain ground elsewhere; inevitably taking back cities and swathes of land each time we focus efforts in another region. They've infiltrated parts of Afghanistan and other failed states in their expansion to the most destabilized portions of the Middle East.[2] In October 2017, the world was shown the true scope of that expansion

---

1   "CJTF-OIR Monthly Civilian Casualty Report," *Operation Inherent Resolve*, March 28, 2018, accessed April 24, 2018, http://www.inherentresolve.mil/News/News-Releases/Article/1477860/cjtf-oir-monthly-civilian-casualty-report/.
2   Colin P. Clarke, "Expanding the ISIS Brand," *RAND Corporation*, February 19, 2018, accessed April 24, 2018, https://www.rand.org/blog/2018/02/expanding-the-isis-brand.html.

when ISIS-affiliated fighters ambushed and killed four American Green Berets in Niger.[3]

ISIS demonstrates a vigorous capability to recruit and radicalize sympathizers to do their bidding. The U.S. is far from immune to that, as evidenced on Halloween night, 2017, when a radicalized Islamic immigrant ran down civilians in New York City, killing eight innocent people.[4]

It is easy to blame the people of the Middle East for the rise of this seemingly unbridled terrorism we face today. We often fall into a perception that we must inevitably "clean up the mess" that our Middle East allies can't handle on their own. There may be some truth to that, but the perception is far too simplistic.

It is difficult for many to fully comprehend the lives that so many within such war-torn regions endure. Most of us simply do not share the same reality as the people of Iraq, Syria, Afghanistan, and elsewhere who are directly affected by unstable governments and organized terrorism. We must understand their realities, and take the time to see the world through their eyes versus ours. And we must understand that our great advances against ISIS have not come without a cost.

Massive airstrike campaigns have had a necessary and advantageous place in our wars. Airstrikes were vital in pushing out the Taliban government in Afghanistan in 2001. They were detrimental in conquering Saddam Hussein's army at the start of the Iraq War in 2003. And they were the main reason we were able to stem the rapid rise of ISIS in Iraq and Syria in 2014.

However, we would be remiss to ignore the unintended consequences that come from the sheer scale of our airstrike campaigns. With that, we have amassed a certain amount of destruction that we can never truly effectively quantify. Accordingly, many of the areas we've liberated from ISIS have been decimated.[5]

---

3   Amanda Erickson, "Everything we know about the Niger attack that left 4 U.S. soldiers dead," *The Washington Post*, October 20, 2017, accessed April 24, 2018, https://www.washingtonpost.com/news/worldviews/wp/2017/10/20/everything-we-know-about-the-niger-attack-that-left-4-u-s-soldiers-dead/?utm_term=.eea6a103f89d.

4   Shimon Prokupecz et al., "Note found near truck claims Manhattan attack done for ISIS, source says," CNN, November 6, 2017, accessed April 24, 2018, https://www.cnn.com/2017/10/31/us/new-york-shots-fired/index.html.

5   Petra Cahill, "In Battle Against ISIS in Syria and Iraq, Civilians Suffer Most," NBC News, July 8, 2017, accessed April 24, 2018, https://www.nbcnews.com/storyline/isis-terror/battle-against-isis-syria-iraq-civilians-suffer-most-n779656.

We must accept the realities that go along with our chosen strategies. And we must examine if our current strategies, continued as they are, will ultimately bring more harm than good to the people of the Middle East and therefore our own national objectives.

• • •

In 2007, well before ISIS came onto the scene, then-Presidential candidate Barack Obama insisted "We need a comprehensive strategy to defeat global terrorists—one that draws on the full range of American power, not just our military might."[6] But that vision has not been fully realized.

ISIS as a state and organized military force has been largely overwhelmed. As a terrorist organization, however, it is still alive and lethal. We cannot become complacent and irresolute, or we will allow ISIS and others like it to serpent from our grip and shift their strength to wherever we are not. The hunt is not over—it is constantly evolving, and we had better evolve along with it.

If we are to be successful in permanently enabling free and independent nations, with stable governments and military forces capable of fighting terrorism without reliance on the United States, we will eventually have to approach the problem with more than just a military hand. We must act with intelligence and foresight rather than being perpetually reactive with military force.

There is a quote from a famous figure in U.S. military history that I carried with me through my entire military career. Commodore Stephen Decatur was an American naval commander, and hero of the Quasi-War with France, the Barbary Wars in North Africa, and the War of 1812.[7] During a formal dinner toast in Norfolk, Virginia, in 1815 he was said to have proclaimed:

---

6   Barack Obama, "Renewing American Leadership," *Foreign Affairs*, July/August 2007 Issue, accessed April 24, 2018, https://www.foreignaffairs.com/articles/2007-07-01/renewing-american-leadership.

7   Joel D. Treese and Evan Phifer, "Commodore Stephen Decatur: An Early American Naval War Hero," *The White House Historical Association*, December 23, 2015, accessed April 24, 2018, https://www.whitehousehistory.org/commodore-stephen-decatur-an-early-american-naval-war-hero.

Our country—In her intercourse with foreign nations may she always be in the right, and always successful, right or wrong."[8]

• • •

That quote by Commodore Decatur tells me we have an obligation as Americans to constantly reassess, and ensure that our policies and actions throughout the world are consistent with our ideals and values.

The United States is *our* country, right or wrong, and we must never forsake it. But the truest of patriots do not walk swiftly into a fire carrying a flag of blind nationalism. That is the hallmark of our enemies. The truest of patriots take time to evaluate strategies and actions, acknowledge missteps, and adjust as needed. They strive to make our nation and its endeavors always uphold the ideals we all believe in.

When directed through moral intent and firmly implemented policies and strategies, the power and might of the United States can be the greatest humanitarian light in the world. I believe we must always use it to safeguard our country, protect the innocent, and enable a more peaceful and prosperous humanity. Toward that end, let us constantly step back and ensure that is exactly what we are doing.

---

8   Gordon Calhoun, "'My Country Right or Wrong'-What Decatur Actually Said and Why He Said It," *Hampton Roads Naval Museum*, April 5, 2012, accessed January 29, 2019, http://hamptonroadsnavalmuseum.blogspot.com/2012/04/my-country-right-or-wrong-what-decatur.html.

CHAPTER 47

After the Caliphate

DANA PITTARD

The fight against ISIS was fundamentally different than the counter-insurgency operations conducted by the U.S. military in Afghanistan and Iraq previously. Specifically, with ISIS' claim of establishing its own state—its *caliphate*—and seizing territory from existing nations.

On the battlefield, the territory-owning caliphate made ISIS an easier target for us than if it had simply remained a terrorist organization with no intention of establishing its own state. From the U.S. military's perspective, waging war against the ISIS "state" within territory it took from Iraq and Syria played to our strengths. The U.S. military is very good at overrunning enemy states and nations.

ISIS' success in seizing so much land so quickly in 2014 served it well on social media and enhanced its coveted international image that the new threat of ISIS was a force to be reckoned with. The fact remains, however, that ISIS simply did not have the capability to adequately defend its newly won territory, and ISIS leaders were never really prepared to provide sustainable governance to large and diverse populations in their newly captured lands.

The coalition's comprehensive campaign against ISIS on the ground—its targeting of their leaders, finances, and governance as well as the information campaign to deny ISIS' Islamic legitimacy—contributed to weakening and defeating the ISIS caliphate. By placing immense pressure on ISIS in Iraq, Syria, Afghanistan, Libya, and elsewhere, the U.S. and anti-ISIS forces quickly put ISIS on the defensive. Now, ISIS' capability to govern, seize new territory, or even attack areas outside of the Middle East, has become extremely limited.

After the Defeat of ISIS in Iraq and Syria

What should happen after ISIS' defeat? Our strategic end-state has continued to be murky. There are major questions that have still not been answered:

- What is the government, populace, and infrastructure in Iraq and Syria supposed to look like after the defeat of ISIS?
- In a post-ISIS Iraq, will the U.S.-led coalition ensure the Shia-dominated Iraqi government in Baghdad respects the rights of the Sunni minority population?
- In a post-ISIS Syria, will the U.S.-led coalition, as well as both Russia and Iran, press the Assad Regime to power-share and respect the rights of the Syrian Sunni majority population?
- What happens to the Syrian Kurds (YPG), who were crucial to ISIS' defeat—considering Turkey, Russia, and Syria generally view the Kurds as enemies?
- How can we possibly achieve our operational intent or end-state in Iraq and Syria without, in some way, cooperating with Iran and Russia?

ISIS' establishment of a caliphate is significant. The concept of an Islamic caliphate resonated with many Muslims both in the Middle East and throughout the world. It brought forth echoes of the past from the first thousand years of Islam's existence. Accordingly, some believed it was the duty of all Muslims to support the caliphate. Fortunately, most governments throughout the Arab Middle East vehemently denounced the very idea of an ISIS "caliphate."

However, the *ideas* of ISIS were initially supported by many Sunnis throughout the Middle East. This was because the movement was anti-Assad in Syria and anti-Shia in Iraq—opposing the Iranian influence and the Shia-led Iraqi government. The root causes that helped fuel the rise of ISIS in the Sunni areas of Iraq and Syria must still be addressed.

The iron-fisted policies of former Iraqi Prime Minister Nouri al-Maliki between 2010 and 2014 caused many Iraqi Sunnis to become disenchanted with the Shia-led Iraqi government in Baghdad. The Sunni provinces in Iraq ultimately became breeding grounds of support for ISIS. The Iraqi government must develop a more even-handed policy with the Shia, Sunni, and Kurdish provinces. It must do a better job in reaching out to disenfranchised Sunni minority populations. Perhaps the Iraqi government in Baghdad should consider allowing more independence to the Sunni provinces similar to what they currently give the Kurdish region.

Iraq will also need significant monetary assistance from nations throughout the world to help rebuild its infrastructure in a post-ISIS environment. Additionally, the U.S.-led coalition partners and Iran must support security sector reform among all the Iraqi Security Forces.

In Syria, there is little doubt that the unfair policies of Bashar al-Assad and his Alawite minority regime enacted against the Sunni-majority population were one of the main causes of the Syrian Civil War. His government's actions propelled ISIS in Syria. Though the Syrian government appears to be winning the civil war, a brokered peace is desirable in which the Syrian regime remains—ideally without Bashar al-Assad—but shares power with the Sunni majority population.

Russia and Iran must be a part of the conversation of this future brokered peace. Some level of compromise and cooperation between Russia, Iran, and our Sunni Arab allies will be essential in creating stability in a post-ISIS era both in Syria and Iraq.

The single most important strategic objective in the region, though, must be to help end the Sunni-Shia schism and the veritable proxy war that exists between Sunni Saudi Arabia and Shia Iran. That proxy war has been helping to fuel conflicts throughout the region—to include Syria, Lebanon, Yemen, Iraq, and potentially Bahrain. The proxy war has also fueled a huge and dangerous arms race in the Middle East. It is time for normalization of relations between Saudi Arabia and Iran and an end to the proxy war that has helped to spawn, or at least support, ISIS and worldwide Islamic terrorism.

Radical Islamic Terrorism Will Continue After the Caliphate

By the beginning of 2018, with the loss of its largest city of Mosul in Iraq and its capital of Ar Raqqa in Syria, ISIS as a state and caliphate was essentially defeated on the ground. This was the result of the combined efforts of a U.S.-led coalition as well as anti-ISIS forces from the Iraqi Security Forces, Sunni tribes, Iraqi and Syrian Kurds, Turkey, Iran, Russia, and the Syrian Army.

Unfortunately, ISIS may become even more dangerous to the U.S. and the West as a terrorist organization without a "state." The military defeat of ISIS will not end the threat of radical Islamic terrorism or the jihadist movement to the Middle East, the West, or America. ISIS will continue to coordinate and carry out terrorist activities. And it will re-form and survive in places like Libya, Somalia, Afghanistan, and other failed states.

If there is to be peace in the Middle East in a post-ISIS era, America and her allies must remain firmly engaged in the region. We have seen what can happen when the United States leaves an unstable area too early. Our exodus from Iraq in 2011 is perhaps the most palpable example.

Similar to what happened with al-Qaeda, ISIS will be made less militarily relevant over the next several years. But we must continue to keep the pressure on, so their leaders spend more time focused on personal safety and evading the U.S. and its coalition partners than planning and overseeing attacks.

The U.S. must maintain a military and diplomatic presence in Iraq, Jordan, Turkey, Afghanistan, and other selected countries in the Middle East. We should consider, as well, establishing a small semi-permanent base in the Kurdish area of northeastern Syria. President Trump's call for removal of U.S. troops from Syria in early 2019 may have been both unwise and premature. Time will tell. But we must continue to maintain and enhance worldwide cooperation and collaboration against terrorism.

Hope for the Future

In June of 2014, ISIS seemed nearly unstoppable. Then, a small group of Americans and their coalition partners, backed by U.S. and coalition airpower, supported anti-ISIS forces on the ground and changed the myth of ISIS invincibility forever. A relatively small group of professionals helped sow the seeds of a larger campaign waged by the United States and an anti-ISIS coalition that eventually hunted down and defeated the ISIS caliphate in Iraq and Syria.

What that small group of dedicated Americans accomplished in a relatively short period of time could one day become a model for how the U.S. could support partner nations in the future without committing a large military footprint on the ground. We hope and pray that the hard-fought combat lessons from 2014, and the successes and setbacks of our fight against ISIS throughout the region since, will be heeded in the future.

The JTAC

There is an elite community of JTACs across the Department of Defense who strive every day to hone their profession as airpower specialists, and thereby bring the full might of the U.S. and its coalitions to bear upon our common enemies.

To the U.S. Air Force TACP and the elite brotherhood of Special Operations Forces TACP and CCT in which I had the honor and privilege to be a part: it is my hope that this book dignifies and honors all of you past, present and to come.

To the infantry, Special Forces, SEAL, Ranger, and other U.S. and allied combat units who take the Air Force "outsider" on to your teams as brothers: our common sacrifices in war bond us in ways that those who've never known the same will never understand.

—WES BRYANT

The Joint Terminal Attack Controller, or *JTAC*

They are the warriors on the ground providing "terminal control" of combat airpower onto enemy targets. As figurative puppet masters in the coordination and control of airpower in ground combat, JTACs are among the elite few in the U.S. military authorized to independently coordinate and control airstrikes. For nearly every airstrike directed by the U.S. and its coalitions—be it with fighter aircraft, bombers, attack helicopters, or drones—a JTAC is behind it.

Born from the forward air controllers (FACs) of the Korean War and Vietnam, the modern JTAC is charged as the airpower and indirect fires

317

expert for ground combat units. The JTAC integrates, coordinates, and controls close air support (CAS) and airborne intelligence, surveillance and reconnaissance (ISR) assets, along with artillery and other indirect capabilities, into a ground commander's battle plan. As the controller of all air assets in the fight, the JTAC is the vital link on the ground between combat troops and the airpower that supports and protects them.

Rightfully termed the "single greatest combat multipliers on the battlefield," one JTAC can annihilate droves of enemy forces with the firepower at his disposal. In fact, JTACs have been so feared by America's enemies that, during the peak of the war in Afghanistan, the Taliban were known to offer huge bounties against them. JTACs have become so coveted by American commanders that they're deemed a *minimum force requirement* for nearly all combat operations—meaning that any unit pushing into enemy territory on an offensive operation must have a JTAC attached.

The majority of JTACs in the U.S. military are Airmen. Part of the elite ground combat branch of the U.S. Air Force, these JTACs hail from two separate brother career fields.

The *Tactical Air Control Party*, or TACP, is comprised of JTACs who attach to conventional forces such as infantry, armor, and airborne in order to provide maneuver force commanders with airpower. The Air Force TACP have a small component of special operations JTACs—designated Special Operations Forces (SOF) TACP—who provide the same to Rangers, Special Forces, SEALs, Marine Special Operations, and other special operations teams.

Brother to the TACP, the *Combat Control Teams*, or CCT, are comprised of special operations JTACs first qualified as forward air traffic controllers. Doctrinally, CCT have the primary mission of establishing and controlling austere airfields, landing zones, and drop zones. In today's fight, however, their qualification as special operations JTACs is most often in demand.

Among the other services there are a relative handful of Navy SEAL and Army Green Beret, Ranger, and fire support specialists secondarily JTAC qualified. And the Marine Corps has its own JTACs to primarily support USMC maneuver units. Throughout America's modern wars and overseas contingencies, the Air Force TACP have controlled the vast majority of conventional combat airpower, while the SOF TACP and CCT have controlled the majority of special operations combat airpower.

From the start of America's war on ISIS, American JTACs have often found themselves utilized in an entirely different capacity than ever before. Then and since, the JTAC has become a central player in the evolution of modern warfare.

Glossary

AAH: Asa'ib Ahl al-Haq
AFCENT: U.S. Air Forces Central Command
AGM: Air-to-Ground Missile
ALO: Air Liaison Officer
AMRAAM: Advanced Medium-Range Air-to-Air Missile
ANF: Al-Nusra Front
ANSF: Afghan National Security Forces
AQI: Al-Qaeda in Iraq
ARCENT/USARCENT: U.S. Army Central Command
ASOS: Air Support Operations Squadron
ATO: Air Tasking Order
BDSC: Baghdad Diplomatic Support Center
BIAP: Baghdad International Airport
BOC: Baghdad Operations Command
BOG: Boots on the Ground
CJFACC: Combined Joint Forces Air Component Command
CAS: Close Air Support
CCT: Combat Control Team
CDE: Collateral Damage Estimation
CDQC: Combat Diver's Qualification Course
CENTCOM/USCENTCOM: United States Central Command
CF-J: CENTCOM Forward-Jordan
CHU: Containerized Housing Unit
CJOC: Combined Joint Operations Center
CJSOTF-S: Combined Joint Special Operations Task Force-Syria

CJTF: Combined Joint Task Force
CJTF-OIR: Combined Joint Task Force-OIR
COIN: Counterinsurgency
CQC: Close Quarters Combat
CRF: Crisis Response Force
CTS: Iraq Counterterrorism Service
EBALO: Enlisted Battalion Air Liaison Officer
ETAC: Enlisted Terminal Attack Controller
FAC: Forward Air Controller
FAST: Fleet Antiterrorism Security Team
FID: Foreign Internal Defense
FLOT: Forward Line of Own Troops
FM: Frequency Modulation
FSA: Free Syrian Army
GBU: Guided Bomb Unit
GMLRS: Guided Multiple Launch Rocket System
HD: High Definition
HIMARS: High Mobility Artillery Rocket System
HLZ: Helicopter Landing Zone
HUD: Heads-Up Display
IED: Improvised Explosive Device
IFF: Identification, Friend or Foe
IO: Information Operations
IS: Islamic State
ISF: Iraqi Security Forces
ISIL: Islamic State of Iraq and the Levant
ISIS: Islamic State of Iraq and Syria
ISIS-K: ISIS-Khorasan
ISR: Intelligence, Surveillance and Reconnaissance
ITC: ISR Tactical Controller
JFLCC-I: Joint Forces Land Component Commander-Iraq
JSOTF: Joint Special Operations Task Force
JSOTF-GCC: Joint Special Operations Task Force-Gulf Cooperation Council

JTAC: Joint Terminal Attack Controller

KH: Kata'ib Hezbollah

KIA: Killed in Action

LNO: Liaison Officer

MARCENT/USMARCENT: U.S. Marine Corps Forces Central Command

MEDEVAC: Medical Evacuation

MFF: Military Freefall

MIT: (Turkish) National Intelligence Organization

MOAB: Massive Ordnance Air Blast

MoD: Ministry of Defense (Iraq)

MSO: Moderate Syrian Opposition

NCO: Noncommissioned Officer

NCOIC: Noncommissioned Officer in Charge

NEO: Noncombatant Evacuation Operations

NSC: National Security Council

NSF: New Syrian Forces

NSW: Naval Special Warfare

NTC: National Training Center

ODA: Operational Detachment Alpha

OIR: Operation Inherent Resolve

OND: Operation New Dawn

OSC-I: Office of Security Cooperation-Iraq

PJ: Pararescue Jumper (Pararescueman)

PTSD: Post-Traumatic Stress Disorder

QRF: Quick Reaction Force

ROE: Rules of Engagement

ROMAD: Vietnam era: Radio Operator, Maintainer, and Driver | Early 2000s: Recon, Observe, Mark, and Destroy

RPG: Rocket-Propelled Grenade

SATCOM: Satellite Communication

SCUBA: Self-Contained Underwater Breathing Apparatus

SDF: Syrian Democratic Forces

SEAL: Sea, Air, and Land

SERE: Survival, Evasion, Resistance, and Escape

SFUWO: Special Forces Underwater Operations

SOCCENT: Special Operations Command Central

SOCOM: Special Operations Command

SOF: Special Operations Forces

SOFA: Status of Forces Agreement

SOF TACP: Special Operations Forces Tactical Air Control Party

SoP: Show of Presence

SOTF: Special Operations Task Force

SOTF-A: Special Operations Task Force-Afghanistan

SOTF-I: Special Operations Task Force-Iraq

ST: Special Tactics

STO: Special Tactics Officer

TACP: Tactical Air Control Party

TEA: Target Engagement Authority

TOA: Transfer of Authority

TRADOC: U.S. Army Training and Doctrine Command

UHF-AM: Ultra High Frequency-Amplitude Modulation

VBIED: Vehicle-Borne IED

VSO: Vetted Syrian Opposition

YPG: (Kurdish) People's Protection Units

Acknowledgments

The authors would like to recognize and thank Dana's lifelong friend and classmate, Paul Divis, for believing in this book project from the very beginning. In the spring of 2015, Paul helped introduce us to our future literary agent—Jan Miller from Dupree-Miller.

We would like to thank Jan Miller, Yvonne Ortega, and their associates for their patience and believing in our book. Jan constantly challenged us to tell our story vividly, and we will always appreciate her devotion to our project. We also extend a gracious thanks to writer Wes Smith for painstakingly helping us craft a book proposal and mentoring us to write with more description, feeling, and clarity.

We extend thanks to Brigadier General Omar Jones and Ms. Lisa Thomas at the U.S. Army Office of the Chief of Public Affairs at the Pentagon, and Mr. Don Kluzik at the Defense Office of Prepublication and Security Review, for helping with the Department of Defense screening of our manuscript for classified content.

We are grateful to so many family and friends for reading our early manuscripts and giving timely and critical advice to make the project better. We'd like to specifically thank colleagues and friends who helped through their consult and support: Army GEN (Ret.) David Petraeus, Army LTG (Ret.) James Terry, Army COL (Ret.) Tim Kehoe, Marine COL Eduardo Abisellan, Marine COL John Barnett, Army COL Clydea Prichard-Brown, Army LTC Brian Ducote, Navy LCDR Aaron Vernallis, Air Force MSgt (Ret.) Marshall Bonham, Mr. Dave Broyles (writer/producer), Mr. James Dolan (CEO), and Chris Pittard.

Finally, we would like to thank our publisher, Anthony Ziccardi, our managing editor, Maddie Sturgeon, and the team at Post Hill Press. Thank you for believing in us, working so hard to get things right, and publishing our story.

About the Authors

Dana J.H. Pittard, Major General, U.S. Army (Retired)

Co-author Dana Pittard retired from the U.S. Army in 2015 at the rank of Major General after thirty-four years of active duty service. From a young age, he has had a passion for the art of war and military history.

Pittard was a highly decorated combat leader and commanded units at every echelon from platoon through division, including multiple combat tours in Iraq and the Middle East. In 2014, he was chosen to lead the initial U.S. response to halt the aggressive spread of ISIS in Iraq.

Dana has earned a B.S. from West Point, a master's degree from the School of Advanced Military Studies at the U.S. Army Command and General Staff College, and attended the John F. Kennedy School of Government at Harvard University as a Senior Fellow. He is currently a vice president with a manufacturing company in Indiana where he lives with his wife, Lucille, and their two sons.

Wes J. Bryant, Master Sergeant, U.S. Air Force (Retired)

Co-author Wes Bryant retired from the U.S. Air Force in 2018 at the rank of Master Sergeant after twenty years of active duty service. In 2014, as a senior Special Operations Forces Tactical Air Control Party-Joint Terminal Attack Controller (SOF TACP-JTAC), he was part of the elite special operations task force chosen to secure Baghdad and northern Iraq against the newly emerged threat of ISIS.

Embedded with Special Forces teams under a Navy SEAL task force, Wes was the tactical lead for a contingent of special operations JTACs to first set foot in Iraq to stop ISIS. As the senior enlisted JTAC to establish the *BIAP Strike Cell*, Bryant coordinated and controlled the first airstrikes against ISIS in the Baghdad region. He later deployed as the senior Special Tactics JTAC for special operations task forces hunting ISIS in Syria and Afghanistan.

Wes earned a bachelor's in Asian Studies from the University of Maryland University College. He's been a lifelong writer, amateur philosopher, and avid student of the martial arts. He currently pursues writing and editing, and teaches Chinese Kung Fu and Tai Chi in his community in North Carolina, where he lives with his wife, Katie, and their two daughters.